Salvadoran Imaginaries

LATINIDAD

Transnational Cultures in the United States

This series publishes books that deepen and expand our knowledge and understanding of the various Latina/o populations in the United States in the context of their transnational relationships with cultures of the broader Americas. The focus is on the history and analysis of Latino cultural systems and practices in national and transnational spheres of influence from the nineteenth century to the present. The series is open to scholarship in political science, economics, anthropology, linguistics, history, cinema and television, literary and cultural studies, and popular culture and encourages interdisciplinary approaches, methods, and theories. The series grew out of discussions with faculty at the School of Transborder Studies at Arizona State University, where an interdisciplinary emphasis is being placed on transborder and transnational dynamics.

Matthew Garcia, Series Editor, School of Historical, Philosophical, and Religious Studies; and Director of Comparative Border Studies

For a list of titles in the series, see the last page of the book.

Salvadoran Imaginaries

Mediated Identities and Cultures of Consumption

CECILIA M. RIVAS

RUTGERS UNIVERSITY PRESS

NEW BRUNSWICK, NEW JERSEY, AND LONDON

LIBRARY OF CONGRESS CATALOGING-IN-PUBLICATION DATA
Rivas, Cecilia M., 1978–
Salvadoran imaginaries : mediated identities and cultures of consumption / Cecilia M. Rivas.
  pages cm — (Latinidad : transnational cultures in the United States)
  Includes bibliographical references and index.
  ISBN 978–0–8135–6462–3 (hardcover : alk. paper) — ISBN 978–0–8135–6461–6 (pbk. : alk. paper) — ISBN 978–0–8135–6463–0 (e-book)
  1. Salvadoran Americans—Social conditions. 2. El Salvador—Emigration and immigration. 3. United States—Emigration and immigration. 4. Transnationalism. I. Title.
  E184.S15R58 2014
  305.868'7284073—dc23   2013021943

A British Cataloging-in-Publication record for this book is available from the British Library.

Visit our website: http://rutgerspress.rutgers.edu

Manufactured in the United States of America

For my family

CONTENTS

ACKNOWLEDGMENTS

This book is about connections in a rapidly changing society, and about the meanings of a community that aspires to be culturally and economically borderless. Even across significant distances, the contradictory comfort and anxiety developed around these connections characterizes the many facets of contemporary El Salvador. The transnational is, in turn, constitutive of national imaginaries.

There are many individuals in El Salvador and the United States whose encouragement and generosity helped me appreciate these connections and realize this project. First, I have many people to thank in El Salvador, especially the journalists, call center employees, and other interviewees whose insights and experiences are so important to this book. Although in most cases I cannot mention them by their real names or identify them directly with their workplaces, these individuals should know that their assistance and kindness is deeply appreciated, and that I learned a great deal from our conversations. Thank you for allowing me access to your places of work.

I began this project while at the Department of Ethnic Studies at the University of California, San Diego. I thank Charles L. Briggs for his support and generous advice. I am grateful to Ramón A. Gutiérrez, Daniel Hallin, Jane Rhodes, Denise Silva, and Elana Zilberg, for their thoughtfulness and guidance. I thank Faye Caronan, Tere Ceseña, Monika Gosin, Julie Hua, Ashley Lucas, and Gina Opinaldo for their friendship. In many, sometimes indirect, ways they have contributed something to this book. I thank Jackie Griffin for staying in touch and for her sound advice.

I am certain that this would be a very different book without the influence and encouragement of many wonderful colleagues at the University of California, Santa Cruz. For sharing valuable ideas and carefully reading and discussing various parts of this book, I am deeply grateful to Rosa-Linda Fregoso, Norma Klahn, Olga Nájera-Ramírez, Marcia Ochoa, Cat Ramírez, Felicity A. Schaeffer, and Pat Zavella. I thank Marcia and Felicity for their memorable welcome to Santa Cruz, and for our many ongoing conversations. I thank Jonathan Fox for sharing countless interesting articles and other information about migrants in Mexico. I thank many colleagues and friends whose kindness, good humor, and exemplary scholarship always inspire me: Mark Anderson, Gabriela Arredondo, Neda Atanasoski, Cindy Cruz, Guillermo Delgado, Sylvanna Falcón, Adrián Félix, Dana Frank, Shannon Gleeson, Herman Gray, Beth Haas, Sri Kurniawan, Gina Langhout, Flora Lu, Lourdes Martínez-Echazábal, Eduardo Mosqueda, Héctor Perla, Juan Poblete, Jennifer Poole, and Megan Thomas. I thank all the members of the Popular Cultures and the Bodies, Borders, and Violence Research Clusters at UCSC for our enthusiastic, productive meetings. I thank Alessandra Álvares, Jill Esterás, Annette Marines, Dana Rohlf, and Marianna Santana for their support.

I thank Wanda Alarcón, Gloria Chacón, Tania Cruz Salazar, and Sarah B. Horton for their friendship and for many interesting conversations that helped me think through some of the ideas discussed in this book. A very special thank you to Susan Bibler Coutin, Robin DeLugan, Cecilia Menjívar, Ellen Moodie, Ana Patricia Rodríguez, and Elana Zilberg for their generous advice and their inspiring scholarship on El Salvador.

I have greatly benefited from insightful comments and questions at several professional meetings and other events. In particular, I thank Noel B. Salazar, Mimi Sheller, and Alan Smart for their comments on my work on call centers as part of a panel at the American Anthropological Association meeting (2009). I also thank the Center for Cultural Studies and the Chicano/Latino Research Center (both at UCSC) for the opportunities to present early versions of chapter 4. I thank Ray Cummings for his perceptive comments on an early draft of the manuscript.

I thank Carlos Vélez-Ibáñez for his interest in this book project, and Lisa Boyajian, Marilyn Campbell, and especially Leslie Mitchner at Rutgers University Press for their expert, reassuring guidance throughout this process. I thank Gary Von Euer for copyediting and helping me refine the manuscript. I appreciate the anonymous reviewer's close engagement with my manuscript and the suggestions that helped me strengthen it.

Several institutes and research units supported my fieldwork in El Salvador and the completion of this project. While I was at the University of California, San Diego, grants from the Institute for International, Comparative and Area Studies (IICAS) and California Cultures in Comparative Perspective (CCCP) supported my research trips to El Salvador. The Center for the Study of Race and Ethnicity (CSRE) supported me through a research assistantship. The UCSD Division of Social Sciences and the Center for Comparative Immigration Studies (CCIS) also provided important support. At the University of California, Santa Cruz, I thank the Division of Social Sciences for supporting my research through a Junior Faculty Research Grant, a Social Sciences Division Research Award, and a Non-Tenured Faculty Development Award.

I am very grateful to many friends and family for their good wishes and for their willingness to share important information, news, laughs, and meals during my stays in San Salvador at different stages of this project. My greatest thanks in this journey will always be to my parents, Maribel and Rafael, and to my brothers, for their example, their support, and for the times we have spent together.

Salvadoran Imaginaries

Introduction

Imaginaries of Transnationalism

At the Houston airport the flight will not board for another hour. Behind me, two women talk about their reasons for going to El Salvador. "We only go for problems. We have come because we have problems, and return to solve some other problem," one of them says. "I don't hear anyone say they are going there to take a great vacation," she adds dryly. The other woman chuckles in agreement. Everybody has "problems," and according to her, physical distance from El Salvador does not make them disappear.

Seated across from me is a well-dressed young woman. I will call her Claudia. She is traveling by herself, and two seats away from her a small group of women wait. A few men—their husbands or other male relatives—are standing apart, talking. Looking around the lounge, one of the women exclaims, "¡Cómo se parecen todos los salvadoreños!" ("How alike all Salvadorans seem!"). She continues, talking about how easy it is for her to tell who is a Salvadoran, presumably not just in this San Salvador–designated waiting lounge, but anywhere, because of a characteristic friendliness or happiness. "Es que se les nota una alegría," she says of her compatriots. To make sure she does not think I am some sort of unpatriotic stranger, I look up from my book and smile at her comment. "And do you live here in Houston?" she asks Claudia.

To initiate a conversation, there are two questions one could ask in this (or any) airport lounge where travelers await their flight to El Salvador: "¿Dónde vive?" and "¿Hasta dónde va?" The first, "Where do you live?" refers to place of residence, now usually in an urban area of the United States; the second question, "How far are you going?" to the final destination in El Salvador after a long day of travel and arrival at Comalapa Airport. The final point of arrival is usually the *cantón* (rural village) or city that most Salvadoran migrants left years, even decades, ago. These apparently simple questions layer individual orientations, memories, subjectivities, and migration histories onto the map of El Salvador. This flight between Houston and San Salvador is one of many daily connections to a circuit of airports and global airline routes. The luggage carried on these flights is a bulky mixture of gifts and necessities, reflecting consumption habits and acquired obligations.

A third question often overheard in these lounge conversations is "How long have you been here?" a sometimes not-too-subtle yet necessary question that tries to establish a timeframe for transnational migration and life in the United States. "Ya me hice ciudadana" ("I have become a citizen"), Claudia replies to her new acquaintances. Now we can understand more about her—she has been in the United States long enough, for about ten years, and has become a naturalized U.S. citizen. She is traveling to El Salvador to pick up her mother and return with her to the United States on Monday, a very short weekend trip. "I'm sure she's all packed and ready by now," she tells us, visibly content and with anticipation. Her mother is to spend four months with her in Texas. Within minutes Claudia and the women exchange their phone numbers in El Salvador, and plan to attend a church group meeting together on Saturday; the women and their husbands are traveling to attend a celebration related to this group. Their plan may or may not materialize, but many networks develop in this way— through negotiation, chance meetings, common destinations, and possibilities for mutual exchange (Menjívar 2000).

As I sit waiting for this flight to San Salvador, preparing for a four-week research trip and the Christmas holiday with my family, I am unavoidably drawn into the everyday lives of my travel companions at this gate—Salvadorans who negotiate the spaces between El Salvador and the United States, whose documents attest to their citizenship and residency status, allowing them to fly between these countries, between obligations to family, work, friends, and "problems" in El Salvador. These situations and spaces gather importance in the construction of a sense of place and belonging. For example, the abstract form of Salvadoranness expressed here by the woman sitting near me—be it happiness or another common trait or experience—is somehow understood by those of us waiting for this flight. Although obviously this trait is not uniquely Salvadoran, it quickly establishes some ideas around which "we" (the Salvadoran passengers waiting for a flight) engage in conversation—about where we are going, where we have been, and who we are.

There are many differences, similarities, and parallels in the lived experiences of transnationalism across the Americas, from El Salvador to other countries in the region. In many cases, migration from Latin America to the United States is rooted in the political violence, exclusion, and deep economic crises that have affected the region. A closer look at migration from Latin America to the United States reveals multiple and shifting identities linked to class, ethnicity, language, and context of arrival among migrants, a group that despite its diverse origins across the hemisphere has been (for various social and economic reasons) homogenized as "Hispanic" or "Latino" in the United States (Dávila 2001; Dávila 2008). The migration paths and diasporic histories of Mexicans, Dominicans, and other peoples of the Caribbean and Central and South America are emblematic of the cultural diversity, struggles, and challenges of the region. The richness of Latin American migration inflects the specific Salvadoran experience—in El Salvador and in the destinations and new homes of migrants—and our understandings and representations of this transnational imaginary. Migrant connections to countries of origin signify the enduring historical significance of nationalism and national identity for many Latin Americans (Miller 2006, 201). This is especially important as migrants pursue dual and even multiple citizenships, strategically and by necessity.

In addition, this persistent imagination of connection and national loyalty shapes perceptions of the effects of migration in the "home" countries of migrants. Latin American governments acknowledge their economic dependence on remittances, and try to find ways to channel these flows of income into productive investments and consumption (in contemporary El Salvador, the view that dependence on remittances from abroad makes people in the home country lazy and unproductive also plays into these campaigns). Many Latin American states have an interest and role in engaging and incorporating migrants for cultural, political, and economic reasons (Calderón Chelius 2004; Flores 2009; Schmidt Camacho 2008). Media portrayals (for example, in newspapers, television, and film) play a role in the representation and constitution of migrant lives and public opinion (Santa Ana 2002). Along with other consumer products, food, civic celebrations, and crafts, these representations of migration are a vital component of identity. Chronicles and breaking news attract reading publics, shaping opinions, identifications, and understandings of transnational dynamics.

Transnationalism presents inconsistencies of flow, negotiation, and attachment. Analyzing the political economies of home in Caribbean Brooklyn and Native American Minneapolis, Rachel Buff observes: "There exists a social contradiction between nationalist ideas of citizenship and an increasingly transnational economy" (Buff 2001, 13). Transnational imaginaries are contradictory and seem to make sense in specific contexts. They are formed and converge in important ways: around shared, relational, and sometimes even hemispheric meanings of return and connection to the home country, around debates of the economic and social processes and consequences of migration, and around deep local changes due to globalization. Juan Flores notes the multiple, transformative aspects of migration and return, and how "modern diasporas and diasporic identities are not singular and exclusive, nor limited to a group or individual sense of social placement" (Flores 2009, 16).

Salvadoran Imaginaries

The intertwined narratives of transnational migration described by Claudia and the other travelers are more than fleeting small talk among Salvadoran compatriots at the airport. I have overheard, observed, and frequently participated in these exchanges while at many airports and in other places over several years of traveling between the United States and El Salvador. These exchanges are part of a larger conversation and social memory, ranging from competing expressions of solidarity and national pride, to hopes and aspirations, to rapid social change and widespread perceptions of post–civil war insecurity in El Salvador. In sharing these experiences, Salvadorans become part of a social imaginary, defined by Charles Taylor as a "common understanding" that "enables, through making sense of, the practices of a society" (Taylor 2002, 91). The concepts of transnational imaginary, social imaginary (Taylor 2002), or migrant imaginary (Schmidt Camacho 2008) are employed to emphasize how practices of media, consumption, and migration are co-constitutive in unevenly producing certain (unequal) global subjects. People engage transnational practices, and become their subjects, in different ways and with particular expectations.

Shared experiences and transnational practices are part of the imaginary, of this "constructed landscape of collective aspirations" (Appadurai 1996, 31). The imagination has a significant role in contemporary social life, as Arjun Appadurai notes: "The imagination is now central to all forms of agency, is itself a social fact, and is the key component of the new global order" (Appadurai 1996, 31). Gustavo Morello writes about two productive imaginaries in Latin America, engaged in a struggle for mutual recognition: the imaginary of elites that have shaped Latin American institutions and versions of Western modernity, and the imaginary of popular and ordinary life. Individually, neither can provide a complete "best account" of Latin American modernity (Morello 2007, 637).

Examined together, the competing imaginaries of the elite institutions and of their popular counterparts can provide us with an understanding of their possibilities as spaces of negotiation, and of why—and how—a constructed landscape is able to accommodate so many apparently contradictory aspirations and versions of national belonging. However, we must be aware and critique the use of "high" and "low" as fixed categories, since "to think in this way is to rigidify the cultural field, eliminating whatever is transitional, hybrid, multiple, or ambiguous" (Rowe and Schelling 1991, 193). Instead, we must analyze the presumed hierarchies of these terms. The Salvadoran imaginary is shared by a large group of people, through direct exchanges, in mediated news accounts, and in multiple other sites of representation, work, consumption, and identity formation. Everyday, ordinary practices—like waiting and talking at an airport lounge or exchanging phone numbers with the idea of meeting again—structure these imaginaries as they link these dispersed Salvadoran communities.

The assumption that transnationalism and economic globalization create a field of equal and available opportunities and market choices for those involved in these processes begs scrutiny. Not everyone participates in these processes equally. Global economic structures place El Salvador as a peripheral and marginal nation, dependent on migration and foreign investment as a way into participation and incorporation in the global economy (Booth, Wade, and Walker 2006; Landolt 1997). Globalization, in its economic, cultural, and social dimensions, broadly indicates "contradictory transformations—in economic organization, social regulation, political governance, and ethical regimes—that are felt to have profound though uncertain, confusing, or contradictory implications for human life" (Ong and Collier 2005, 3). El Salvador becomes globalized in relationship to other countries, particularly the United States, through cultures of migration, consumption, and labor needs, such as service work. Labor and migration have been transformative forces in the Salvadoran social landscape for decades, and especially since the unprecedented displacement of people during the 1980s civil war. As a "corporative regime" (Escobar 2007, 60), El Salvador depends on emigration and on maintaining emotional and cultural connections with *salvadoreños en el exterior* ("Salvadorans abroad") as a strategy for encouraging or even guaranteeing the flow of remittances and nostalgic links to the home country.

Migrant aspirations and portrayals of the "American Dream" in the media, consumption in shopping malls, and service work (such as bilingual call centers) are facets of Salvadoran transnationalism and, importantly, highlight exclusions from this process. Transnationalism is a productive and contradictory process that is visible in some areas of contemporary El Salvador, where cultures of increasing consumerism, emigration, and dependence on remittances (Rodríguez 2004), along with the 2001 dollarization of the economy and use of English in transnational workplaces, have become features of postwar identities and everyday life.

These sites of the Salvadoran imaginary are spaces of interpellation, where people learn to self-regulate and become subjects. While Salvadorans abroad are connected and claimed to the nation through media portrayals of migration, Salvadorans who live within the geographic borders of the Salvadoran state are imagined as "consumers and citizens" (García Canclini 2001) of San Salvador's shopping malls; others are envisioned as a workforce of bilingual, transnational, and exportable voices, as call center training and hiring practices suggest. In postwar El Salvador, these experiences are socially situated and shaped by economic development strategies, technological advances, and ideas about the linguistic and professional capacities of Salvadorans.

In the news portrayals and sites of representation analyzed in this book, "who is Salvadoran" is not simply a legal question of citizenship, place of birth, nationality law, and passport eligibility, as might be defined in the constitution and immigration legislation of El Salvador. Beyond this identification with a political and legal system, the stories of migrants, consumers, and English-fluent Salvadorans become legible in a system of representation and in a culture that has developed and sustains this transnational imaginary, shaping our knowledge and expectations about these processes and practices of globalization. In this regard, mediated identities become important as we read across texts and places and the people involved in them; we move from media to mediations (Martín-Barbero 1993). As Roger Silverstone indicates, "we should be thinking about media as a process, as a process of mediation" (Silverstone 1999, 13). What does mediation do, and what are the implications of this process? "Mediation involves the movement of meaning from one text to another, from one discourse to another, from one event to another. It involves the constant transformation of meanings, both large scale and small, significant and insignificant, as media texts and texts about media circulate in writing, in speech and audiovisual forms, and as we, individually and collectively, directly and indirectly, contribute to their production" (Silverstone 1999, 13).

Mediated identities encompass a range of expressions of "who is Salvadoran." These expressions are complex, and present as transformative definers of belonging in various narratives of culture, patriotism, suffering, employment opportunity, and movement across borders. Migrant narratives are key. From the news stories of emigrants who remember their country of origin with nostalgia and a sense of idealization, to the stories of migrants who face danger near the railroad tracks of southern Mexico and of deported and repatriated bodies, these are important instances where Salvadoran migrants become newsworthy in Salvadoran media despite their physical absence from the country's territory. The characterizations are sometimes celebratory and often intense, in that they convey strong feelings regarding the circumstances and effects of migration.

Via interviews with newspaper reporters and close readings of journalistic texts, I examine and interpret the meaning and function of these newspaper portrayals. This analysis is important because it reveals both a perception of why emigration from El Salvador is necessary, and a sense of how journalists, through their work, actively participate in this production of meanings around a dynamic and mediated culture of migration. Migration is presented as a daily news topic to Salvadoran readers; in turn they are a public that is brought into being as part of the social production and circulation of news. In these journalistic spaces, the Salvadoran public is not simply reading about reflections of what the reality and "true life" of migrants might be. They are, instead, assumed to be an essential and interactive part of the migratory process, reading about their friends, relatives, and compatriots, almost constituting a conversation similar to the one that I participated in within the relative comfort of the airport lounge in Houston.

In this mediated world, the Salvadoran public is immersed in perceptions of change—that is, in a powerful idea about the transformation of El Salvador, its postwar relationship to Salvadorans in the United States, and the contradictory meanings about the elusive opportunities that exist (or, at least, are imagined to exist) within and beyond the country's borders. Migration is widely acknowledged as the principal way to expand life and employment opportunities, and as a fundamental source of income for many Salvadoran households. This view is not merely anecdotal: it is voiced and documented in a growing body of insightful scholarship on El Salvador that discusses the migratory phenomenon historically, sociologically, and in contemporary ethnographic studies (Machuca 2010).

This book examines the Salvadoran imaginary and the profound social changes and aspirations involved in the construction of a culturally and economically borderless nation. It reads across multiple layers: representations made possible by transformative uses of communication technologies, literary and journalistic narratives of migratory experiences, longing for and rejection of the idea of transnational belonging, and the relationship between private and public spaces in recent Salvadoran history. In large part, this book is inspired by and anchored in the idea and relevance of everyday practices, and by the patience and resilience that is often required of common Salvadorans in connection to the national and transnational spaces they aspire to inhabit. Furthermore, the postwar period continues to reference an uncertain temporality: the often-confusing attempt at categorizing a "before" and "after" in a history of violence and insecurity that includes the civil war and the decades after the 1992 Peace Accords. In this regard Beatriz Cortez suggests that while the term *postwar* refers to the end of civil wars in El Salvador, Guatemala, and Nicaragua (thus pointing to specific national, even temporal, contexts) the idea of a postwar sensibility refers to something beyond defining this particular historical moment, and intends to draw a contrast with the sensibility of the revolutionary projects that circulated throughout the isthmus during the twentieth century (Cortez 2010, 23–25). The civil war years, the undemocratic decades that preceded them, and the aftermath of the Peace Accords continue to inflect politics, cultural production, and contentious memories in many countries of the region.

Focusing on the intertwined effects of inclusion and exclusion from transnational processes, I analyze how everyday and at times seemingly disparate sites of experience and media representation—customer service call centers, news reporting about migration, shopping malls, and literature—produce and commercialize the paradoxical idea of connection accentuated by distance in contemporary El Salvador. This idea acknowledges the complex relationship between narratives of migration, mobility, expressions of nationalism, consumption, and the promotion of postwar foreign investment. In most cases the realities of physical distance—in migration and outsourced service work—accentuate the needs for connection. Salvadoran imaginaries are constituted within this complexity, and their meanings are shaped as part of a culture in the narratives of the continuous and the ordinary that make up everyday practices. I argue that this connection accentuated by distance is a constitutive characteristic of Salvadoran transnational identity and that the transnational is, in turn, constitutive of the national. Furthermore, this book explores how some people and places come into representation as part of a legitimated narrative of the transnational and Salvadoran imaginary, while other sectors remain unacknowledged and excluded from this condition.

This is the story of how 20 percent of Salvadorans live outside El Salvador, a country of approximately six million people, and of how media and state institutions represent and seek to maintain the symbolic and economic significance of emigrant loyalty. It is the story of ordinary Salvadorans in the postwar period, of the necessity of their search for opportunities and a better life in the United States, or—for a relatively small group of bilingual Salvadorans—a job opportunity in the call centers. For others it is about a search for secure spaces of social life that, in a context of generalized and diffuse violence, seem to exist only in consumption and privately owned shopping malls. The particular significance of these sites is shaped as part of a larger culture in the narratives of everyday life and media. They are connected and emblematic of the interactions people collectively engage in as part of daily life in a globalized world: Internet and telephone communication, consumption of daily news and commodities, and the imagination of community.

In this book I present interpretations and readings of media, images, and events, examining how they are contextualized and layered, and how they come to make sense in constituting Salvadoran imaginaries. I examine news circulation and media portrayals of migration in the "Departamento 15" section of the high-circulation Salvadoran daily newspaper *La Prensa Gráfica* and the "En el camino" ("On the Road" or "On the Journey") section of the digital newspaper *El Faro*. I analyze the novel *El asco: Thomas Bernhard en San Salvador* (1997), by Horacio Castellanos Moya, as an example of literary production and as a representation of the emotional (and cynical) dimensions of Salvadoran postwar culture and sensibilities. I discuss hiring and training practices in the call center sector in San Salvador. This relatively new and dynamic sector "is a perfect example of globalization in El Salvador," as a friend in San Salvador noted. I also trace the significance of spaces of consumption in San Salvador, especially shopping malls. These varied research sites are linked as they coexist, intersect, and highlight forms of citizenship, belonging, and participation; they are also connected as sites of particular forms of exclusion and inclusion in transnational El Salvador. Clearly, the meanings of these sites and representations are not closed or fixed. I analyze and interpret these news stories, spaces, and media images in relationship to each other, as moments in time, and in relationship to broader discourses of nation-building, while mindful that images have important, central purposes as part of research (Aguayo and Roca 2005).

How I present this work is grounded and shaped by my relationship, subject position, and access to this field, with the awareness that El Salvador has changed since I lived there and continues to change, and as a Salvadoran who now lives and works in the United States. I lived and attended school in San Salvador and first moved away to attend college in Maryland in the mid-1990s. Education has been an important part of my experience in the United States. In 2002 I began my graduate studies in California, and I traveled to El Salvador whenever possible, four times between 2004 and 2006. The length of each research trip to El Salvador varied; in sum, during those years I spent approximately ten months in San Salvador.

During 2005 and 2006 I conducted interviews with human resources managers and customer service agents employed at several call centers in San Salvador. I interviewed journalists who covered migration issues for *La Prensa Gráfica*. I conducted research at the newspaper's archives, and throughout my time in San Salvador I (or one of my relatives) purchased it daily, in time constructing my own archive of migration-related news, call center employment advertisements, and other relevant news and editorials. While in San Salvador in 2005 and 2006 (and in more recent, shorter trips in 2011 and 2012), I conducted my observations at the shopping malls. I chose three malls to focus on, based on their location and my academic interest in their history and architectural features—although I could have visited many other shopping malls in San Salvador.

As someone who grew up in San Salvador, I had a good knowledge of the city and shared in a social memory of many political and cultural events. I returned to a welcome situation where I was carrying out research while living close to my family after nearly a decade of living in different cities of the United States and other countries. They, along with the interviewees, became part of a world of interesting and revealing connections between research about a society and everyday social life. Friends sometimes shared their contacts if possible. For example, a former neighbor and one of my close friends knew people who worked at call centers; both were valuable contacts during my research. In other cases, I telephoned the call centers after seeing their advertisements in the employment section of a newspaper, and made contacts without being introduced by someone else; on several occasions this resulted in an interview. In the case of my interviews with the journalists, from the first time I called the newspaper they were open to being interviewed, and the person in charge of *Colecciones* ("Collections") allowed me to access the newspaper's archives.

Reflecting on the trajectory of this project, I am grateful that many people opened their doors to share their impressions, their concerns, their optimism, and their knowledge with me. The world of the jobs and careers of some of my friends and acquaintances became fascinating, although I understood when sometimes my interviewees preferred not to reveal too much about themselves. With this in mind, I have changed the names of the people I interviewed, and in most cases, to maintain confidentiality I do not identify them directly with their workplaces or with specific call centers. I conducted most of the interviews in Spanish, and all translations into English of the interviews, Salvadoran news articles and documents, and excerpts from the novel *El asco* are mine. Translations into English of other material are also mine, unless otherwise noted.

Research Sites and Organization of the Book

As spaces where Salvadorans come together and make sense of globalization and what surrounds them daily, the call center, the mall, and the newspaper open up new ways of recognizing and engaging the transnational field. Yet while some people can "freely" participate in these places, these are also sites of constraint and exclusion. This is why I juxtapose and examine them closely, asking how and why some media representations, work cultures, languages, and practices constituted in these sites have become part of the dominant narrative of globalization and modernity, while others are marginalized.

In arranging these chapters, I have considered the differences and convergences of each site—how each in its own distinctive way shows a facet of Salvadoran transnationalism, institutional efforts, uneven globalization, and the predominance of powerful narratives of identity, belonging, and exclusion. I begin the book with a discussion of media institutions and news coverage of migration, because the story of this intersection of social processes and forces has much to tell about the construction and imagination of El Salvador as a nation without borders. In chapter 1, I discuss the context and creation of "Departamento 15" and the processes of news production, circulation, and representation of Salvadoran migrants in *La Prensa Gráfica*. The meaning of "Departamento 15" exceeds the political project of Salvadoran media and political institutions. This fifteenth department is not simply a question of a borderless and viable political map for the twenty-first-century state, but something that is both more metaphorical and more tangible. The texts and representations in the mediated space called "Departamento 15" delineate greater cultural, economic, and emotional attachments as part of the "imagined community" (Anderson 1991) of transnational El Salvador, what one of the journalists I interviewed described as "finding the Salvadoran in the story, even if this person is very far away."

I analyze media texts in order to discuss inclusion and exclusion from transnationalism, and the notion that the public of this section takes on its own character, addressed as a national entity. The "Departamento 15" section was first published in El Salvador in 2000, and it is dedicated to news about the various Salvadoran communities outside the country (including major cities in the United States, Canada, Europe, and elsewhere). *La Prensa Gráfica*'s Internet edition circulates beyond the borders of El Salvador and the Central American isthmus, demonstrating how traditional ideologies of news production are shifting as transnational communities of readers, websites, and other innovations in this imaginary gain importance and affect our relationship to news.

Apart from serving as the well-known title of a news section, "Departamento 15" has multiple meanings in my research. The news section re-spatializes El Salvador by creating a transnational "fifteenth department," a complement to the country's fourteen departments (administrative units similar to states). "Departamento 15" symbolizes the Salvadorans who are included in this diasporic space, whether they like it and are aware of it or not. This additional department thus alludes to a political-social-cultural identity that is linked to (or, at least, within reach of) the Salvadoran state and interested media institutions. Via close readings of advertisements and articles from "Departamento 15," I examine in chapter 1 the mediation and circulation of this identity project.

In chapter 2, I analyze the consequences of social and political processes on the migrant body, in particular the invisible violence of family separation and the devastating bodily injuries suffered by Central American migrants in southern Mexico. In contrast to the portrayals of inclusion and patriotism highlighted in the previous chapter, here I focus on the narratives and images of suffering that might create subjects worthy of reclaiming, at least symbolically and sometimes in reality, for the mediated spaces of the nation.

In addition to my analysis of a selection of stories about the process of repatriating injured Salvadoran migrants from Chiapas, Mexico to El Salvador as featured in "Departamento 15," I also examine the work of a team of journalists and press photographers from *El Faro* (the first Latin American digital newspaper) and their news section "En el camino," a project that documents migration and the harsh conditions Central American migrants encounter in southern Mexico—ranging from robberies and accidents on trains, to abuses of young girls and women. In these media images the Guatemala-Mexico border becomes a material and dangerous reality. Based on this journalistic work and on the portrayals of Central American migrants, I argue that the representational space of the *transmigrante* (the migrant in transit through Mexican territory) becomes significant to the construction of El Salvador as a continually violent place, even in the absence of civil war. I also discuss an online forum where readers of "Departamento 15" comment and engage in dialogue about the relationship between violence and their own decisions to emigrate. These narratives and memories of violent migration continue to inform the formation of the in-between, transnational space inhabited by Salvadoran migrants during (and beyond) their multiple border crossings.

The first two chapters of this book demonstrate how the texts, images, and representations produced by these media institutions delineate greater cultural, patriotic, and emotional attachments as part of the imaginary of transnational El Salvador. I focus on themes and ideas such as nation, connection, sacrifice, and family separation to illustrate how imaginaries are shaped and produced by narratives that become common or normalized as part of Salvadoran society. Readers might see themselves in some of the news portrayals while not in others—this is not just a matter of omitting (or simply censoring) news stories of Salvadorans who are not "model" or "ideal," but of negotiating complex meanings even around journalistic representations of poverty, undocumented migration, deportation, and gang violence.

In this regard, print media, the written word, and portrayals of return and feeling for the nation are critical to our understanding of the "hold" of the Salvadoran imaginary—"the novel and the newspaper fostered imagined communities through their integrative relations to time and space" (Shohat and Stam 1994, 101–102). Chapter 3 offers a close reading of the novel *El asco: Thomas Bernhard en San Salvador* (1997), by Horacio Castellanos Moya, as an example of literary production and a representation of the emotional dimension of Salvadoran culture, the national imaginary, and identity since the late 1990s. I examine the main character's return to El Salvador and his transgressive (and, to some, offensive) *asco* ("disgust") for Salvadoran society in order to discuss the intertwined narratives of disdain, reluctant return, nostalgia, and sense of obligation (however ambivalent) to family and friends that are central in *El asco*. Clashing ideas such as transgression, nostalgia, and disgust speak to the less idealistic aspects of postwar and contemporary sensibilities, linking the novel to discourses about migration and the possibilities for El Salvador such as those previously described in the newspapers. This analysis unveils a paradoxical and provocative notion: that disgust is an emotion which is foundational to certain artistic expressions, critiques of patriotism, and extensive (and deep) collective feelings within the Salvadoran national imaginary.

Edgardo Vega, the protagonist of *El asco*, returns to El Salvador to bury his mother and try to sell her house. After eighteen years of living in Canada, Vega feels tremendously disgusted by his country of birth. This is not, I argue, a simple feeling expressed lightly or in an offhand manner. Rather, disgust in this novel is deeply rooted, felt, and brought on in relation to all aspects of Salvadoran culture in their complexity and fascination. In this chapter I analyze the way Vega tells us about his disgust, this moral, visceral, bodily emotion. I address the ambivalences around national belonging and connection to El Salvador, including the question of how different sites and situations present us with paradoxical instances of connection accentuated by distance. *El asco* grapples with the commonly held notion that certain aspects of Salvadoran history and culture, such as food, places (for example, childhood home and tourist attractions), and ways of socializing are invariably productive of migrant nostalgia. Vega mocks these feelings of nostalgia, actively differentiating himself from (and feeling superior to) those who ache for El Salvador and for memories of "better times." I argue that he certainly remembers, and his disgust is marked by a sense of himself as an estranged Salvadoran, someone who remains paradoxically connected by this profound aversion to his country of birth.

Along with the "Departamento 15" and migration chapters, my analysis of *El asco* points to the diversity of migratory and transnational experiences, understandings of class, and marginalization discussed throughout this book. Since chapter 3 analyzes literary representations of emigration, detachment, and repulsion along with the "aesthetic of cynicism" (Cortez 2010) as a critique of neoliberal and revolutionary projects in postwar El Salvador, it is fitting to place this chapter before my discussion of call centers in chapter 4. In some cases, bilingual agents in the call centers might operate precisely within some of the rapid social changes, situations of undesired return to El Salvador, constraints, commercialization, and expectations of contemporary Salvadoran society that the novel identifies and critiques.

Chapter 4 discusses hiring and training practices in the call centers of San Salvador. As an example of global labor flexibility, foreign investment, connectivity, and technology, this sector also highlights El Salvador's locality as a place that must be strategically and continually imagined, branded, and situated as attractive to foreign investors. I was initially drawn to this idea, and to researching this sector, when I began to hear about this topic in engaged, enthusiastic conversations with friends (and friends of friends) who were job searching in San Salvador during the late 1990s and early 2000s, and to see more frequent job announcements for call center positions in the employment sections of major Salvadoran newspapers. Call centers became more present in the employment opportunities landscape of San Salvador, especially since 2004.

Through my interviews with employees and human resources managers, I provide a snapshot of call center work, a global, mobile industry located in a specific time and place—San Salvador during the first decade of the twenty-first century. This snapshot of employment includes young, middle-class Salvadorans (and those who aspire to belong to this group) who have a good level of education, denoted primarily by their access to English language lessons. This cultural and linguistic capital qualifies them to apply for call center jobs, for which fluency in English is a requirement. Return migrants, among them deportees from the United States, are also part of this sector. The stories and assumptions behind their English-language fluency reveal uneven experiences of language learning and processes of globalization. Through a discussion of hiring and employment practices in the call center, chapter 4 addresses the symbolic aspects of how this sector becomes part of a transnational agenda, emblematic of the ongoing process of deep transformations in the ways Salvadorans relate to service work and to new understandings of globalization, risk, and neoliberalism.

As the research project developed, in the interviews with call center employees I focused more closely on questions of language, hiring, and advertising related to this workplace. These questions allow for a discussion of the relationships among English-language fluency, perceptions of accents and ways of talking, changing work cultures, and the aspirations of young Salvadorans. Put succinctly, the call center is emblematic of the relationship between El Salvador and the United States, and of the complexities of local, urban Salvadoran cultures in relation to globalized consumer cultures. This labor site is one of many versions of the imaginary of El Salvador as a nation without borders. In this discussion, aspirations and a contradictory sense of location gain importance. Critical to my analysis, interviewees expressed mixed, nuanced feelings: an optimistic sense of being inspired and connected to the global as they remained situated and constrained within local conditions. These are signals of an awareness of opportunities that could be available elsewhere; however, staying in El Salvador means adjusting to new structures of flexible labor.

As a form of foreign investment, call centers bring transformative practices of globalization to local conditions. I analyze the interviews with managers as narratives of becoming global, as the call centers "export voices" and value linguistic and technical skills. In addition, I analyze media coverage of call centers in El Salvador, particularly job announcements and articles about this industry that appeared in *La Prensa Gráfica*, as an example of how these sites intersect and are materially connected. In call centers, the problems of faraway callers are resolved with a "Salvadoran touch." They are important and complex sites where narratives and ideas of Salvadoran laborers and a "Salvadoran brand" are constructed and contested nationally and in relation to transnational labor and consumption practices. In the context of El Salvador's postwar social and economic transformations, the branding of the country as attractive for foreign direct investment is intertwined with formations of language ability and outsourced service work. Call centers are not unique to El Salvador, however I argue that they are connected to the Salvadoran transnational imaginary in unique ways that highlight the importance of connection and distance.

Chapter 5 traces the significance of shopping malls in San Salvador and develops the idea of an imaginary of consumer-citizenship within the constraints of insecurity, common understandings of safety, and economic exclusion. Consumption, leisure, and socialization spaces have gained salience as new and recently remodeled shopping malls have altered San Salvador's physical and social landscape. I focus on three shopping malls located in San Salvador and nearby municipalities. In considering these spaces of consumption and leisure, I situate the shopping malls as part of the imagination of the national and the global, where Salvadoran consumers are presented with "choices" that both constrain and liberate. The growth and expansion of shopping malls highlights interesting contradictions in Salvadoran economic conditions. Why are there so many malls in a country where a significant percentage of the population lives in poverty? Who, ideally, shops here? I closely analyze the idea that shopping malls in San Salvador are private spaces with public character, where visitors can consume while temporarily escaping the violence of the streets, an important means by which the nation is currently defined.

A discussion of fear and violence in the social imaginary adds depth to predominant understandings of shopping malls as idealized spaces of social interaction, since the public spaces of the streets and parks are perceived as dangerous. As much as the shopping malls in San Salvador might be spaces for emergent patterns of cosmopolitan consumption, I argue that a greater aspect of their presence in the city is that they are spaces where consumers can envision an escape from violent imaginaries. In the shopping mall, visitors can imagine the fulfillment of all sorts of wishes—window shopping and perhaps even owning things that come from different parts of the world, the experience of global influences and trends within local consumption patterns. Malls can be sites of fixed and calculated exchange, and postmodern sites of shifting identities, tourism, kitsch, the negotiation of taste (Bourdieu 1984), and the commercialization of fragmented subjectivities: "the shopping mall is a distinctive sign of the global dissemination of late capitalist economies" (Friedberg 1993, 111). As part of the transnational imaginary, malls are "socially regulated paths" for the life of things (Appadurai 1986, 17). As this chapter demonstrates, malls are forms of urban development, exclusion, and reconfigurations of the relationship between consumption, cities, and violence. People are free to visit the mall, yet constrained in their ability and means to shop.

Shopping centers are landmarks of the expansion of San Salvador and its surrounding areas. Beyond this striking physical change in the city's skyline, I argue that malls also mark a new way of imagining and (un)bounding urban spaces of citizenship and belonging in postwar El Salvador. The shopping mall which many of us may be familiar with is a generic building type that became popular in North America during the twentieth century (Hardwick 2004; Jacobs 1984). A few shopping malls were built in San Salvador during the late 1960s; some of these have been remodeled as the decades passed. Many more small and medium-sized shopping centers have sprung up since the 1990s. In this chapter I focus on a large mall built in the early 1970s and on two newer, upscale shopping malls—commercial and architectural projects that have gathered greater attention (and foot traffic) since they opened in 2004. My qualitative discussion highlights characteristics and observations I have made in the course of my field research, and the extent to which spaces of consumption constitute and influence social relationships. In the Salvadoran imaginary, consumption becomes part of a discussion of notions of security and modernity, of the mall as a privately owned yet quasi-public space. This imaginary of mall consumption can be productively read against an imaginary of fear and urban violence that visitors to the mall seek to escape, at least temporarily. Street vendors, part of the informal sector, emerge in contrast to this exclusive imaginary. I consider their presence and marginalization not simply as an isolated account of El Salvador's visible economic inequality, but as emblematic of asymmetric and competing notions of public space, legitimacy, and opportunity.

Overall, the chapters are integrated as complementary narratives of mediation, circulation, and the construction of a borderless nation. They present stories of loss, disgust, migration, actual border crossing, strategic opportunities, and consumption. They highlight the complex, productive tensions within the Salvadoran imaginary, and the interaction and constant contestation between people and institutions. Idealized constructions of El Salvador—as a country shaped by the loyalty of migrants, consumer "choices," or strategically located investment opportunities—in the sites I researched make us question hierarchies of power and influence, of who is able to make and circulate these versions of postwar El Salvador. The visibility of this idealized, solid story of openness to transnationalism contrasts with the fragmented, tense migratory experiences of Salvadorans in transit through Mexico, of literary expressions of disgust, and of Salvadorans caught in often-alienating, even marginal, jobs.

As I traveled between El Salvador and the United States, I reflected upon these competing definitions and on my relationship to these narratives as someone who could access and research these sites. I belong in these spaces to different degrees, with freedom, while also with constraints and attachments. The chapters that follow are about media, branding, migration, and the creative remaking (and crossing) of borders in an attempt to encompass multiple stories and imaginaries, a perceived "truth," about Salvadorans. Sometimes the narratives work. Sometimes we even accept that they "make sense" as they seem to successfully explain a reality that satisfies our hunger for daily news or our need to cope with the everyday by establishing parameters of what is normal. And, crucially, they sometimes expose the rifts of millennial, neoliberal El Salvador, reminding us that the Salvadoran imaginary is contingent upon and situated in a shifting moment and place—in this case, a country and a transnational community that can be constantly re-imagined and remade.

1

Tracing the Borderless in "Departamento 15"

"El periodismo es el mejor oficio del mundo" ("Journalism is the greatest trade in the world") read the banner at the top of the website of the Asociación de Periodistas de El Salvador (APES) in 2010. This phrase is borrowed, appropriately, from journalist and novelist Gabriel García Márquez's 1996 address to the assembly of the Inter American Press Association (IAPA).[1]

In his address García Márquez notes several deep transformations of the media landscape that have influenced his beloved *oficio* as he has known it for decades. Chief among them is the emergence of journalism schools throughout Latin America and the profession's increasing reliance on technology—particularly recording devices, which García Márquez refers to as *un loro digital* ("a digital parrot") in his address. In contrast, he mentions that journalists of his generation learned on the job, empirically in newsrooms. They constructed their craft and relied on notepads and excellent listening skills—now replaced by the digital parrot.[2]

In García Márquez's view of a previous era of journalism in the Americas, vocation and passion for the work are presented as the key elements that make this "the greastest trade in the world." Despite this long-standing perception of status, ethics, and respectability in public discourse, it is paradoxical that the work of journalists in contemporary Latin America is dangerous even as most of the region has transitioned from dictatorial regimes to democracy, especially since the 1980s and 1990s. Censorship and other dangerous limitations on press freedoms persist even if sometimes they are not as overt as they were during times of repression and regimes of exception and suspension of constitutional guarantees. "Peace" and "postwar" are sometimes overused and overlapping words in the neoliberal context of Central America, where a growing sense of everyday physical danger and fear

emerge as facets and manifestations of a new subjectivity and sense of individual insecurity. Media sometimes give voice to these subjectivities and the
imaginary of urban fear, even replacing the deficiencies of the state apparatus: "It does not go without saying that the media has started to make up
for the state system—at least in collective imaginaries—which has become
incompetent when it comes to facing corruption and social violence. The
media acts as both the prosecutor who makes accusations and the judge who
responds to the very same charges, since the legal order operates with impunity" (Rotker 2002, 10).

This sense of danger and everyday fear continues to test the passion, ethical
compass, professionalism, and vocation of journalists. The IAPA maintains data
and documentation concerning violence against journalists and restrictions to
freedom of the press in its annual country reports. The 2009 country report for
El Salvador, for instance, highlighted the murder of Spanish-French photojour-
nalist Christian Poveda, who during his time in El Salvador had been working on
La vida loca, a documentary about gangs that operated in some areas of San Salvador.[3] More recently, the IAPA reports have highlighted crimes and censorship
against Honduran and Mexican journalists as they cover the political and social
violence in their countries, violence that is related to drug trafficking, human
rights abuses, and unstable state institutions as it feeds a climate of impunity,
political instability, and insecurity.

In El Salvador, the lack of personal security can be both newsworthy subject and occupational hazard of the reporter's daily work, as much as it is the
preoccupation of the everyday Salvadoran. This has been the case for decades,
particularly since the 1980s civil war. Mark Pedelty unveils this relationship
between terror and newsworthiness in War Stories, his ethnography of foreign
correspondents in El Salvador. Pedelty discusses the work of journalists from
media institutions in the United States and Europe, tracing their relationship
to their work and to the contrasting perspectives of Salvadoran journalists who
had a different social and political connection to their nation's violence. Clearly,
reporters of all nationalities took risks, in part because they knew that it was
important for their professional identity as war correspondents. Pedelty provides us with a sense of narrative time and place, "a place which so fascinates
and horrifies these reporters that many have lingered long beyond 'the story.' It
is a space within which they have developed their identities as Salvador reporters" (Pedelty 1995, 22; emphasis original).[4]

The Salvadoran civil war ended in 1992 and international media attention
turned to other important conflicts—Bosnia, Rwanda, the Middle East. However, something had shifted within Salvadoran national media culture and society. This shift includes the ways in which media institutions not only report
on, but also produce and commercialize a postwar transnational imaginary. I

examine how the transition from war to postwar along with transformations in the Salvadoran state and society impacted print news media's coverage of Salvadoran communities abroad, especially in the United States. Via close readings of the section "Departamento 15," I examine media representations and how the Salvadoran daily *La Prensa Gráfica* constructs Salvadorans as model transnational citizens in the global division of labor. This primary concern with media representations and notions of national belonging informs the theoretical approaches and questions I pursue. What are the images that predominate in the construction of this particular narrative of migrant Salvadorans? How has this narrative become newsworthy, and how has it circulated in El Salvador and beyond? What is the nature and function of these representations? How do the journalists of "Departamento 15" report on the lives of Salvadoran emigrants, and how might this be indicative of how this postwar generation of journalists views their profession?

To begin to address the question of postwar journalism, it is important to note that since the 1980s, journalism and communication programs have become increasingly professionalized and more visibly established in Salvadoran universities, for example, in the Universidad Centroamericana "José Simeón Cañas," known as UCA, and the Universidad de El Salvador. The mass media landscape has shifted. Radio had always been an important resource, used by various organizations, the Church of El Salvador among them, in "its criticism of the traditional structures of social and political domination" (Sol Arriaza 1988, 93). Radio stations that had by necessity operated underground during the war (for example, Radio Venceremos among others) moved their transmitters from their undisclosed, secret locations in the remote mountains of Morazán to San Salvador. They explored access to new audiences with commercial formats, which varied considerably from their wartime news and music programming. Now, protest songs from Cuba and South America played alongside Top 40 and adult contemporary hits from the United States (López Vigil 1994; Moodie 2010, 80). New television channels emerged during the 1980s and early in the 1990s, including channels twelve, twenty-one, and thirty-three. Use of the Internet was becoming more common, and *El Faro*, Latin America's first digital newspaper, was founded in San Salvador in 1998. These developments represented a significant diversity in the roles of mass media and added to the variety of programming, editorial practices of news programs, and the postwar media landscape. Since the civil war years, many new (and renewed) media outlets challenged a censored and "weak" news culture, the legacy of a military censorship program instituted in 1955 during the presidency of Colonel José M. Lemus (Alisky 1981, 217; Rockwell and Janus 2003, 35).

Print media, especially newspapers that had been associated with right-wing political ideologies throughout the twentieth century and overtly during the civil war, sought to move away from the perception (sometimes well founded) that they were linked to specific political parties and economic interests in this transition from war to postwar. *El Diario de Hoy* and *La Prensa Gráfica*, newspapers with an estimated average daily circulation of 100,000 each, modernized their newsrooms due to a generational shift and a perceived change in public opinion in the postwar 1990s and into the twenty-first century. Rick Rockwell and Noreene Janus have analyzed the transformations of these major media institutions—these included new and colorful layouts, glossy magazine supplements, and a younger generation of editors and journalists. They refer to these transformations as "newly respun corporatism" (Rockwell and Janus 2003, 30), surface changes that have not altered the fundamental editorial leanings and opinions that continue to characterize Salvadoran media, especially its dominant newspapers. They provide this assessment of the challenges that the region's journalists and media institutions face: "All too often, under the cover of peace accords or masked by the hype that comes with more commercial systems, the media in Central America have only superficially appeared to be changing in ways that would bolster democracy. All is not bleak, however, because progress has been made" (Rockwell and Janus 2003, 11). Discussing the conditions and emergence of watchdog journalism in South America, Silvio Waisbord explores the critical relationship between democracy, multiple coexisting journalisms, and economic/market factors, suggesting that "the relationship of democracy to watchdog reporting is far from simple. . . . Still, political democracy offers better conditions for journalism, opens room to tackle controversial issues red-lined by military censors or vetoed by editors, and makes it possible for reporters to take jabs at state officials without necessarily fearing for their physical integrity" (2000, 64). These assessments of media, news reporting, and transition to democracy in Central and South America raise timely analytical questions about how media institutions can or will become more open to different opinions and topics regarding the social and political future of El Salvador.

In 2006 *La Prensa Gráfica* unveiled further changes in its image: "this redesign is more than a way of diagramming and presenting the pages, that is, it is about the presentation of the new philosophy of *La Prensa Gráfica*, which faces global journalistic challenges in the new information age."[5] Whether changes are merely cosmetic and profit-driven, or part of a novel and deeper global multimedia philosophy, how and why can these media institutions continue to be substantially influential in Salvadoran daily life? Is it enough that they have made visible and sophisticated changes to their print layouts, and especially online editions, by including discussion boards, comments threads, and other forms of engagement with readers on their websites?

In his analysis of television news in the United States, Daniel Hallin notes that the modern concept of journalism and news reporting that presently predominates in many media institutions—as he argues, one that is ready to "take technical knowledge as a model for the reporting of news" (1994, 19)—is relatively recent and closely connected with commercial media in a capitalist system that has emerged since the nineteenth century. In this model of technical knowledge, objectivity as an ideal of news reporting and as the primary claim of the professional journalist becomes a mark of modernity and a staple of editorial independence. This analysis of emerging professionalism tied to strong commercial interests in part describes the media system in El Salvador, although I must add that the situation is more nuanced, complex, and marked by the country's historical remains and specific material conditions. Conservative media form part of an economic and social elite, and thus are resourceful and able to represent their values, aspirations, and opinions as constitutive, accepted "national" opinion and news in this complex media landscape.

The 1990s presented a new, changing media landscape because the country had been substantially transformed, from war in 1980 to the Peace Accords signed in Chapultepec, Mexico, in January 1992. As El Salvador transitioned into the postwar period, the Salvadoran state, United Nations peacekeepers, newly formed political parties, and other actors had a stake in upholding the Salvadoran peace process and its new institutions for nation-building as a success (DeLugan 2012; Dunkerley 1994; Moodie 2010). Also, during this decade, market liberalization was held up as a policy solution to the economic and social challenges that Latin America faced (Levine 1992). In 1990s El Salvador, new market policies encouraged and resulted in the privatization and restructuring of ANTEL (Administración Nacional de Telecomunicaciones, or National Telecommunications Administration) and other public utilities and services (for example, the pension funding system), in addition to banking reform (a privatization process of nationalized banks). On 1 January 2001, during the administration of President Francisco Flores, the "Ley de Integración Monetaria" (Monetary Integration Law) officially permitted the U.S. dollar to circulate freely alongside the Salvadoran currency, the colón, as legal tender in El Salvador. Although the colón, named after Christopher Columbus, had been the official Salvadoran currency since 1892 (Herodier 1997, 36), it was quickly replaced. Soon—that is, within weeks—Salvadoran consumers became accustomed to the new coins and bills, the quarter dollar became the *cora* in the popular pronunciation of Salvadoran speakers, and the U.S. dollar predominated in everyday transactions. In short, what Rockwell and Janus call the "newly respun corporatism" (2003, 30) was not limited to changes in news culture, layout presentation, and music formats at newspapers, radio stations, and other media institutions. It was part of larger shifts in culture, finance, and consumption, and affected these spheres in what seem to be unlikely ways. Since the macroeconomic climate seemed stable and energized by peacetime, the government actively promoted foreign investment.

Looking beyond these borders, many Salvadorans could begin to ask—since this now seemed feasible in the Salvadoran imaginary—if their compatriots, especially the many who had emigrated due to the civil war, would realistically want to return. Since so many of them had fled the country clandestinely during the 1980s, seeking relief from poverty, threats, and political fear, it seemed that nearly every Salvadoran family knew somebody in the United States. Nobody was untouched by the war.

During the 1980s, *El Diario de Hoy* and *La Prensa Gráfica* did not report on this emigration in a consistent, systematic way. The political, economic, and divisive ideological concerns of the conflict absorbed the energies of the war reporters, the political capital of editors and owners, and the logistical resources of these newspapers. The civil war was fought within El Salvador's borders, and sometimes negotiated in centers of power beyond these boundaries. It was fought primarily in remote (and historically forgotten) rural areas of northern and eastern El Salvador, where guerilla warfare and other strategies developed as the war progressed (Binford 1999). A few times—for instance, during the November 1989 *ofensiva*—it was fought in the capital's most exclusive and most marginalized neighborhoods. In part, political ideology and established censorship practices explain the absence of news about emigrants from these conservative publications throughout the 1980s.

Many of the emigrants who lived undocumented lives in the United States were assumed to sympathize with the political left or to be part of a growing solidarity effort in support of the Frente Farabundo Martí para la Liberación Nacional (FMLN). Even if this assumption was not always substantiated, these newspapers avoided drawing attention to the causes of these groups. The efforts of Salvadoran organizations, activists in exile, and their allies in the United States (and other countries) to gain political asylum and other protections drew attention to their causes of international solidarity and respect for human rights of displaced and disappeared Salvadorans (Coutin 2000; Gosse 1996; Perla 2008). While only a small segment of migrants might have been involved in these efforts, this was often a vocal group. Many migrants, however, simply sought to stay away from politics once they left El Salvador. They sought to leave the trauma of war behind and make a living elsewhere, and for this they were simply not considered newsworthy. Emigrant Salvadorans had vanished from the horizon of this media landscape as they crossed the multiple borders that led them to other parts of Central America (for example, Costa Rica and Honduras), Mexico, the United States, Australia, Sweden, and other parts of the world. It is hard to say that in the history of the Salvadoran media system rural, poor, and urban working-class Salvadorans were represented in these newspapers in the first place anyway—"because only 7 percent of the Salvadoran population get information from the newspapers on a daily basis, these publications reflect the concerns of the nation's elite" (Rockwell and Janus 2003, 41).

Is it possible that the media system had now shifted at least a bit, to be able to include Salvadoran communities abroad as part of its everyday news? Would these emigrants return, at least symbolically? What would El Salvador look like then? And here, tracing along these questions, is where one story of representation, commercialization, *La Prensa Gráfica*, and "Departamento 15" as a section begins.

A Story of Representation: Covering Our People Abroad

"Departamento 15" has multiple meanings in my research: primarily I discuss it as a space of media representations and the name of a news section about Salvadoran migrants, published in print and online by *La Prensa Gráfica*. "Departamento 15" is also a fluid space of people and the things that matter to them, an ethnoscape beyond the pages of the newspaper, productive of meanings, cultures, and materialities about transnational El Salvador, "a virtual imagined community of sorts, conceptualized by transnational communication networks" (Rodríguez 2005, 20). The phrase itself is a reference to the fourteen departments (the political divisions) of El Salvador; it even has a nice ring to it when said slowly in Spanish—Departamento Quince. The other fourteen departments of El Salvador are not officially or popularly referred to in this numerical manner (unlike, for example, regions or zones in other parts of Latin America). Departments in El Salvador are named after place-names from the pre-Columbian era (Cuscatlán), Catholic saints introduced during the conquest and colonial period (Santa Ana, San Miguel, San Vicente, San Salvador), post-independence Central American leaders (Morazán), and modern aspirations and ideas (La Libertad, La Unión, La Paz—liberty, union, peace). Whether I categorize them intentionally and neatly or not, these names stand as markers in this landscape, evoking moments in Salvadoran history. "Departamento 15" seems like an especially appropriate name for this emerging and undefined space of migrant transnational El Salvador. It is a somewhat "messy" space that "we," the Salvadoran public brought into representation, cannot fully take for granted. It breaks with conventions of the names of places within the modern, territorially integral nation, while it also acknowledges something special about the numerical continuity that links fourteen departments to this otherwise unnamed fifteenth space.

"Departamento 15" symbolizes the Salvadorans who, whether they like it or not, are included in this diasporic space, as an additional department, thus alluding to a political-social identity linked to (or, at least, within reach of) the Salvadoran state and its institutions. I argue that "Departamento 15" means more than this political and economic project of the Salvadoran state. This fifteenth department is not simply a question of a viable political map for twenty-first-century Salvadoran state and media institutions, but something that is both more metaphorical and more tangible. The texts and representations in "Departamento 15" delineate greater cultural and emotional attachments as part of the "imagined community" (Anderson 1991) of transnational El Salvador.

I refer to specifically arranged texts and representations, and concentrate on "Departamento 15," the news section of *La Prensa Gráfica*. This section has existed since April 2000 and its main focus is news about Salvadoran migrants. Among many topics, "Departamento 15" has published stories about social and cultural events organized by Salvadoran organizations (for example, hometown association fund-raisers and consular activities), features about notable Salvadoran migrants, and news about U.S. legislation that might affect the immigration status of Salvadorans in the United States (for example, extensions of Temporary Protected Status and information about work authorization, legal permanent residency, and naturalization). Sometimes the news section includes discussions of Salvadoran laws that might affect the Salvadoran citizenship status of those abroad—for instance, the debates surrounding voting rights for Salvadorans abroad or information about how to access Salvadoran consular services in cities across the United States. These topics delineate migrant lives that are clearly and purposefully lived in the United States, yet remain connected to key—and newsworthy—aspects of Salvadoran culture and the Salvadoran state.

Scholars of El Salvador have discussed the significance of some of these issues and practices for Salvadorans, and have debated the degree of importance of the national state in the contemporary social lives of migrants. Focusing on Salvadorans in the Los Angeles metropolitan area, Beth Baker-Cristales argues that the state functions as an important cultural formation, one that continues to influence the everyday lives and interests of Salvadorans in this important migrant destination in southern California. A compelling aspect of her "ethnography of a variegated and complex population" (Baker-Cristales 2004, 2) is that it presents and closely attends to multiple and intersecting forms of migrant social organizing, particularly along the lines of class, political affiliation, and ideas of the nation. The assumed connection of migrants to the Salvadoran state—and the assumed stability of this concept and related ones such as citizenship and nationality—must be further interrogated to understand the complex nature and function of Salvadoran media institutions and their coverage of migrant issues that were for the most part underreported until the postwar years.

In this regard, Susan Bibler Coutin raises significant questions about the presumably coherent concepts that are part of the immigration system (such as nation and citizen), stating: "In drawing attention to gaps between immigration as a conceptual system and as a social reality, I do not mean to suggest that if we revise our immigration categories or make some policy adjustments, then these gaps would be closed. Rather, I argue that the immigration system *creates* the very disjunctures that seem to undermine it and that, moreover, these disjunctures can be key to the immigration system's coherence" (2007, 5; emphasis original). In my analysis of "Departamento 15" as a news section I highlight these created disjunctures of Salvadoran citizenship and of what makes sense in Salvadoran migration practices. The section presents one way of understanding the complexities of Salvadoran migration, it is one form of representation, one way of making and incorporating what, for instance, is undocumented, unauthorized migration into official, national news for Salvadoran readers. Now we are no longer simply reading about the stories of people who left El Salvador clandestinely and were excluded and forgotten by the nation and the state. Instead, this is professionalized journalism in a postwar media landscape, reporting on the rupture and aftermath of their departure and why knowing the emigrant should matter to Salvadorans in El Salvador. The section's significance is that it presents the gaps of the transnational as national concerns; it draws attention to these puzzle pieces and to how they do not always fit neatly, and ultimately to "ways that incompatible realities are true simultaneously" (Coutin 2007, 5).

As a Salvadoran researcher I am aware of class, level of education, immigration status, and the effects this variable mixture of freedoms and structural constraints can have on the lives and opportunities of Salvadoran migrants. This awareness is important when examining the complex assumptions and realities about migrants' political affiliations, their rural or urban origins, the extent of their transnational family obligations, and their socioeconomic status presented in "Departamento 15." As a product of Salvadoran media culture, "Departamento 15" seeks to construct meaning and continuity along these disjunctures of class and migration status. Many of the stories I discuss portray facets of successful migration, ideally leading to eventual social and legal acceptance by the host country. Narratives of forced displacement, denial of political asylum, detention, and removal (deportation) proceedings endured by Salvadoran migrants during the 1980s and beyond are part of a diverse Salvadoran immigrant experience recounted by migrants themselves in U.S. courts (Coutin 2000), by deported youth in San Salvador (Coutin 2007; Zilberg 2004; Zilberg 2011), and by reporters and the audiences that become part of this cycle of news.

I first interviewed the journalists of "Departamento 15" in August 2005. I arrived at their offices with my own "digital parrot," a small matte silver voice recorder that looked like a then-fashionable flip phone (this was prior to the dawn of smart phones with colorful touch screens). By this time, the news section had existed for about five years. When I contacted one of the journalists to ask if I could speak with any of them, she was very welcoming. We arranged a group interview with an editor and two reporters who were part of the section staff in San Salvador. On the day of the interview one of the journalists brought lunch for everyone, including me—a gesture all of us appreciated. In the first moments of my recording I can hear the sounds of wrapping being removed from ham-and-cheese croissants. A few months later I conducted an interview with a journalist who was involved in the website of *La Prensa Gráfica*. On both occasions, I conducted the interview in a conference room of the main offices of the newspaper, located across the street from the U.S. Embassy in a neighborhood called Santa Elena. This physical location is interesting. "Departamento 15" is produced across the street from the Consular Section, where day after day (excluding weekends and holidays) Salvadorans queue to apply for U.S. visas.

La Prensa Gráfica has not always been located along this nice, ample boulevard. The first issue of the newspaper, then called *La Prensa*, circulated on 10 May 1915. It was founded by José Dutriz (1877–1946) and his elder brother Antonio (1873–1936), and its first offices were in a house located in downtown San Salvador. At the time, the brothers owned and operated a successful printing and typesetting business, Tipografía La Unión (Dutriz 2002, 12–13). In October 1928, the newspaper began to circulate every day of the week, including on Sundays—with this, it became the first true daily in Central America.[6] In 1929, the newspaper moved to a larger office building, still located in downtown San Salvador. In El Salvador, this was the first building constructed specifically to house a newspaper's offices, presses, and other specialized machinery.[7] It remained there for sixty-seven years. In August 1939, the newspaper took the name *La Prensa Gráfica* (Dutriz 2002, 7). In July 1996, the Dutriz family moved the enterprise from downtown San Salvador to its present location in Santa Elena, Antiguo Cuscatlán (Dutriz 2002, 17).

Like this new and modernized location, the journalists of "Departamento 15" are representative of a younger generation. Several of them are graduates of El Salvador's prestigious Universidad Centroamericana "José Simeón Cañas" (UCA). In addition to their *licenciatura* ("bachelor's degree"), one of them had also earned a degree in journalism in the United States. As one of them put it, they decided to become journalists "in a moment of inspiration." This sense of journalism as a vocation or a calling was part of how they presented themselves to me. One of them had been pursuing studies in medical school before deciding to switch to journalism; another was previously a sociology student. While they work at a newspaper that for most of its near-century of existence has been traditionally associated with conservative and/or center-right politics (at least as considered in the context of the Salvadoran political spectrum), it is worth noting that these might not necessarily be politics they share or personally support. Sometimes during my interview it seemed to me that they were ambivalent about whether or not to clarify this for me, about what sort of ideological map to provide me with. It was subtle—but as a Salvadoran of their generation (or close), I think I have an understanding of this ambivalence or form of expression. Their work may in part be a vocation or a calling, but it is also a profession that relies on ideas of objectivity. In general, we did not discuss current political events (commonly understood as the tensions between political parties or the controversy of the day), even as we tacitly acknowledged their quotidian importance. However, I cannot say that our discussion was not in some sense political—after all, we were discussing migration, one of the major contemporary social issues for El Salvador, and could not be detached about its importance.

While we ate the croissants, we eased into a discussion of their work. "I know this can be a strange question," I prefaced, "but what is your typical day like?" "We don't have that! But I can try to describe what today looks like for me so far, and [the others] can tell you about their own day . . . maybe?" the editor replied.[8] Together they composed an outline of their newsroom routine: checking for (and aggregating) international news and wire services, perusing major national papers of the United States (for example, *New York Times* and *Los Angeles Times*), conducting interviews over the phone, contacting Salvadoran consulates in different parts of the world, attending meetings, making sure their articles and related images have a space in that day's edition, and making last-moment changes in headlines. The journalists of "Departamento 15" rely on technology (mainly the telephone and the Internet) to maintain contact with their correspondents and carry out much of their work, what one of them aptly described as "finding the Salvadoran in the story, even if this person is very far away."[9] This is the daily beat of these reporters. They are engaged through technological connections that often do not require them to leave the offices in Santa Elena, yet allow them to find and communicate with distant migrant communities and other sources.

To reporters with more "traditional" beats—those who cover crime and protests in the streets of San Salvador, the day-to-day politics of Casa Presidencial and the legislative and judicial branches, or sporting events at the stadium on Sundays—this might seem like immobile reporting since the journalists of "Departamento 15" do not routinely interview people face-to-face or chase after their sources at press conferences. However, they do seek sources locally and beyond as their profession requires—these include policymakers, academics in Salvadoran universities, organizations such as the United Nations Development Programme, and government ministries that attend to Salvadorans abroad (in particular, to cultivate contacts with the Salvadoran consulates in the United States). The production of "Departamento 15" and the work of reporting described by the journalists involves the creation and circulation of codes of shared meaning—a complex work of encoding and representation, a way to "'make sense of' the world of people, objects and events, and how you are able to express a complex thought about those things to other people" (Hall 1997, 16). In the case of a newspaper section such as "Departamento 15," representation includes the daily ritual of "finding the Salvadoran," of creation and reading, encoding and decoding of messages and news—a reinforcing and reworking of what a culture of migration is supposed to mean for Salvadorans everywhere. To exist in a relevant way, "Departamento 15" demands a daily renewal of attention from the migrant Salvadoran public it claims to represent. In this imaginary, migration is one of many shared, common experiences among Salvadorans.

As it portrays the Salvadoran emigrant who seeks—or, ideally, has success-fully established—a life in the United States, "Departamento 15" reclaims this emigrant for a Salvadoran nation-building and identity project. Representations acquire new meanings over time. This process reworks daily stories of migration, reshaping ideas of citizenship, Salvadoranness, and belonging. Paradoxically, it also fixes stereotypical qualities of Salvadorans, for example, as invariably nostalgic for their home country, or as hard workers—stereotyped as the "Ger-mans of Central America" (LaFeber 1993, 10). In El Salvador, these stereotypes might be perceived as positive demonstrations of pride and love of country. For example, news items about Salvadoran Independence Day celebrations in Los Angeles or New York are displays of this mixture of nostalgia, patriotism, and national identification. Features about Salvadoran migrants who own their business and have thus realized their own version of the "American Dream" are part of these portrayals of hard work and migrant entrepreneurship.

During the 1980s, a Salvadoran newspaper section such as "Departamento 15" did not exist, although it was during this period that Salvadoran emigration to the United States reached unprecedented proportions. This makes the emer-gence of "Departamento 15" even more interesting. It is motivated by older his-tories of migration, by the necessity and narratives of migrants who emigrated during the harshest years of the civil war and have now lived in the United States for twenty-five years or more. However, it is adapted to current narra-tives, to the present reality that emigration continues at levels comparable to or higher than those of the 1980s civil war. As a journalist explained during our interview: "The section was proposed as that link between the country and the communities of Salvadorans abroad. [For example] that people here in the country become aware that the community in Sweden gathered and celebrated something. . . . The other objective is to reunite the Salvadorans who at a given moment were separated from their families and from their country."[10] "Depar-tamento 15," then, is a representation of the accepted reality of migration in Salvadoran daily life. To search for the Salvadoran in the story is to search for him or her everywhere, especially among those who aspire to emigrate, those who continue to leave, and those who do not have immediate plans to return to El Salvador.

Salvadorans who feel comfortably settled in the United States or apprehensive about socioeconomic conditions in El Salvador and therefore express no longings to return (Morán-Taylor and Menjívar 2005, 108) are now hailed as subjects of the borderless nation. As Salvadoran national culture is increasingly permeated by migration, Salvadoran emigrants are reclaimed to a representational space where they are acknowledged as an essential part of Salvadoran society. Paradoxically, these emigrants are pulled back, virtually at least, by their movement away from El Salvador. As the diasporic becomes the national, "Departamento 15" produces meaning through its choices of newsworthy, patriotic themes.

As a news project, "Departamento 15" turns emigrants into transnational citizens, addressing a shortcoming of the state and Salvadorans at "home." Imagination, time, and space are interdependent and vital to these narratives of movement and nation. Mikhail Bakhtin's notion of the chronotope, used to describe "the intrinsic connectedness of temporal and spatial relationships" (Bakhtin 1981, 84), is relevant in this analysis of narratives of migration insofar as it can be borrowed from literary criticism to understand the stories of migrant communities and how these are presented in print media and journalism. Time is significant in the imaginings of national consciousness and distant communities. Benedict Anderson's discussion of the emergence of nationalism further addresses the importance of time: ideas of simultaneity and homogenous, empty time are embedded in the modern imaginings of the nation. Anderson emphasizes that each member of the nation "has complete confidence in their steady, anonymous, simultaneous activity" (Anderson 1991, 26). In a project of print media such as "Departamento 15," this confident imagination of the nation is key. We do not have to know everything that is happening to Salvadorans, but some imagination is enough; this community "is imagined because the members of even the smallest nation will never know most of their fellow-members, meet them, or even hear of them, yet in the minds of each lives the image of their communion" (Anderson 1991, 6). The representations of Salvadorans abroad ("en el exterior," as is often said) signal a new relationship between time and space in which being Salvadoran is not solely linked to residing within the geographic boundaries of El Salvador. Through media images, Salvadorans are linked within larger national imaginaries built in the postwar period and in this transnational migrant space.

How to represent this time and space? "Departamento 15" first appeared on the pages of La Prensa Gráfica on 3 April 2000. An advertisement announcing the creation of this section, dated 31 March 2000, illustrates this point. It reads "Nuestro país no termina en las fronteras" ("Our country does not end at

the borders").[11] The name of the section is telling in its direct reference to Salvadoran space and geography. For the newspaper, Salvadorans abroad come to
represent the fifteenth administrative unit. This direct claim to transnational
space is enhanced by the logo of the section—this logo is literally a sign, an
interstate highway marker numbered "15" as an emblem of location, a destination, and a recognizable media brand (figure 1). Representing a transnational
space, the sign-logo "Departamento 15" is placed against a backdrop of clouds
and sky, without a particular or fixed location, without a stable grip. It appears
to be disembodied even as it is claiming actual migrant bodies as subjects of
this new transnational space.

While this sign in the early advertising for "Departamento 15" marks a
space, one that stands in for real people living in real locations, it also acknowledges that often there is no specific, definite ground or location for this space.
Where do Salvadorans belong? How does this text map the location of this public? The advertisement explains:

Departamento 15

The new section of *La Prensa Gráfica* where you will find the most interesting histories that reflect the living conditions of Salvadorans abroad.

Appreciate their successes, their accomplishments and entrepreneurial initiatives that cultural exchange has provoked.

Look for it this Monday the 3rd in the Departments section

Covering our people abroad[12]

This newspaper advertisement presents the Salvadoran immigrant experience
as one of hard work, success, and entrepreneurship, composed of "the most
interesting histories" (or stories). It also appears as if the newspaper's mission is to educate Salvadorans within El Salvador about the lives of Salvadorans
beyond the borders (*fronteras*—because the country does not end there, as they
announce in their slogan). The ad's text connects time and space in multiple
ways, especially in its emphasis of why Salvadoran readers should be interested
in the stories of "Departamento 15". It delineates and assumes a particular mode
of circulation and address—a local readership that sees this advertisement on a
Friday at the end of March and, of course, can expect to find the first issue of the
new section the following week, on the first Monday of April. "Look for it this
Monday," the ad states. This will become a new element of the reader's already
routine, habitual consumption of the newspaper.

In addition, the advertisement suggests that Salvadorans should appreciate the positive results of wartime and postwar emigration—in this instance
La Prensa Gráfica refers to this as "cultural exchange," the transformations
that occur when people form transnational lives. Clearly, Salvadoran migrant

FIGURE 1. Our country does not end at the borders. Advertisement for "Departamento 15," *La Prensa Gráfica*, 31 March 2000, 17.

culture is imagined as distinct from the culture of the country's borders, and worthy of appreciation. Thus the section aims to be educational, to help with the establishment of a Salvadoran spatial and temporal relationship, an explanation of cultural exchange and transnational space, "an aesthetic of cognitive mapping—a pedagogical political culture" (Jameson 1991, 54). To "cover our people abroad," then, becomes a matter of educating Salvadorans within the borders; a transnational project of reclaiming emigrants entails a national project of attracting and informing the readership of "Departamento 15." Also in this advertisement, the use of the pronouns "their" ("their accomplishments") and "our" ("our people abroad") construct semantic borders—in this case, emigrants are outside, and not only literally. They are not among the imagined audience for this advertisement.

"Departamento 15" is published in print and online. In both cases, the section has its own pages and designated layouts within the publications. If one turns the pages of the print version of *La Prensa Gráfica* (as I did repeatedly in the course of my archival research and in my daily purchase of the newspaper while in San Salvador), one will usually find the "Departamento 15" pages after the "national" news section. The pages of "Departamento 15" are easy to identify, since they are adorned with the highway sign marked with a "15," as shown in figure 1. The logo, a distinctive sign of this emerging transnational brand, is visibly placed near the day's headline or main story. This particular branding and media ownership of a representational space of migration is part of the reclaiming of the migrant subject for a postwar social and cultural national project.

Although the section has its own pages, many articles that could fit into other areas—business, arts, sports—are also marked with the highway sign-logo "15" and placed in sections beyond "Departamento 15." Since its first issues in the year 2000, "Departamento 15" articles seeped into other sections of the newspaper's print edition, sometimes defying editorial and territorial boundaries. "'Departamento 15' is the axis that traverses the entire newspaper," one of the journalists explained during our interview, pointing to the present salience of migration in Salvadoran daily news—this news seems to be a backbone, in which relevant ideas about globalization and El Salvador's place in the world make sense and take form.

The journalist's characterization of the section as an axis, as a point of orientation, is appropriate. The news articles about migration intersect with news about different points within the country's borders, including Salvadoran rural areas. For example, these stories might include those of *campesinos* who left their hometowns and now live in urban areas of the United States, and might participate in a hometown association event now featured in "Departamento 15." This transversal news placement is already a test of the viability of portrayals and of "Departamento 15" as a created and shared code for an imagined community of readers, regardless of location. "Departamento 15" represents a transnational flow into national and departmental news—through media representations in *La Prensa Gráfica*, Salvadorans in U.S. cities reach their relatives and friends in urban areas, towns, and even remote rural villages in El Salvador.

The news story "Buscando nuevos horizontes" is an example of this possible reach, of "searching for new horizons" in the media representation of migrants. As one of the first "Departamento 15" articles to be published, on 3 April 2000, this piece works as a statement of purpose for the new section. The article attempts to "endow the individual subject with some new heightened sense of its place in the global system" (Jameson 1991, 54). "The rest of the world is the space of development for 20 percent of our people," the article begins. "Departamento 15" is presented as a space that will raise awareness, sensitivity, and public opinion about the "economic, social, and cultural" weight of Salvadorans who live abroad:

> Because of the cultural contact they have had in other countries, they are [a] source of inspiration and scientific, technological, entrepreneurial, and cultural experience. They are much more than their value in remittances, almost the only exclusive reference [we had of them] for many years. Here we want to disseminate [information about] the living conditions of Salvadorans abroad because it is important to sensitize and generate greater public opinion about the economic, social, and cultural weight they have in national life.[13]

"Buscando nuevos horizontes" states that 20 percent of the Salvadoran population needs to seek greater opportunities outside El Salvador. It makes this emigration pattern seem natural, the progression of an increasingly globalized Salvadoran nation. "New" transnational horizons become nationalized spaces for the opportunities of compatriots, spaces cited in this article as the "natural extension of our small territory of twenty thousand square kilometers"; further, the article estimates that "more than two million Salvadorans have left for more than two million reasons," referring to the estimated 2.4 million Salvadorans who live abroad.[14] While reasons for migration can be individual at some level, this process does not happen haphazardly, but is rooted in a history of prior contact and intervention between the "sending" and "receiving" countries, which forge transnational ties even before people migrate.

This is not to suggest a simple, linear relationship between autonomous, bounded countries defined only by the "legal" or "illegal" movement of bodies. A portrayal of migration as a process of purely individual choices and opportunities would erase other institutional factors associated with neoliberalism or structural adjustment in Latin America, policies which are often associated with a rise in economic inequality. A critical transnational perspective (Espiritu 2003) encourages us to look beyond purely individual reasons for leaving El Salvador. It compels us to reexamine the one-way perspective that prevails in paradigms of migration, assimilation, and assimilability in the United States, in order to critique global structures and unequal relationships that shape migration patterns.

A photograph accompanies the article "Buscando nuevos horizontes." It shows a woman next to a sign that reads: "Parking for *salvadoreños* only." The sign looks like a novelty item, a customizable sign that we might see at a souvenir store, or one that could adorn a door or a wall in a home. In the textual arrangement of "Departamento 15," it serves as a marker of place and belonging, a space where anyone who is *not* Salvadoran "will be towed." The woman carries a measuring tape on her shoulder. Perhaps she is a garment worker. The caption that accompanies the photograph reads "Pueblo de migrantes," but gives us little information about the woman in the picture. Surely she has a location, one that falls within the discourses of a global division of labor and the imaginary of "a migrant people." *La Prensa Gráfica* emphasizes her identity as a migrant, immobilized in this image as she "searches for new horizons."[15]

"Departamento 15" attempts to construct a reality of Salvadoran life in the United States to produce and organize an understanding of an imagined transnational community. To accomplish this, however, it must proceed from and exploit anything that seems to be an unusual and newsworthy assumption regarding Salvadoran immigrants in the United States. Articles about migrants' intense longing for Salvadoran food (or something along those lines) cannot justify the existence and longevity of a news section about what they do every day, and cannot hold the serious interest of a reader in San Salvador. What is particular or strange about Salvadorans abroad, and what makes them Salvadoran? Michael Warner argues that a "modern social imaginary does not make sense without strangers. A nation, market, or public in which everyone could be known personally would be no nation, market, or public at all" (Warner 2002, 57). In other words, there has to be a strangeness of the *salvadoreños* in the United States for them to be newsworthy and to continuously feed the Salvadoran cultural imagination.

To shape this imaginary, the journalists of "Departamento 15" engage a range of provocative and contradictory stereotypes. From portrayals of Salvadorans as particularly loyal and attached to their country of origin, to accounts of the forced return of deportees or of violence against migrants, stereotypes are reductions of the essential characteristics of Salvadoran migrants and their circumstances. The journalists are, indeed, in the process of making and representing strangers and compatriots. As Stuart Hall notes, "*stereotyping reduces, essentializes, naturalizes and fixes 'difference'*" (Hall 1997, 258; emphasis original). Desirable qualities of what it means to be Salvadoran and a migrant, such as an exemplary work ethic and love of country, are presented as very distinct from less acceptable (but sometimes still represented and newsworthy) qualities such as illegality, criminality, or perceived resentments and differences of opinion due to political views, wartime displacement, and traumatic flight from repression.

La Prensa Gráfica is able to introduce "Departamento 15" as the logical "axis" of the newspaper and to refer to emigration and the transformation of El Salvador as "cultural exchange" (as it does in figure 1). In this case, the struggle of transnational Salvadorans is summarized in one sentence, for example: "Con su partida, en fin, ha cambiado la identidad salvadoreña, ha cambiado su vida y la nuestra" ("with their departure, then, Salvadoran identity has changed, their life and ours has changed").[16]

In this case the news section clearly demarcates an us/them dichotomy while in other instances it focuses on creating a *nosotros*, an "us" that is selectively used to facilitate the "bonding together of all of Us who are 'normal' into one 'imagined community'" (Hall 1997, 258). The use of exclusive terms (in this context, these pronouns) places Salvadorans within and outside El Salvador in different spatial and power relationships, with differential access to the resources and institutions of the Salvadoran state. Between oppositions such as us/them we are dealing with what Jacques Derrida describes as "a violent hierarchy. One of the two terms governs" (Derrida in Hall 1997, 258). A strategy of "splitting" and excluding the different or the misfit is part of stereotyping, "part of the maintenance of social and symbolic order" (Hall 1997, 258). From the newsroom in San Salvador, textual arrangements of language (including the use of pronouns) and photographs echo these theoretical interventions of cultural studies, and in practice become constitutive of impressions of migration and distance from the state. Textual arrangements raise important questions about the uneasy limits of this social order, which lie somewhere between accepting the transnational migrant as a "national Salvadoran," and claiming this migrant by insisting on their emigration and their remittances as a "natural extension," a fact of life.

Three days after this first issue of "Departamento 15," on 6 April 2000, *La Prensa Gráfica* published responses from its readers under the headline "La recompensa de ser pioneros" ("The reward for being pioneers"), where the "pioneers" are both the newspaper section and the migrants it covers. Aaron from Canada wrote, "'Departamento 15,' sincerely many thanks for making us part of Salvadoran society, for giving us a place. We are far away but the heart is always [in] El Salvador." José wrote from Las Vegas, "It was about time that a national news media outlet took us into account and who better than the best Salvadoran newspaper. I congratulate you, and keep on." Pedro from Vancouver noted, "We are the first virtual department of the world!"[17] These responses reveal different spatial cues and locations—José imagines himself as a recipient and reader of national media; Aaron feels far away, yet included in Salvadoran society; while Pedro celebrates a new and unique "virtual" department.

Readers' responses are a reminder that the text of "Departamento 15" is not fully closed, and that a reading of a text can be interpreted and reinterpreted in various ways: "Language (communication) is both material and social. It is therefore mutable. Makers and users, writers and readers, senders and receivers can do things with communication that are unintended, unplanned for, indeed, unwished for" (Newcomb 1984, 39). While many response messages accommodate the prevalent meanings of Salvadoran migration portrayed in these pages of "Departamento 15," other messages from Salvadoran readers abroad break or subvert the idealized narrative. They aim to create a more nuanced space of inclusion for other histories, and to expand the definition of nosotros, the "us" in the Salvadoran transnational experience, by including their stories and perspectives as they respond to the work of journalists. For example, Héctor from California writes, "[I]t is time to recognize the invaluable contribution that Salvadorans have provided to El Salvador through many years, and this sentiment is shared by many of my compatriots abroad. We are fed up that we are only seen as a source of income, for even the exit from our country was traumatic enough for us, not to mention leaving our families, friends, and memories behind, to arrive to such strange places. Thank you for this section."[18]

Despite the limitations of space and access, many messages in this print edition try to insert alternative histories. The response by Héctor, with its reference to a "sentiment shared by many of my compatriots abroad," demands something *beyond* recognition for working hard and sending money home. It demands restitution of family, friends, and memories. But who can provide this type of restitution? To what extent can "Departamento 15" be an effective means of restitution and recovery of memory? The section gains a symbolic value, similar to a war memorial, as it reconstitutes and claims migrants to the Salvadoran imaginary.[19]

The article on "new horizons" considers the possibility of the return of emigrants, introducing complex elements of nostalgia, connection, and imagination of community. "Departamento 15" aims to be a space for the generation of public opinion and response in order to "imagine how much we would gain if they returned. To imagine how much we are wasting. And to imagine how we can make the most of their successful experience, their organizational initiatives, their social, economic, and political links and contributions."[20] The return of successful Salvadorans is imagined as a benefit, an expansion of exploitable global resources that would greatly enhance the national community. The news section is invested with a special power—through its circulation, portrayals, and responses it establishes transnational connections. The newspaper can provoke the imagination of return and migrant nostalgia. In turn, this emigrant community also thinks about searching and responding, perhaps in an effort to link this newfound space of a transnational "Departamento 15" with some sense of recovery of a disrupted past.

It is necessary, however, to note that in other "Departamento 15" stories, the idea of return has been viewed as negative for the well-being of the nation, as in the cases of deported gang members identified in Salvadoran media as extortionists and corruptors of local youth, leading them to crime and gang activity. Here we have at least two constructions of the Salvadoran from "Departamento 15." One is of a highly valued Salvadoran with social and economic resources that are in great demand—the product of hard work, creativity, and honesty. He or she has skills gained elsewhere in the world, and postwar El Salvador needs these skills and good citizenship.

Another possible construction is that of the deportee, particularly (but not exclusively) the criminalized and racialized *marero* ("gang member") who has already been "banished from the kingdom," the United States (Zilberg 2002, 232; Zilberg 2004; Zilberg 2011). Deportation adds meaning to (and in many cases, stigmatizes) the migrant experience of many Salvadorans. The gang member is spatially and socially dislocated, a misfit, unlike the meaningfully located migrant and loyal transnational citizen of El Salvador. Lives are split and shaped by these stereotypes, forms of violence that lead to misrecognition. "Departamento 15" implies or presumes a national unity, and through this process it attempts to dislocate the elements of the transnational imaginary that seem undesirable. Meanwhile, many Salvadorans remain symbolically close, sharing in Salvadoran society and this journalistic space.

A Story of Circulation: "Practically as if They Were Here"

For a few months during 2002 and 2003, *La Prensa Gráfica* (including, of course, "Departamento 15") circulated in print in many cities of the United States. The project was ambitious, its early stages illustrative of how *La Prensa Gráfica* envisioned and constructed a public(s) beyond geographical borders.[21]

On 9 September 2002, the print version of *La Prensa Gráfica* circulated in El Salvador as it had for decades—and simultaneously it also circulated in Houston, San Francisco, Los Angeles, Washington DC, and New York.[22] The following day an editorial chronicled the event as "Una expansión histórica" ("A Historical Expansion"):

> Starting this Monday, our newspaper will, on a daily basis, reach the hands of Salvadorans in the mentioned cities, and with that possibility our compatriots will be able to feel closer to the realities [of the *patria*], practically as if they were here. This is a fact that transcends market policies and logistical efforts: it is the concrete result of a rapprochement that we have been dreaming about for a long time, as the realities and the interaction between Salvadorans here and Salvadorans there have become stronger and more organic.[23]

The news stories, editorials, and responses surrounding this event highlight how this sense of "historical expansion" involves Salvadoran readers in this project of circulation—how it shapes everyday practices and a public while sharing a vision with them. By addressing Salvadorans in the United States, migrants and the newspaper become accomplices and partners in this project. According to Michael Warner, the nation "includes its members whether they are awake or asleep, sober or drunk, sane or deranged, alert or comatose. Because a public exists only by virtue of address, it must predicate some degree of attention, however notional, from its members" (Warner 2002, 61). The editorial considered here is a perfect example of an imagining of an attentive public, a group with a national (Salvadoran) interest.

The editorial quoted above is meaningful in its allusion to history, to a past of separation and displacement. The newspaper's circulation in the United States is the tangible result of a dream of rapprochement or reunification. Circulation, as Michael Warner notes, is a significant analytical category in the study of print media and modern nationalism: "public discourse has presupposed daily and weekly rhythms of circulation. It has also presupposed an ability—natural to moderns, but rather peculiar if one thinks about it at all—to address this scene of circulation as a social entity" (Warner 2002, 69). The editorial builds on this notion of circulation and the existence of a modern and transnational social imaginary, recognizing the reality of "interactions between Salvadorans here and Salvadorans there."[24] In other words, it acknowledges the strength and social significance of transnational ties, and the need to expand to the Salvadoran communities in the United States to reach as many compatriots as possible. This reach imagines Salvadorans in urban areas of the United States as if their daily lives were located in El Salvador, close to its realities, an unquestionable part of the social entity—*practically as if they were here.* U.S.-based readers of *La Prensa Gráfica* and its "Departamento 15" section are thus drawn into this daily circulation project and this media landscape.[25]

Circulation in the United States is, in part, a response to new locations and changing habits of news consumption, a fact acknowledged in the editorial: "The necessities of information grow and change in an accelerated manner; and the fundamental imperative lies in serving the citizens in a better, more opportune, and broader way, wherever they may be."[26] The idea of "historical expansion" recognizes, symbolically at least, the space where *citizens* do not necessarily live within geographic, territorial boundaries. Now, an entity called "the Salvadoran public," regardless of location, is claimed as a social totality, imagined and served by its own national newspaper. The basic purpose of the newspaper's redefined circulation project, its editors and publisher claim, is to "serve as a permanent link, in this age when distances of all kinds give in to the uncontainable advances of technology."[27] This emphasis on permanence, connection, and a sense of belonging in an era of rapid technological innovation, transnational movement, and instability seeks to bind Salvadorans as a national category of desirable readers of Salvadoran news. In turn, this transnational Salvadoran public/community participates in a global division of labor, as immigrants in large global cities. This variety of capital and possibility is acknowledged in the editorial:

To be able to have all that informative material on a daily basis will make the links between the co-nationals and their communities fresher and more vigorous. Our country is, percentage-wise, the one with the most population in the United States. That enormous contingent of Salvadorans who live and work [in the world's] most developed society constitutes a force of extraordinary cultural and economic power, acting in a decisive manner upon the destiny [of the *patria*] and in the configuration of the modern identity of our national conglomerate.[28]

Salvadorans have left their country and eventually settled in other areas of the world. Following the paths of its potential readership, the newspaper expands beyond territorial boundaries. By addressing them, this public emerges and now becomes mediated, visible "in relation to texts and their circulation" (Warner 2002, 50). The newspaper attempts to give new life to and refresh the connections between Salvadorans abroad and the communities they left behind. Salvadorans in the United States are reclaimed as part of a postwar national project—to rebuild and modernize El Salvador, to influence the country's destiny and its "configuration of modern identity."[29] However, in this imaginary, the text of "Departamento 15" alone is not enough to create a public (Warner 2002, 62). *La Prensa Gráfica* as a text is not an isolated creator of this social totality, but is in conversation with existing (and transforming) discourses about postwar El Salvador.

Discourses of state modernization and of postwar reconciliation, democracy, migration, and globalization are already in circulation, combining to form an imaginary where Salvadorans in the United States, for years invisible and unaddressed, are now acknowledged. For example, the 1999 report *Temas claves para el Plan de Nación: Consulta Especializada* ("Key Topics for the Plan of the Nation: Specialized Consultation"), authored by a group of consultants, including policy specialists and academics, outlines a vision for postwar El Salvador. The first chapter, "Sociedad sin fronteras" ("Society without Borders," or frontiers), immediately incorporates "salvadoreños en el exterior" as necessary for the project of nation-building:

In the world there are now formidable challenges for small countries. Globalization provokes a growing internationalization of national processes. . . . El Salvador has resources to connect better to the world. At the same time, it has conditions to enter another stage in its history. During the twentieth century there had never been so many favorable aspects to initiate the eradication of poverty and emerge from underdevelopment. There is an unequaled human experience, accumulated by the hundreds of thousands of women and men living abroad, who still maintain links with their communities of origin.[30]

"Globalization provokes a growing internationalization of national processes," this proposed plan for the nation argues, sounding uncannily like *La Prensa Gráfica*'s editorial, "Una expansión histórica." In both spaces of knowledge and information (one, of academic research and policy specialists, the other of journalists and editors), the opportunity to connect to the outside world exists through the Salvadorans who already reside outside El Salvador. They can provide the way out of poverty and underdevelopment—not solely through their remittances, but because of their "unequaled human experience," as cited above. In this view, migrant connections are logical and will facilitate the most "favorable aspects" for national development—something that is still to come in the aftermath of the country's armed conflict. Similar discourses of opportunity and local development through engagement with the transnational field and the experiences of Salvadoran immigrants permeate the texts of "Departamento 15," "A Historical Expansion" and similar editorials, and the *Plan de Nación*. In the case of the plan of the nation and the historical expansion of the newspaper's circulation, these ideas are connected by the time and space represented in "Departamento 15," one that presupposes a public that is receptive to the ideas of historical progression tied to economic advancement. As José Roberto Dutriz, executive director of *La Prensa Gráfica*, expressed in a 10 September 2002 article regarding the project of circulation in the United States: "With this effort, *La Prensa Gráfica* situates itself within the process of globalization, and crowns an example for the Salvadoran economy."[31]

A news report of the time recounts how the newspaper circulated in 2002 and reached stores in New York City and nearby areas. According to this story, the newspapers arrived and sold very well, as a Salvadoran grocery store customer in Hempstead expressed: "'It was about time, you are going to sell this very quickly because we are always looking for it.' . . . 'You have had a great idea,' he said, and immediately took an issue. Ten minutes later, ten people in that same place took their issues and started reading them."[32] In addition, readers from different cities in the United States e-mailed their messages to *La Prensa Gráfica*, commenting on this project of circulation. These messages were published in the newspaper. For example, José from Dallas, Texas, wrote, "I congratulate the Dutriz group for such a good project, I feel proud to be as Salvadoran as *La Prensa Gráfica* and I will carry the name of my country with pride, just like *La Prensa Gráfica* does today."[33] Ramón also e-mailed his response, commenting on this event, "This is one of the greatest dreams that Salvadorans have reached: to be well-informed with our own newspaper. I congratulate you, I feel very happy to be a pure Salvadoran."[34] Meanwhile, Alfredo wrote from California, "I feel very proud to know that the newspaper of El Salvador is here now. For me as a Salvadoran-American it is one more achievement of our people [*pueblo*]."[35]

This project of daily circulation began in 2002 and lasted into 2003, but did not continue. In an interview, an employee of the newspaper stated that although this was clearly an innovative project on the part of the newspaper, many long-term logistical aspects had not, as the employee put it, "been fully thought out," and the newspaper turned to other projects for the section "Departamento 15." The question of distribution was particularly challenging, this employee said, because (in the employee's view) the newspaper did not at the time pay enough attention to publicizing its sales points in the relevant urban locations in the United States.[36] We can agree that this is not necessarily a negative outcome—beyond being one media institution's experiment with notions of circulation, newsworthiness, and national pride, this project raises many practical and interesting questions about the viability of print media in the Internet age and assumptions of circulation in connection with modern ideas of national territorial borders. What does it mean for print media to actually cross these borders, into the territory of another country? Where would the newspaper be sold? How would migrant readers find out where to buy it, and would they take the time and effort to become devoted daily buyers and readers of these print issues? How much would each newspaper cost, in order to justify the expense of printing in San Salvador and shipping it to sell in Houston, San Francisco, and other cities? Clearly, it is one thing to portray migrants on the pages of "Departamento 15" as Salvadorans who live "practically as if they were here"—and an entirely different enterprise to attempt the daily ritual of print media readership on a transnational scale.

As this print circulation project was phased out, the importance placed on the presence and materiality of the newspaper—as far as circulation and sales in the United States were concerned, of course—gave way to an emphasis on the Internet as a more feasible and accessible intervention. The website of *La Prensa Gráfica* was first launched in 1996, and in 2003 it received a significant overhaul in both its design and content. During its first years the website was simply a mirror image, a reflection of the print issue—reproducing the masthead, headlines, print articles, and photographs, but not much more. But this design began to change in 2001, when two strong earthquakes hit El Salvador in January and February. At that point many Salvadorans in the United States and other parts of the world turned to the website for up-to-date information, as a journalist of the newspaper's electronic edition explained in our December 2005 interview in San Salvador:

> It wasn't until 2001, with the earthquakes, that the website did everything it could, in a moment of emergency. Because it served as a link between the communities abroad and Salvadorans who were here, enduring this national emergency. That is when we really saw the value that the Internet had . . . the value of having an informative website, and

where we started to definitively separate the print edition from the electronic edition. Because we saw needs that later became permanent, for
example having interaction with the reader, which we did not have with
the print edition. With the earthquakes, we started to see that great need
that people [in the United States] had of communicating with people
here. . . . So, that interaction began there. And it was there, too, that we
parted with the idea that this had to be only a mirror edition [of print].
We started to use other types of resources. . . . Well, more basic things
that the web was able to support at the time. Although by 2001 most
websites of large newspapers already had incorporated audio, video, we
in the region [Central America] were just starting with that. And even so,
we were like the pioneers in starting to launch this type of thing, which
in the beginning was trial and error. What do people like most? What can
they use most? What is most appealing to people? What really gives the
best results among our readers? But really, without a study of our readers . . . something that could tell us what they really want . . . this pretty
much worked by pure intuition. And pure ingenuity.[37]

Since those beginnings characterized by intuition and the webmaster's creativity, the publishers, editors, and journalists have emphasized the redesign
and development of the layout of *La Prensa Gráfica* as a whole, focusing on the
entire website of "Departamento 15" and its multimedia components. During
the final months of 2002, the newspaper hired a Mexican firm to consult in the
redesign of its layout, including the print and electronic editions, to carry out
a survey of readers to find out about their needs and preferences, and to assess
the traffic to the newspaper's website.

The newspaper, particularly the electronic edition, has changed considerably since 2002. While its colors and design echoed those of the print version,
the redesigned website could now support a wide range of its own unique features and products, most notably chat rooms, slideshows of Salvadoran monuments, audio, video, and special supplements that were only published online.
The special issues for Mother's Day, Easter, the August festivities, and other Salvadoran holidays were created for online consumption because "we conducted
a study of our readers, and realized that during those dates, people expected
something special from us because they keep a very special memory" as one of
the journalists noted.[38] This point is important, as it marks a transition between
what is perceived as stereotype or cliché and what is upheld as evidence. That
holidays are meaningful was no longer mere intuition—it was solidified as
market research, vital business information. This was no longer an assumption about a diasporic public in the imaginary. Now, survey data in hand, it
had been demonstrated that the newspaper's website had an interested readership in the United States.[39] Many Salvadorans in the United States might never

have purchased the print edition, or even known that for a short time it might have been available near them, but now they were clicking in to this Internet address that was easy to remember—daily, perhaps, and especially on days that reminded them of times spent in El Salvador. As one of the Internet journalists explained, "we had to renew the sections of the website. And the most important feature was 'Departamento 15' . . . to specifically satisfy the needs of all these readers who were abroad, of this nostalgic market of news."[40]

As part of this objective of community connection with this market, "Departamento 15" developed subsections (or "minisections" as one of the reporters called them) to enhance the website. One of these is named "Busco a . . ." ("I search for . . ."). This message board can link Salvadorans abroad, those who have lost contact with people they knew in El Salvador, to the newspaper's spaces of circulation. Every day, new messages from Salvadorans searching for old friends or long-lost relatives are posted on the "Departamento 15" website (as it existed at the time of my interview with the journalists), and some of these announcements are eventually published in the print version of the newspaper, in a fashion similar to readers' responses or letters to the editor. "Departamento 15" and its readers/respondents open a dialogue; the newspaper "gives voice" to the readers and their messages, and declares in its title, "Find your loved ones through 'Departamento 15.'"[41] The section gains the ability to *produce* the return of the migrant through media and reestablishment of personal connections. "Departamento 15" journalists referred to "Busco a . . ." as a free and "public" service, an important and rewarding aspect of their work as communicators, as one of the journalists elaborated:

> This section of encounter, of search for people is another of the sections that we all like. That satisfaction of someone [a reader of "Departamento 15"] calling to say, "Thanks because I found the person I was looking for, I found my friend, I found my father." . . . In the end one realizes that this is a public service, really, although the state does not pay us we are servants of our own Salvadoran community by uniting them, by informing them, by linking them to each other. . . . We will unite Salvadorans who left with their country, family, and friends, but also abroad we will unite communities.[42]

As my interviews with the journalists indicate, at times they speak of their work in "Departamento 15" as a *public service*, situated in a relationship with the Salvadoran people and as part of a state and media project of reuniting communities everywhere. Although the newspaper is privately owned, this service is "public" and aimed primarily at the emigrant community. "Busco a . . . ," letters to the editor, and readers' responses enable "Departamento 15" to project and gauge its reception by Salvadorans, both at home and abroad, serving as confirmation of its own popular reach and its ideological construction as a public, informative service that reunites people (and is a necessary mediating link between the nation and its diaspora).

Ultimately, a combination of research, common and sometimes stereotypical knowledge about Salvadorans in the United States, and response to national emergencies such as the 2001 earthquakes justifies this great investment in developing a multimedia site and aggregating news and other content online to reach Salvadorans wherever the Internet is accessible. I raised a question regarding the appeal of media convergence and investing in an Internet presence to a journalist, who replied:

> All of us want to be seen all over the world, right? We want to be part of that world because now we have realized that it exists, and that it is closer than we think. . . . I think that the universality of the Internet is what ends up being so attractive for everyone. Because, for example, *La Prensa Gráfica* emerged online with that idea: to open a window that otherwise would have remained closed. Because with paper it is difficult to reach all the countries where Salvadorans are. . . . Each medium, separately, needs a very specific and complicated support in order to be diffused, but that is not so much the case with the Internet. So, yes, we have our press that might cost millions of dollars, but we also open a site on the Internet.[43]

Although the print edition of the newspaper no longer reaches Salvadorans in cities across the United States, *La Prensa Gráfica* online is accessible beyond the borders of El Salvador. Convergence of multiple media is key to this online project, as is the relative logistical ease of infrastructure, updating, and maintenance of the website. With its daily portrayals of migrants on the website's news, "Departamento 15" is present in this media world and continues to link Salvadoran communities regardless of their physical location. José, for example, lives in San Francisco and sent his comments to the editor. Describing his daily ritual of interaction with Salvadoran news, something that requires access to the newspaper's website, he writes, "Personally the first thing I do every day is turn on my computer and read *La Prensa Gráfica*, accompanied by a cup of coffee. Congratulations!"[44]

The online responses posted by many readers point to a sense of pride in Salvadoran nationality and culture, and highlight the positive receptions of this news production and circulation project. The newspaper "alludes to its own popularity" (Warner 2002, 70) by publishing the responses and comments of its readers. "Departamento 15" offers some hints as to how the circuit of culture and decoding of meaning develops: references to "our newspaper" and "the newspaper of El Salvador" are evidence of the connection between mass media and its transnational public.

Through the responses of readers we can sense a positive reception of "Departamento 15" by migrants who anticipate that this will be a space where they can participate in Salvadoran society. These responses have mutually constitutive purposes. One, they reinforce a journalistic claim to a specialized kind of knowledge of the subjects portrayed in "Departamento 15." At the same time, the readers are called upon to validate and confirm that knowledge. For instance, the subheading of "The reward for being pioneers" pointedly asks the readers to participate in this exchange: "Your participation is invaluable in this section, and confirms to us that we are on the correct path."[45] Two, while publishing the comments and responses, the newspaper continues to justify its existence as an authority and service that "gives voice" and has the power to produce and represent a community of readers who in turn send messages and perpetuate this cycle and dialogue.

Conclusion

The representation of Salvadoran migrant productivity and daily life outside El Salvador expands the national borders, revealing a transnational social imaginary. A persistently imagined yet indefinitely deferred return to El Salvador is central to the cultivation of community and the perpetuation of a newspaper readership interested in migration. As a postwar media product, "Departamento 15" circulates as a representation of the notion of migrant longing and reunited communities. This circulation is not always an easy project. Crucially, not every project of circulation crosses borders in the same way—the Internet can reach Salvadorans more than print editions, and readers express diverse responses to this ideological hailing.

Focusing on the newspaper's construction of Salvadorans in the United States as exceptionally patriotic and hard-working allows us to comprehend the discourses that facilitate their representation as model transnational citizens in the global division of labor. While in these cases representation as a concept is most immediately linked to media representation and stereotypes, via close readings of editorials and advertisements I also suggest the presence of broader political and social meanings in these texts. Imagining and representing the audience of Salvadoran migrants in national media culture and in the transnational imaginary has been a dynamic process for *La Prensa Gráfica*. Tracing this shift, I show how in early advertisements for the "Departamento 15" section, the idea of "covering our people abroad" implied and celebrated unity and learning about migration while clearly expressing the semantic borders of us/ them. Early interventions into transnational circulation imagined Salvadorans in urban centers of the United States as Salvadorans who could still be involved in the daily rituals of buying and reading the newspaper in their local newsstand, "practically as if they were here." While this was a welcome novelty, this assumption of circulation presented physical and logistical barriers. In response to these obstacles and with new knowledge of its readers, the newspaper recognized the importance of interacting with readers via the website. Instead of assuming that publics remain passive and disengaged, it was critical to innovate and introduce multimedia to facilitate a dialogic, interactive relationship.

Throughout, Salvadorans outside the borders of El Salvador are addressed and become a public—they are included as part of a social totality and a transnational project in the postwar media landscape. In addition, it is important to contextualize the emergence of "Departamento 15," along with related discourses of postwar reconstruction and globalization, as plans for the economic and social future of El Salvador. While I point to the emergence of new transnational spaces and responses in the news section, it is not to suggest that media representation of Salvadoran emigrants has been immediately followed by political or other kinds of representation for them within the spaces of El Salvador. In Salvadoran media, Salvadoran migrants have emerged as figures that embody desirable traits of citizens in postwar society. They are people who work hard, take risks, and care for their families by sending remittances and in many cases getting involved in hometown associations or other projects that maintain their connection to their place of origin. The main concern is reclaiming this complex history of the migrant as a contributor to the national economy and culture. However, this project cannot be carried out by a single media institution—it has also been developed and sustained by migrants for practical reasons, as a survival tactic for many families who depend on remittances and networks of friends and family. The sections of readers' responses and frequent references to the possible social and economic contributions of Salvadorans abroad create a field of meanings and perceptions of a shared past and possible future in a borderless El Salvador, a way of representing national identity and expanding the role of the press in constituting and mediating citizenship and the nation.

These spaces of imagined community encourage collective national remembering—or forgetting—and reclaiming of citizenship in a modern nation (Ashplant, Dawson, and Roper 2000; Gómez-Barris 2009; Hobsbawm and Ranger 1992). The response section reminds us of the possibility of openness, alternative histories, and dialogue that may develop in "Departamento 15." These statements of openness and inclusion, while subject to critique, are part of how "Departamento 15" journalists view their work and incorporate the words of migrants—the section wants to include them and serve this community in a mutually constitutive project of representation, mediation, and recognition.

2

The Desperate Images

"La verdad circula por todas partes" ("truth circulates everywhere"), *La Prensa Gráfica* proclaims in a publicity campaign. A 2003 advertisement from that campaign is particularly striking. The photograph shows a group of young men wearing caps and carrying backpacks, barely discernible in the darkness. The men are jumping on a train, presumably on their way north, toward the Mexico-U.S. border. One of the migrants points and looks directly at the camera—perhaps with a mixture of defiance and fear—while his companions are busy finding their footing. The staff and readers of *La Prensa Gráfica* meet his gaze, the captured moment in a full-color, two-page advertisement—the uncertainty of migration, the instability of a moving train, the darkness and danger associated with undocumented travel. "To search within and outside our borders, to follow the facts no matter what the consequences, to transmit the news with actuality is our job" the advertisement states next to the photograph.[1]

A second image evokes similar uncertainty—a news *crónica*, this one by Óscar Martínez of the digital newspaper *El Faro*, chronicles only a few of many nights in the *centros botaneros* (bars and dance clubs) of Chiapas, Mexico. Also in the darkness, undocumented Central American girls and women (most of them between the ages of ten and thirty-five years) work as waitresses or dancers, and in many cases are forced into prostitution. Most of the young women interviewed by Martínez left extremely abusive conditions in their homes in Central America. Coming from a context where domestic violence was the most common familial relationship (something witnessed and experienced since their childhoods), women like "Keny" and "Erika" intended to make their way through Mexico, and eventually to the United States. Instead, somewhere after crossing the border between Guatemala and Mexico their bodies acquired a different value as single migrant women, and, significantly, as Central American

49

women. They are the victims of violence and sexual assaults, their money and identification documents are stolen, and all that remains is a body to be traded for an existence now far from their migrant aspirations. The trade is elemental, merchandise reduced to bare life, and Martínez describes it eloquently in his chronicles: "There is . . . an expression coined in this path of the undocumented: *cuerpomátic*. It refers to flesh as a credit card with which one can obtain security on the journey, some money, so your travel companions will not be killed, a more comfortable train ride . . ." (Martínez 2010, 86; emphasis added).

The migrant body is likened to a credit card, even to an automated teller machine. The word *cuerpomátic* suggests hybridity of body and machine. It also suggests the possible and real dehumanization of migrants, as if somehow they are commodities and able to readily set their feelings aside for the sake of mere survival during their journey. These bodies are used and burdened with emotional and physical pain, and with debts that sometimes are deferred into uncertainty and eventually cannot be repaid.

Through textual analysis of news items and the images they evoke, this chapter takes a closer look at histories of violence and family separation, and also examines media portrayals of amputated and repatriated bodies as contested symbols of social relationships and migration in the Salvadoran transnational imaginary. Many of these news stories are drawn from the section "Departamento 15" of *La Prensa Gráfica* and from the news section "En el camino" (a title that can be translated as "On the Road" or "On the Path" or "On the Journey"). "En el camino" is the result of in-depth reporting carried out primarily in 2008 and 2009 in southern Mexico, produced by journalists and photographers of *El Faro*—a Salvadoran online newspaper founded in 1998, and Latin America's first completely digital newspaper. This section of *El Faro* includes investigative news stories, chronicles, interviews with migrants and Mexican authorities, photo essays, and editorials. A book of chronicles and a photography book, based on the reporting and photo essays, were published in El Salvador in July 2010 (Martínez 2010; Ponces, Arnau, and Soteras 2010). This discussion of "En el camino" is of significance for developing an analytical understanding of competing narratives and imaginaries of Salvadoran migration. I also discuss an Internet forum/bulletin board. On this site, Salvadorans in the diaspora engage in "crime storytelling" (Moodie 2010) and develop emerging ways of commenting on their experiences and making sense of the violent causes of their emigration. The analysis of a string of comments and exchanges from this online forum reveals a particular knowledge of violence, even one specifically related to El Salvador as "a relationship to terror" (Pedelty 1995, 2).

Media portrayals of migrants in the news sections of *La Prensa Gráfica* and *El Faro* are situated within particular, even paradoxical, contexts. The news items are published in El Salvador, where many of the journalists are based. They are, however, addressed to transnational audiences: to readers who reside in El Salvador and to multiple audiences of migrant communities (primarily in the United States, but also in Canada, Mexico, Australia, and Europe). A complex transnational field emerges in this circuit of texts, where as "spectators and subjects of images, we engage in and are subject to complex practices of looking and being looked at" (Sturken and Cartwright 2001, 106). In these acts of viewing and making meaning of images and news, at times we may be invited to look at portrayals of migrants in difficult conditions; in other instances we are able to identify with their situation and with them as Salvadoran and more broadly as Central American and Latin American.

Salvadoran migrants in the United States draw upon a diversity of collective memories and patriotic symbols to construct their histories of migration and their complicated relationship to a state that has rarely (or never) been able to guarantee their personal security and rights. In light of this possibility of reconnection, Susan Bibler Coutin (2010b, 49) develops the notion of "re/membered communities" to analyze how Salvadorans in the diaspora relate to each other and to El Salvador as a place of origin and longing. Journalistic projects emerge as part of these "re/membered communities," as discursive and mediated manifestations of these nostalgic relationships, circuits of culture, and possibilities of connection.

"Departamento 15" and "En el camino" are spaces where viewers can make multiple meanings around portrayals of migrants. These projects of journalism and circulation assume the existence of a receptive public, and the possibility of claiming this Salvadoran emigrant reader for the nation—even when this Salvadoran has been away from El Salvador for many years. Given this project of inclusion, it is interesting to note that the same journalistic spaces that have portrayed Salvadoran transnational movement, migration, and borderless imagination must also include stories of deportation, death, mutilation, and accidents that befall Salvadoran migrants in the course of their trip through Mexico and to the United States. What, if anything, distinguishes the stereotypical nostalgic Salvadoran of civic national imaginings from the amputee and deportee, from the gang member, or from the mother who, out of necessity, leaves her children behind? Why do these distinctions matter when we (as viewers of these media representations) engage in the construction of meanings of migration and its contradictory, sometimes violent, processes?

The exploration of these contradictions is central to this analysis of "Departamento 15," the journalism of "En el camino," and the transnational spaces it claims for the nation. The transnational space of fluidity and exchange is constituted by its constant need for "others"—Salvadorans who are denied mobility in the course of their difficult journey, sometimes in the most dramatic forms. Immobility (in some cases, injury, detention, and eventual deportation or repatriation) and family separation are disruptive of the idea that the experience of migration and borderless transnationality is equally lived and accessible to every Salvadoran. Anna Tsing argues that metaphors of "flow" and "circulation" transform problematic processes with profound human consequences into feel-good, quasi-natural processes. She argues that transnational migration, one of the "flows" we address as we study globalization, "is movement stimulated through political and economic channels" (2000, 338). Tsing defines and engages "friction" as a nuanced view of flow and global connections, in which "heterogeneous and unequal encounters can lead to new arrangements of culture and power" (2005, 5).

As "flows," representations of bodies rely on "historically determined (and therefore socially acceptable) images that permit a distinction to be made between the observer and the Other" (Gilman 1988, 7). We can think of the body as "simultaneously a physical and symbolic artifact, as both naturally and culturally produced, and as securely anchored in a particular historical moment" (Scheper-Hughes and Lock 1987, 7). The portrayals of experiences of violence and deportation are situated in a history of "nonexistence" and "illegality" of Salvadoran bodies in transnational migration (Coutin 2000). Stories of tragedy and family separation existed during wartime, as personal family histories that extended, unavoidably, into the postwar moment. During wartime (1980–1992), various narratives of violence, illegality, and refugee status were ignored and eventually reconstructed to pursue asylum and residency claims, which previously had been legally and politically denied (Coutin 2000; Montes 1987). This chapter analyzes the portrayals of injured Salvadoran migrant bodies—how these are produced, mediated, and "re/membered" intertextually and in connection to wartime and postwar emigration. These images exist between the emergence of migration as a survival tactic during the 1980s, and the everyday struggles and necessities of the twenty-first-century neoliberal Salvadoran state.

In this discussion, it is important to remember that these individual narratives and histories of movement exist within larger social and economic structures. They are linked to what is already a messy, complex narrative of migration—that the civil war ended in El Salvador has hardly changed the dangerous nature of the migrant path through Mexico, or the adversities at the U.S.-Mexico border. These partial accounts exist through time, spaces, and media—and thus "no stories are innocent: they inevitably are structured through past texts" (Moodie 2010, 8). Franco Basaglia's notion of "peace-time crimes" further compels us to imagine the intertextuality and sense of time that connects these narratives. Nancy Scheper-Hughes examines this notion of "peace-time crimes" in order to "imagine a direct relationship between war time and peace time . . . a continuity between extraordinary and ordinary violence" (1997, 473). Cecilia Menjívar discusses the complexity of multiple forms of violence against women in postwar eastern Guatemala, finding that violence becomes normalized through a range of interpersonal, structural, and symbolic practices. Crucially, this analytic framework shows us how different forms of violence intersect, and how "although it is important to interpret particular situations as forms of violence, it is equally significant to trace links to broader structures, lest we inflict even more harm on the vulnerable" (2011, 28). To imagine and "re/member" (or even to "securely anchor") a hurt and amputated migrant body in this temporally and geographically scattered community of Salvadorans is an uneasy task, even as we account for the intent of postwar state projects, or for media institutions and their concerned, outraged, and patriotic audiences. Veena Das describes "how feelings of skepticism come to be embedded within a frayed everyday life so that guarantees of belonging to larger entities such as communities or state are not capable of erasing the hurts or providing means of repairing this sense of being betrayed by the everyday" (2007, 9; also see Hume 2009).

These everyday, normalized stories of injury and migration become important because they remind readers of a broader national community of Salvadorans. Ellen Moodie (2010) writes compellingly about crime storytelling and the "big stories and the stories behind the stories" that contextualize the everyday personal narratives of ordinary citizens within larger processes of postwar transition, democracy, and disenchantment. She considers that the personal experiences of Salvadorans and their generalized—and often accurate—perception that the postwar years are "worse than the war" has shaped new ways of knowing and relating to the nation and how people "imagined a common shape of their world" (Moodie 2010, 14).

Stuart Hall argues that mass media manufactures ways of "making sense" of events and crises, and of defining who is allowed to take part in an increasingly closed circle of news production (Hall et al. 1978). Stereotypical, legible portrayals are part of this simplification of people's circumstances. According to Hall, a stereotype arises from a combination of fear or repulsion and curiosity, and seeks to contain/manage the subject by flattening its characteristics (Hall 1997; also see Bhabha 1994, 66). Stereotypes have both positive and negative effects as they are socially produced and as they circulate in the media. For instance, this is how we arrive at cases of reduction and idealization of the complexity of Salvadoran transnationalism to a set of clear-cut cultural practices and portrayals of a "migrant people," including the assumption that the vast majority of Salvadorans in the United States are represented through these practices regardless of location, urban/rural origin, or time of arrival. Stereotyping "classifies people according to a norm and constructs the excluded as 'other'" (Hall 1997, 259). It results in a practice of othering to justify ideas of superiority and inferiority. Similarly, stigma is quite literally a bodily marker of social identity, and its effect is to exclude and "type-cast" individuals (Goffman 1963). This stigmatized and injured body is a marker of difference and a contested symbol of violent emigration.

In media narratives, stereotyping and stigmatization function as forms of social control, evidenced in the portrayal of productive and civic transnational bodies or in cautionary tales of dangerous migration. Control (or the lack thereof) also arises in the narratives of who is involved in violence against migrants—in the interrelated ideas of who is the victim and who is the perpetrator. Susana Rotker, in her analysis of narrative and urban violence in Latin America, considers the powerful idea of the "potential victim" as a subject who is denied mobility and who cannot enjoy the state's full guarantee that he/she will be protected from harm. Anyone could be the potential victim—"The potential victim is middle class, wealthy, or poor: it is anyone who goes out and is afraid" (Rotker 2002, 16).

In newspaper accounts, Salvadoran unity is often emphasized through the common and naturalized understanding that emigration, with its resulting remittances and transnational ties, is a survival tactic for Salvadoran families and essential for a viable nation-building project. The importance of the family as a social unit is reproduced, this time transnationally, as families are split by migration and forced to negotiate great geographic distances, anxiety, and the tense choices between parental presence and remittances or gifts (Dreby 2006; Horton 2009; Kent 2010).

A presumed common diasporic identity is set against life-altering, traumatic stories in which failed attempts at migration disrupt the "normal," homogenizing transnational "us" presented in "Departamento 15." In addition to their newsworthiness as stories of tragedy, the migrant experiences in "Departamento 15" and "En el camino" have a disciplining value, which accounts for their presence in the news sections. Like the news features focusing on patriotic Salvadorans in a transnational space, which produce an idealized, didactic narrative of migration, national belonging, and merit, stories focusing on the emotional strain of family separation also produce meaning(s). They seek to discourage undocumented emigration, yet reinforce the idea that for many Salvadorans the "American Dream" is worth the life-threatening risks described in the news. Stories of tragedies and repatriation of victims also serve to reclaim, symbolically and in reality, emigrant bodies to the sovereignty of Salvadoran territory.

In the stories portrayed in these news sections, the process of migration is interrupted and ends unexpectedly. The undocumented journey through Mexico involves many risks. Many of the cases discussed in "Departamento 15" and "En el camino" focus on the southern region of Mexico, especially Chiapas, where the migrant and train routes converge as migrants cross the first border between Central America and North America. Near the train tracks and in the surrounding countryside, Central American migrants are assaulted and detained. They are killed and their bodies are repatriated. They fall (or are pushed) off trains and suffer serious injuries; sometimes their limbs are mutilated.

The route through Mexico has long been described as dangerous and risky for the undocumented travelers of the isthmus. During the 1980s, Central Americans fleeing wars were already the targets of unscrupulous *coyotes*, thieves, and extortionists who took advantage of their disorientation, undocumented status, and traumatic experiences with authorities in their countries of origin (Cruz Monroy and Barrios Juárez Badillo 2009; Menjívar 2000, 58–76). Crimes and human rights abuses against Central American migrants leaving repressive regimes during the 1980s echo in the present-day conditions of violence in border areas such as Mexico-Guatemala—just as in the militarized U.S.-Mexico border we see the redeployment of the low-intensity conflict (LIC) doctrine from 1980s Central America (Dunn 1996).

The geographic distance between families and the physical incompleteness and social stigma of amputation and deportation remind us of the complexity of Salvadoran migration and its effects. Tragic and visibly violent circumstances are what earn many Salvadoran migrants any newsworthiness, and by extension any presence in the representational spaces of the transnational imaginary. However, this violence is built on the more subtle (and invisible) experience of separation and uprooting itself. Stories of maternal suffering, or of violence and bloodshed along the multiple, physical, national borders Salvadorans must cross to reach the "American Dream," stand in stark contrast to the world of patriotic celebrations and entrepreneurial success presented elsewhere in the borderless transnational space of "Departamento 15."

Separation and Sacrifice: "Everything That I Am Doing Here Is for Them"

"Departamento 15" often addresses concepts of family separation and sacrifice in its stories. These themes are especially present in accounts of Salvadoran women who emigrate and leave their children behind, often in the care of grandmothers or sisters, in the hopes of earning enough money to eventually reunite their families in the United States. A family life of living together and sharing the same geographic space is denied and sacrificed, and "transnational motherhood" comes to shape family dynamics and notions of obligation and virtue (Dreby 2006; Hondagneu-Sotelo and Avila 1997; Horton 2009).

In a "Departamento 15" story titled "Sacrificio y lágrimas de una madre emigrante" ("Sacrifice and tears of an emigrant mother"), we learn about Noemí, a Salvadoran woman who lives in the United States and will spend Mother's

Day without her children. She has not seen them in two years. The story was published on Mother's Day, and in the context of this celebration it is featured prominently in the news section and becomes emblematic of the struggles of transnational mothers. A picture of Noemí accompanies the story. She is wiping a table at the restaurant where she works as a waitress. Noemí communicates with her children, and with a greater audience of Salvadorans, through "Departamento 15." She tells the reporter, "I have nobody here and I wish, through *La Prensa Gráfica*, to tell my children that I love them very much, that I miss them and that everything that I am doing here is for them."[2] Although her message will circulate widely to readers on this special day, it is intensely personal, for her children. She speaks of her loneliness to multiple audiences. Who knows if this newspaper will reach the hands of her children? Although the phrase "everything that I am doing here is for them" may seem vague, it is clearly felt. Perhaps it is the simplest and best possible way to explain the complexity of transnational motherhood. Noemí avoids the complicated task of explaining her reasons for migrating to her children and the journalist—that, after all, is in the past and now unseen. Further, instead of dwelling on her present situation in the United States, she leaps to a moment of optimism, even joy, about the expected gains and the eventual reward for her sacrifice. Her loneliness on this Mother's Day ("I have nobody here") is a small price to pay for "everything" for her children.

In another story, "Cecilia," an undocumented woman—who did not want her real name published in the newspaper—paid twelve thousand dollars to reunite with her children after six years of separation. When she left El Salvador, her first son was eight years old, the second was four, and the youngest was only a few months old. After arriving in Washington DC, she worked two, three, and sometimes even four jobs. Finally, after many years, she saved enough money to hire a *coyota* (in this case, a "smuggler" who is female) to bring her children from El Salvador.

However, for twelve thousand dollars the coyota could bring only two of Cecilia's three children. The coyota decided and informed Cecilia that only the two older children (now aged fourteen and ten) should make the journey, because according to her if they waited any longer the border crossing would be riskier for teenage boys. The coyota took the money without specifying when she would finally bring the children to Washington DC, "because that depended on their luck on the border."[3] Cecilia is a transnational mother who is negotiating great distances, multiple jobs, heavy financial obligations, debt, and uncertainty. However, she is not presented as somebody who has the ability to make particular kinds of life-altering choices for her children. Her choices are constrained by her need to hire (and learn to trust) a coyota in order to see her sons again. It is up to the woman who will travel with Cecilia's children to decide on their safest route to the United States, and who will make the trip—a choice dictated by their ages, the dangers and high costs of the trip, and by their "luck on the border." Could it be more fitting that the coyota made these "choices" and left the end result up to "luck," relieving Cecilia of making the decision to leave her youngest child in El Salvador without his brothers?

After paying thousands of dollars, Cecilia could only wait for their arrival; at this point she became materially powerless and unable to protect her sons in their journey. But she worried, had them in her thoughts, and spent emotional energy on them. She "cried every night out of fear that her sons would not make it" and "prayed to God asking Him to protect them on their way."[4] Finally, after one month, her children arrived safely: "The tight hug, the uncontainable happiness, thousands of questions and tears of emotion filled the mother and her two sons, in spite of the memory of the youngest brother who stayed behind."[5] Because of him, Cecilia continues to work, and hopes to save five thousand dollars to someday see her youngest child again. "God will help me," she says, "He will guide me until we are all together."[6]

Sometimes children and teenagers do not wait for their parents (or other family members) to earn the money to travel, and instead decide to migrate on their own. They take on what are usually seen as adult roles and risky decisions as they negotiate the transitory social construct of youth: "Human transit does not only refer to physical mobility, but also existential. To pass from child to youth, from youth to adult, and from adult to old age means a change of identity. . . . Upon migration ways of being, and of understanding and living, are transformed. Furthermore, for migration youth becomes paradoxical, for while the body is in conditions for the challenges the journey requires, inexperience exposes its protagonists to situations of abuse, injustice, and pain" (Cruz Salazar 2011, 233).

Eight-year-old Jonathan had not seen his parents in five years. Two weeks after he had disappeared from his aunt's house in El Salvador, the Border Patrol found him in Arizona. His mother (who lived in Los Angeles) arrived at the detention center and claimed him. She said, "I did not know he was coming here, he is a hyperactive boy."[7] Jonathan had a very straightforward explanation for his decision—he said he decided to travel because "he felt lonely in El Salvador and wanted to be near his parents."[8] However, at the time of publication of this article in "Departamento 15" (December 2004), Jonathan had received a deportation order and had to appear in court. This could frustrate his hopes of reunification with his parents and his one-year-old, U.S.-born sister, whom he is just beginning to know. Jonathan's limited access to his parents, his undocumented status, and his possible deportation contrast with his younger sister's U.S. citizenship and the relative security and stability of her household. This is symbolic of global inequalities even between siblings.

In another story, seventeen-year-old Margarita left her home in La Libertad (near the Salvadoran coast) without telling anyone of her intention to reach her mother in Los Angeles. "Young woman survives the dangers of undocumented travel"[9] describes Margarita's journey through the Arizona desert to reunite with her mother. This meant leaving her grandparents and younger sisters behind, and risking her life. After traveling through Guatemala, she set out from Sonora, Mexico, with other migrants. Later, she separated from the group as they walked through the Arizona desert, and she ran out of food and became desperate. Margarita recounts this stage of her journey for the newspaper: "I walked for about seven hours, toward the highway, ready for the *migra* [U.S. Border Patrol or other immigration authorities] to find me. I did not want to die."[10] As the day ended, the lonely, hungry, and exhausted teenager faced the extreme temperatures of the desert night. Yet Margarita did not lose hope, as the news article describes in detail:

> The cold [weather] that had taken over her body could not put out the flame of faith in the heart of Margarita, a young Salvadoran who endured the low temperatures of the Arizona desert only to see her mother again and find a better future for her and her family. When she walked alone in the desert and could no longer feel her body and strength waned, Margarita could only ask for help to the one who according to her never fails her, "God, let immigration catch me, but I do not want to stay here," it was then that a coyote and a group of immigrants appeared and brought her to the city of Gardena, California.[11]

Margarita's migration narrative emphasizes the dangers of her journey, invoking images of a young woman alone in the cold desert night. Despite facing extreme temperatures she keeps a "flame of faith" in her heart as she hopes to reunite with her mother. When she prays to God, she asks for the Border Patrol to find her. Instead (and as if on cue), a coyote and his group find her and lead her to California. As a melodramatic narrative of imminent danger and crucial salvation, Margarita's story is a "perpetually modernizing form," part of "an evolving mode of storytelling crucial to the establishment of moral good" (Williams 2001, 12). The readers of "Departamento 15" can relate to Margarita's journey, sympathize with her suffering, and even rejoice in her survival and reunion with her mother and the timely arrival of a coyote who guided her and others through the desert to her destination—her own version of a promised land. A new mode of Salvadoran belonging claims Margarita to the pages of the newspaper: "a second model of citizenship has emerged around the visible emotions of suffering bodies that, in the very activity of suffering, demonstrate worth as citizens" (Williams 2001, 24). It is through enduring pain, suffering, and a dangerous journey that the Salvadoran migrants portrayed in these articles are "re/membered" (Coutin 2010b) to their families and the nation as young, often inexperienced migrants who take great risks to see their parents again.

Margarita's mother stated, "It is a miracle that she is alive. What she did was something crazy. I will not bring my other daughters this way."[12] Margarita said that one of her companions was another young Salvadoran, a pregnant teenager. "She was coming here to give her child a better future. I never saw her again," she said.[13] In connection with this text and its circulation, five days later "Departamento 15" ran a story about Mirna, a pregnant teenager who crossed the border after several weeks of travel. "I was very lucky I was not caught," Mirna admits in the story, as she holds her newborn baby and "dries her tears remembering her sister, her grandmother, her uncles and cousins, who stayed behind in La Unión, in eastern El Salvador."[14] Mirna's mother paid fifty-five hundred dollars for the trip, and has now incurred debt with friends.

Even a happy ending to a migratory tale is complicated in these cases. The accumulation of thousands of dollars in debt, as in the case of Mirna's mother and countless other travelers and cuerpomáticos, indicates the high financial costs of migration. Mirna's tears as she remembers her relatives, the cold numb hands of Margarita in the desert, and Cecilia's tears and nervousness embody "friction" (Tsing 2005) and the bodily, affective, and economic costs of migration. Stories of suffering in the migratory passage continue to inflect narratives of success as immigrants; as stories that are directed, in part, to audiences of migrants and their friends and relatives. Suffering and tears become "evidence of a subjectivity worthy of recognition" (Williams 2001, 24). At the same time that they become complex subjects, women such as Noemí and Mirna become gendered subjects of news. These examples point to the gendered aspects of migration, where ideas of sacrifice, altruism, and suffering for children are more dramatically expressed through accounts of women's migration and representations of lasting family relationships, enduring both as "reunited" and "separated."

In these stories, it is mostly women who bear the responsibility for reuniting with their children, regardless of the risk and at any cost. Alternatively, they endure transnational motherhood as they sacrifice completely to make sure their children have "everything." Women in migration in particular seem to become subjects who embody and demonstrate both anxiety (crying and awaiting the outcome of the coyota's decisions) and fortitude (multiple jobs and resignation to loneliness) in media portrayals.

On one level the accounts described above serve as cautionary tales for Salvadorans (especially women) who may be desperately considering undocumented travel. People who will never experience this journey, and those who experienced their journey weeks, years, or decades ago (and now live in the United States) also read these stories. Yet the transnational imaginary depends on the permeability of borders—on Salvadorans being able to cross into other countries, on the Internet and other technologies that enable mobility and "flows." Stories of family separation, danger, and violence against migrants can be interpreted as the perception of a threat to a predominant social order. The Salvadoran imaginary depends on migration and transnational practices, what have become the "normative outlines of our society" (Hall et al. 1978, 66). As families suffer separation and individual bodies are injured, violence in its multiple forms extends to representations of social bodies and the body politic (Scheper-Hughes and Lock 1987).

The Mutilation of the American Dream

Presently, emigration is taken for granted as the antidote to a lack of economic opportunity in El Salvador and as a guarantee of stability and income for transnational families, even as they are emotionally affected by lengthy separations. As the Salvadoran migration pattern continues to exist and become a normal and everyday practice, the transnational space of "Departamento 15" cultivates a reading public, fostering a concern for the daily life of the Salvadoran migrant. An interest in keeping a body count of migration emerges: how many Salvadorans are in Houston, Washington DC, or Los Angeles. To this we add stories of how many have been deported from the United States, how many dead and wounded have been repatriated from Mexico, and how many who made it to the United States at the appropriate time have applied for an extension of Temporary Protected Status (TPS) or petitioned to become legal permanent residents in order to live and work in the United States.

Migration is a contradictory practice, one that highlights the multiple dimensions of globalization. To survive life in El Salvador, thousands of people risk their lives by crossing multiple borders to the United States. As an extension of a pattern that increased because of armed conflict since the 1980s, migration and violence—along with accidents and repatriations—still force Salvadorans to "disappear." This is the price paid for a perception of Salvadoran postwar stability. As Nancy Scheper-Hughes argues, "Internal 'stability' is purchased with the currency of peace-time crimes" (Scheper-Hughes 1997, 473–474). The repatriation of injured bodies carries valuable symbolism during wartime (Ashplant, Dawson, and Roper 2000) and beyond, in "peace-time." When the injured migrant is repatriated to El Salvador, he or she is physically recovered from disappearance, to the *patria* and its imaginary of belonging. Media portrayals of these issues, for example those found in "Departamento 15" and in *El Faro*'s news section "En el camino," compel us to question the various categories of value assigned to migrant and repatriated bodies. Provocatively, the journalists of "En el camino" sometimes refer to Central American migrants as "los migrantes que no importan" ("the migrants who do not matter") to emphasize their vulnerability—although, clearly, these migrants are newsworthy and the central reason for this project. The point is to question regimes of value, and to read further into the assumptions of who "matters" in this journey.

Two story lines tend to predominate in the reporting of "Departamento 15" as the Christmas holidays approach. One is the narrative of return of relatives, holiday celebrations, and the continuity of cultural and emotional ties between Salvadoran immigrants, their families, and their country of origin. Another story line presents a less optimistic situation for the Salvadoran migrant. For example, a headline reads: "Twenty Salvadorans dead in 2003: They died in tragedies that occurred in southeastern Mexico."[15] The photograph for this article about migrant tragedy and death is captioned: "Victim: family and friends carry the casket with the remains of Jenri Daniel Márquez, eighteen years old, who died last May 8, run over by a train in Ixtepec, Oaxaca."[16] This caption directs the readers to a geographic point of tragedy where Jenri the young migrant became a victim, where his movement toward the United States abruptly stopped. The long stretch between Tapachula, Arriaga, and Ixtepec is the setting for many of these news stories about crimes and human rights abuses against migrants (Martínez 2010).

Jenri is one of many known cases of Salvadorans who die near the Mexico-Guatemala border region every year. Lucas Asdrúbal Aguilar, at the time the Salvadoran consul in Tapachula, Chiapas, reported the body count: "Six were run over by trains in attempts to board; a similar number, in highway accidents; five, in violent assaults; two of natural causes, and one asphyxiated inside a trailer."[17] The consul adds that all the bodies, except one, "had been repatriated to their place of origin with the aid of Mexican [and Salvadoran] authorities."[18] Also included in this 2003 report are the cases of twenty-one Salvadorans who were repatriated after suffering accidents during their journey through Mexico. Eight of them had their legs amputated, and the rest suffered knife or bullet wounds during assaults and robberies. These represent only a very small number of the nearly twenty-five thousand cases of reported returns (repatriations or deportations) from this region during the year 2003.[19] Meanwhile, many cases of assaulted and missing migrants are not acknowledged or not investigated by local police or other authorities—and in many instances, migrants do not denounce crimes against them due to mistrust and fear of deportation.[20]

On the same page of this issue of the newspaper, an article entitled "Eleven gang members [arrested] for mugging" also draws attention.[21] Gangs such as "Mara Salvatrucha" are mainly made up of young Central Americans—sometimes they are also deportees, also caught between El Salvador and the United States. In many cases the gang member refuses (yet is forced) to return as a "failed" migrant, and cannot return to El Salvador as the heroic subject of migration.

But in "Departamento 15" and in many of the chronicles of "En el camino," he returns as a hyper-masculine image, shirtless, tattooed, angry, caught up in violence, and ready to defend the territory of his affiliation. In media discourses the gang member is stigmatized by his marginal lifestyle, status as a deportee, and tattoos (Martel Trigueros 2007; Zilberg 2004; Zilberg 2011). Meanwhile, the Salvadoran migrant—a compatriot, and a "potential victim" (Rotker 2002)—is marked by undocumented status and the violent experience of the migration journey. Both are trapped within larger structures of power and global inequality that compel migration and lead to encounters such as José Ismael's, an experience shared with the reporter from the confinement of bed number fifty-six in the Tapachula hospital:

> [José] narrated that he left Ciudad Dolores, in the department of Cabañas . . . with the objective of returning once more to Los Angeles, in California, from where he was deported two years ago. "In the area known as El Ahorcado (south of Tapachula) we the undocumented (about thirty people) were assaulted by gang members, we came on the train from Ciudad Hidalgo; but because I resisted, they hit me with machetes on the back and two gunshots in the head with homemade weapons," he said. He added that he was thrown from the train, and later aided by some *campesinos* that passed by where he lay. Later, the young Salvadoran was able, on his own, to arrive at the Jesús El Buen Pastor shelter in this city and speak by telephone with his mother in El Salvador. . . . On his body [José] has a tattoo of the number eighteen, which confirms his belonging in that gang which operates in El Salvador. The compatriot accepted that he was processed some years ago in the correctional for minors in El Salvador.[22]

The excerpts from José's story show a violent migration narrative, yet they conform to a representational strategy where the "other" can be reclaimed as a compatriot in the pages of "Departamento 15." We learn about José's current lack of mobility—hospitalization due to bullet wounds received while on the train traveling north with a group of migrants. We also learn about a history of gang membership and that he had been deported from the United States, one of many "experiences of forced transnationality" between the Americas (Zilberg 2004, 776). A few days later, José was "practically expelled from the hospital," although the bullets were still in his head, because there were no neurosurgeons to extract them.[23] José will be repatriated to El Salvador; a second return rooted in violence is about to take place. The news stories trace the reclaiming of a now-victimized Salvadoran, injured migrant, and gang member. José's movement is a series of expulsions: from the United States, from the train, from the hospital. He admits his membership in the "Mara Dieciocho," or Eighteenth Street Gang, since his tattoo shows his loyalty to this group. In addition to the tattoo, José is marked by deportation from Los Angeles, violence in Chiapas, and repatriation to El Salvador—a layered identity and violent history of transnational movement that complicates the notion of nostalgia and homesickness for El Salvador. José, after all, wanted to return to Los Angeles—a Salvadoran city outside El Salvador's borders, and a powerful site within the transnational imaginary. Where is José's nostalgia and sense of belonging located? José's tattoo confirms his belonging to a transnational gang, but his experience of violence in Chiapas transforms him into a "reclaimable" Salvadoran subject, and a good son who telephones his mother in El Salvador as soon as he can. A few days after he had left the hospital, another story about José appeared in "Departamento 15." The headline states: "Consul and migrant are mugged." In November 2003, the Salvadoran consul accompanied the still-convalescent José on his repatriation journey. They took a bus together from Chiapas to Guatemala. In the town of Escuintla, Guatemala, some men boarded the bus, ordered the driver to slow down, and proceeded to rob the passengers. Eventually the consul and José arrived in Guatemala City, where they boarded another bus and completed the repatriation process.[24]

The intersection of gang violence, mugging, and undocumented migration covered in this reporting is particularly newsworthy because of its symbolic and disciplinary value. The bodies of the gang member and the migrant are closely linked as outcomes of longer historical processes of poverty and exclusion, yet represented as two distinct sectors of society in relationship to a crisis of border violence. The story of José and the consul's mugging can be imagined to cause a collective outrage over a larger crisis: the eruption (or "epidemic") of gang violence and other abuses against migrants and those who try to aid them. It is a crisis of Salvadoran (and other Central American, and Mexican) bodies involved in assaults and murder against each other, "a fundamental rupture in the social order. The use of violence marks the distinction between those who are fundamentally of society and those who are outside it. It is cotermi-nous with the boundary of 'society' itself" (Hall et al. 1978, 68). The portrayal of gang violence in Chiapas is closely tied to other themes and front-page head-lines in Salvadoran daily news, such as "Seven gang members die at the hands of rivals"—a told and retold story of unruly Salvadorans attacking each other.[25] Those portrayed as "outside" society—deported gang members in the villages or impoverished urban areas of El Salvador, or near the railroad tracks of south-ern Mexico—are caught up in violence. Those who are "inside" society, on the other hand, engage in postwar reconstruction, help their families, and keep their Salvadoran identity through demonstrations of patriotism. Migrants trav-eling north are caught in the midst of these extremes, marginalized and then reclaimed to the national social imaginary and its symbolic power, in "a con-tinual slippage of categories" (Bhabha 1994, 140).

Pain and War

Óscar is a Salvadoran teenager who in February 2003 decided to travel to the United States with two friends and one hundred dollars in his pocket: "Upon seeing on television the news about the war that the United States could initiate in the next few days against the regime of Saddam Hussein in Iraq, Óscar . . . decided that he wanted to join the army [of the United States]."[26] Óscar's decision to "enlist" was shaped by news and rumors of an imminent war far from his home, and his (mistaken) belief that he could join the U.S. Army to earn a salary that he could send to his family—this salary would be greater than what he earned as a construction worker, hauling sand and repairing roads in Ahuachapán, El Salvador.

Once the group crossed into Mexico and approached the train tracks, Óscar's two friends were able to jump on the train, but he fell. Óscar's injuries were so severe that his legs were amputated and he remained in a hospital in Tapachula for several days. His father traveled to find him there, and with the help of the Guatemalan Red Cross, Óscar was transported to the Guatemala–El Salvador border. Óscar's repatriation from Mexico was painful. The photograph that accompanies this "Departamento 15" article shows Óscar grimacing as Red Cross workers lift him out of an ambulance. "Destiny did not allow my son to go further; now I will have to work harder as a day laborer and bricklayer to be able to buy him a wheelchair," Óscar's father told the "Departamento 15" reporter.[27] In the article, the reporter describes Óscar's father as *acongojado*, as grief-stricken or heartbroken as he spoke about his son's tragedy. This word tries to convey the anguish and overwhelming sense of physical and moral pain that father and son feel. There is no relief in this moment of return—only a sense of loss, and that economic pressures will be greater for this parent who now needs a costly wheelchair for his son.

In the chronicle "La Bestia," journalist Óscar Martínez of *El Faro*[28] vividly describes a fall from "the Beast," the train, and tries to put into words the pain of the migrant's injuries. Here, we read about Jaime, a Honduran migrant who had barely slept during his long train travel through the Mexican countryside. After an exhausting eleven-hour train ride, he decided to continue on another train on the same day, instead of trying to rest. He was desperate, impatient to continue on his journey—"a mortal combination," Martínez writes (2010, 70). After another six hours, tired from sitting on top of the train, Jaime dozed off. When he awoke, he had lost his grip and he was slipping as he heard the deafening sound of the train, rapidly and heavily passing him by. And, as the journalist describes it, Jaime was sure that his life slowed down as he felt himself fall, as if "floating on the air. He, realizing that he was heading directly to the tracks" (Martínez 2010, 71).

"I did not feel pain," Jaime tells the journalist—and then, he realized that something was missing when he tried to stand up. He could see how his mutilated leg ended, in crumpled bones and flesh. He made a tourniquet and tried to walk with the help of a branch. After one hour of walking along the deserted tracks, Jaime fell, feeling dazed. He lay there for ten hours. In the late afternoon, some men found him and took him to a hospital. Martínez describes the feeling of pain, based on his previous observations as a journalist: "This [not feeling pain at first] is normal. The story is repeated in all the mutilated migrants that I have spoken with. At first it does not hurt. Then, sooner or later, the pain makes the muscles of your face contract, and a sudden and intense heat invades your body until it makes you feel that your head will explode" (2010, 71). When Jaime awoke from the surgery, he was hallucinating. For Jaime, the pain arrived that night, in the hospital, as he "dreamt that he played soccer, that he kicked a ball with the foot he no longer had" (Martínez 2010, 72). He woke up from this dream, screaming so loudly that several nurses ran to attend to him.

Dennis Patrick Slattery writes about how "the body wounded is a very mortal flesh remembered in a particularly unique way" (2000, 6). He asks how the wounded body changes the ways we narrate, how we have a sense of place, and how this marked body is formed by experience: "To be wounded is to be opened to the world; it is to be pushed off the straight, fixed, and predictable path of certainty and thrown into ambiguity, or onto the circuitous path, and into the unseen and unforeseen" (Slattery 2000, 13). Jaime's wound, and his dream-memory of soccer and his foot are intertwined with greater notions of "re/membering" in Central American migration. Can we understand Jaime's story and other narratives of migration and accidents through words that are synonymous with pain, and through news articles and images that communicate this affliction? It is difficult to understand physical pain, to grasp the "inherent difficulty of accurately describing any event whose central content is bodily pain or injury" (Scarry 1985, 13). As consumers of news we might be familiar with the stories and portrayals, and as audiences we are often hailed, reluctantly, to read about the pain and injuries of migrants. Perhaps this is reporting about a dimension of violence that is finally unreportable, even unknowable. Pain seems distant, and mediated: "When one hears about another person's physical pain, the events happening within the interior of that person's body may seem to have the remote character of some deep subterranean fact" (Scarry 1985, 3).

Zuleyma's Story

Zuleyma's story further illustrates the dynamics of power and the structural inequalities involved in the gendered portrayals of migration, pain, and suffering. She is a young woman from Cabañas, a department of El Salvador. In

December 2003, Zuleyma and her sister decided to travel to the United States, accompanied by a friend and a larger group of undocumented migrants. Her trip ended in tragedy. Thirty gang members boarded the train where nearly one hundred undocumented migrants, including Zuleyma and her companions, traveled. The gang members proceeded to shoot and strike the migrants with machetes. Several travelers jumped off the train, but were pursued by the assailants. Zuleyma's sister, Hipólita, and a friend, Sandra, were assassinated with guns and machetes.[29]

The following day a "Departamento 15" article in the "Nation" section of *La Prensa Gráfica* discussed how family members of the victims were asking for help from the Salvadoran government to bring the bodies back to Cabañas. It was also revealed that Zuleyma was wounded, and hospitalized in Tapachula.[30] In response to this and similar events the consulates of Guatemala, Honduras, and El Salvador issued a joint statement condemning the violent attacks against migrants: "We convoke the Mexican authorities to stop the violence of gang members against migrants and to reinforce the observation of respect for life and other human rights equally and for all."[31] Another article on the same page is related, in that it provides a response to the article about Zuleyma and the consular statement: "The [Mexican] deputy attorney general . . . announced the capture of ten gang members suspected of assaulting the freight train where two Salvadoran women died and another three were wounded last Tuesday. . . . Among the captured are Salvadorans, Hondurans, Guatemalans, and one Mexican. . . . [He] added that another thirty-six undocumented people who were on the train were sent to the National Institute of Migration [Instituto Nacional de Migración, or INM] to begin deportation proceedings to their countries of origin."[32]

Not only did the Mexican authorities capture ten gang members of diverse nationalities, but they also captured over a third of the train's migrant passengers, to initiate the proceedings to deport them to their countries of origin. While the authorities in Chiapas are policing their borders, the proceedings to repatriate the bodies of Hipólita and Sandra continue. On 12 December 2003, the news sources are no longer Central American consular staff or Mexican officials, but friends and family of the victims. They await the bodies of Sandra and Hipólita in Cabañas. We learn that Sandra was twenty years old and Hipólita, twenty-one. Both were young single mothers and they had two children each, aged between two and four years.[33]

On 18 December 2003, Zuleyma is repatriated along with another wounded man. This is a story of return to the homeland. Speaking about her tragedy, Zuleyma says, "It is good that most of the gang members were detained. I hope they send them to jail so they will not kill again. I will never again leave my home."[34] The social imaginary gives meaning to Zuleyma's experience. Her return is part of a history of emigration and violence. Now she hopes all gang members go to jail, and as for her, she will remain in her home and will never attempt to emigrate again. Zuleyma's tragic migrant experience serves as a cautionary, disciplinary tale for her and many more migrants, and makes sense for the "imagined community" (Anderson 1991) that has followed her story for several days through the pages of "Departamento 15."

Finally, on December 20, the newspaper further reveals Zuleyma's point of view in an article titled "'I was struck with machetes . . .': Survivor of tragedy narrates the nightmare she lived."[35] A large photograph shows Zuleyma with a bandaged arm and her two small children. She has survived to return to Cabañas where her family lives, and to tell her migrant's story. What she narrates is a nightmare, a "ghost story" (Gordon 1997). She has, in fact, pretended to be dead: "They struck me everywhere with machetes. I only covered my head. After receiving two wounds on my head I pretended to be dead so they would stop hitting me. They left me for dead because I stopped breathing when they touched my neck."[36] She has also witnessed the death of her sister and her friend. The final paragraphs of the story describe Zuleyma's extreme poverty and the illness of her young daughter, the causes of her emigration. In the pages of "Departamento 15," she is physically and symbolically recovered from ghostly disappearance, and repatriated to the Salvadoran social imaginary even as this means returning to her former condition of disadvantage and poverty.

I have traced Zuleyma's story in an effort to grasp how the newspaper understands and portrays the complex path of the undocumented, injured, gendered migrant. Her story is one of migration, lost family members, violence, tragedy, repatriation, and return to a life of poverty and marginality in rural El Salvador. Like the family separation stories of Noemí, Cecilia, and Margarita, Zuleyma's story is representative of the intersection of class, gender, and migration status as categories of difference, and highlights the contradictions of Salvadoran postwar migration and the complexities of claiming and reaching all transnational Salvadorans.

Virtual Traces of Violence and Emigration

The narrative of the migrant reaches the readers of "Departamento 15" as a "re/membered community" (Coutin 2010b). The stories become constitutive of a Salvadoran transnational imaginary in that they enable practices, such as reader responses and participation in Internet bulletin boards, around a commonly shared knowledge about emigration and border crossing from El Salvador through Mexico to the United States. Narratives about migrants circulate and find their way to the newspaper's Internet forum in the form of responses and comments such as this contributor's: "I would like to ask for a moment of silence for our compatriots who have lost their lives abroad. They died trying to reach what has always been denied in El Salvador, the right to live in dignity as a human being."[37]

In the "Departamento 15" online forum, memories of violence coexist paradoxically with nostalgic sentiments. This type of message board is a site for the production of community and mediation of experience, and shapes ideas of belonging, interaction, and inclusion as participants "consume the words of others" (Dean 2001, 260). Speaking of diasporic Filipino and Filipino American communities, Emily Ignacio characterizes the Internet as "a transnational space where people from all over the world can converge" (Ignacio 2005, 3). On the multimedia website of "Departamento 15," pictures and words combine with audio, video, and bulletin boards where readers can comment on news articles. The readers of *La Prensa Gráfica* become content producers as they participate in a forum where they can post their opinion on current events and read the opinions of others. They can explore the possibility of emigration in chat rooms where they can seek legal advice on visas and residency procedures, primarily to the United States and Canada. The digital version of the newspaper is a space where Salvadorans in El Salvador and abroad come together and share community and meanings of Salvadoran transnationalism. The Internet becomes a "discursive space where identity is performed, swapped, bought, and sold" (Nakamura 2002, xiv) around the histories of Salvadoran transnational migration presented on this website.

"Interaction with our readers is very important," a journalist for the website for *La Prensa Gráfica* explained in an interview. For her, audio, video, words, and images immediately "converge" on the Internet. She added, "We want to reach other countries [where Salvadorans are] and the Internet allows us to do that."[38] To accomplish this, the newspaper's website has gone through a series of changes and modifications since the late 1990s and early 2000s. In its early days it was primarily a mirror of the print edition. As part of the project of circulation in the United States—a project introduced with the intention of reaching Salvadoran communities abroad and claiming them to a national space—the website innovated and expanded its media content to reach the consumer of news in different ways, and in many respects it became a "new medium increasingly dissimilar from the old one" (Boczkowski 2004, 188). With this reach, journalists also realize that their work is read beyond the spaces of print circulation of El Salvador, reaching Salvadoran publics who respond virtually and from different points around the world. The newspaper website adjusts to (and creates) different locations and habits of mobile news consumption: some people may prefer to view a picture slideshow, or listen to an audio clip, recording, or video, instead of reading the words of the news article alone.

Communities of participants are formed in this site of consumption and interaction. They come to discuss current issues and events in the *foro* ("forum"). They come to know each other and to respond to opinions, sometimes to disagree, and sometimes to agree that they "should just print these comments out and give them to the president," as a journalist told me,[39] an idea that unites the forum commentators in dialogue and a common political participation, however informal. As Jodi Dean notes, "the cybersalon provides political theory with structural and empirical information important for thinking about the democratic possibilities of certain kinds of social and political spaces" (Dean 2001, 264). As a social space, the online forum extends beyond El Salvador, connecting communities of Salvadorans around the world as they discuss news and common issues.

In this sense, the online forum *seems* like a Habermasian "democratic public sphere" because it presents itself as a "universal, antihierarchical, complex, and demanding mode of interaction" (Buchstein in Dean 2001, 246). However, as the memories of violence and migration that are often discussed in the online forum symbolize, this online space is already shaped by critical experiences of inequality, which extend beyond access to the Internet. Discussing the implications of the idea of the public sphere, Jodi Dean argues for a concept of civil society that "acknowledges the inequalities, exclusions, and competing rationalities characteristic of networked societies in an age of globalization" (Dean 2001, 251).

As media institutions claim to have specialized information and knowledge about migration and related issues, we return to the question of how "Departamento 15" and other newspapers attempt to establish themselves as significant sites for shaping citizenship, as spaces for communicating responses to the state, and as institutions of "public service" that connect Salvadorans. Turning to consider the online forum on violence and emigration, how do participants construct violence and relate it to their crucial experience of leaving El Salvador? In May 2005, readers responded to these questions posted on the forum: "Was violence a determining factor in your emigration from El Salvador? What changes has your life had [have you experienced] in another environment?" Within a few days these questions generated a lively discussion (approximately 150 responses when I accessed it). Many of the respondents wrote that the answer was an obvious "yes," adding that lack of job opportunities also motivates emigration. Responding to the question and addressing the other forum participants, someone said, "Reading this forum, it is clear that the causes are economic, because of bad governments and their policies of tyranny, where the poor become poorer."[40]

Other forum participants thought that violence was still the main cause of emigration: "The current wave of violence is an echo of the past war," someone wrote. "My wife and I felt insecure in our own country," added another. There were comments about gendered violence: "Yes, it was violence, but domestic violence because women in El Salvador have no protections." An emigrant contributed his story: "Life had no value if you were a young university student. I came to the United States in 1980." He continued, "The war destroyed my ideals in El Salvador . . . but it is still the tiny piece of land where I was born." Another post tells a similar tale: "my idea was to return in a year or two, when things had 'calmed down' but twenty-five years have gone by. I do not plan to return. I read the newspapers on the Internet because they bring back memories of my childhood, of a reality that will not return."[41]

Linked to memories of violence, other participants on this forum expressed anger and depression about their situation as migrants, about how hard family separations can be: "It is a mix of feelings, anger and questions . . . things in a strange country are not easy [especially because I had to leave my son]." Another contributor also expresses frustration: "our family was separated . . . even today I become angry about everything my brothers and I went through, because of the violence that stalked us. Thanks for letting me vent a little." And a participant echoed this feeling, referring to violence as something that is passed on, projected to the future, by saying, "We [left] violence to our youth, instead of the opportunity to make a life in their own country."[42]

Others joined the conversation: "now we live in racist countries where the governments are not interested in us, after they provoke wars, they drain our best-qualified workforce." Meanwhile, another participant posted his opinion: "I think the biggest mistake that [we] many compatriots have made is to abandon our motherland for a materialism that is only fantasy and falsehood." Finally, someone commented on the violence of the migrant's journey, even in a time of peace, "It tears my soul to see news of hundreds of Salvadoran citizens who are apprehended in Mexico and the border with the United States to be deported. Entire families pawn their future to cross the border. We have become a country of desperate people. . . . Peace was signed but the war is fresh in the minds of Salvadorans."[43]

As demonstrated above, respondents in the online space that links El Salvador and the United States have a variety of conceptions of violence, experiences shaped by their subjectivities and by disparities of gender, socioeconomic status, and time of emigration. In the Salvadoran imaginary, it seems as though everybody can speak about different types of violence, and agree on its link to migration and to a common shared knowledge about conditions in El Salvador (and the extent to which these are currently perceived as violent, especially in the postwar period). On this point, one of the many messages on this forum summarizes this knowledge: "All Salvadorans knew the postwar would be harsher than war."[44] What emerges through the questions posed by the newspaper is a dialogue, a variety of representations and explanations for the connection between violence, temporality, and migration. By asking its readers to comment and to create public opinion, violence and migration become shared codes of meaning in online interactions, as they link Salvadorans around the world to the visible and invisible climate of violence in El Salvador.

The contributions by Salvadorans in this online space of "Departamento 15" reveal anxiety about leaving El Salvador, and an ambivalence, even fear, about returning. These impressions may be related to particularities in the migratory experience of participants, perceptions about the postwar climate, and preexisting inclinations to return to El Salvador. The voices of the content producers circulate and talk back to each other in a virtual space, yet are anchored in memories of separation from El Salvador. In answering a question such as "Was violence a determining factor in your emigration from El Salvador?" the respondents consider individual *and* larger structural, historical, and global perspectives on the movement of Salvadorans across borders. They can consider the "big story" (Moodie 2010) of war and transition to democracy and the subjective, personal narratives that serve to communicate and share nuanced understandings of this imaginary.

The examples above draw attention to the complex processes for which migrants risk their lives, their bodies, and their financial and emotional resources. They produce disciplinary meaning(s) as they are consumed and commented on by the newspaper's readers in print and online. The stories reinforce the idea that for many Salvadorans, improved economic conditions and family reunification are worth the life-threatening risks and financial costs described in "Departamento 15" and "En el camino." These mediated processes describe and illustrate the broader inequalities of globalization—the relatively free circulation of newspapers, capital, and other commodities versus the restricted, risky migration of bodies.

Conclusion

"Departamento 15" does not just present nostalgic pictures of happy immigrants and their families at home. It reports on these complicated representations, drawing the attention of the readers to the contradictions of transnationalism, embodied in separated and reunited families, migrants killed or maimed during their journey north, and Salvadorans returning home in ambulances or caskets.

Like Zuleyma, Hipólita, Jenri, and many others, the migration narratives of thousands of emigrants traveling through southern Mexico often end in tragedy, death, or deportation. Salvadoran migrants are rejected or reclaimed—criminalized, deported, or repatriated to the sovereignty of Salvadoran territory. Their tragedies are reminders of the violence of migration, and of the uneasy "flows" of Salvadoran transnationalism. Postwar stability depends on these "peace-time crimes" (Scheper-Hughes 1997); migration from El Salvador through Mexico is a continuation of wartime emigration—it continues to marginalize certain bodies, and reveals tensions in the Salvadoran imaginary.

In El Salvador, economic and political stability is purchased through normalized survival strategies of emigration and remittances sent from abroad. These become naturalized forms of displacement, economic survival, and exclusion from Salvadoran territory. In some "Departamento 15" stories we see examples of the normalization of transnational ties and of emigration as a characteristic of modern Salvadoran everyday life. Portrayals of Salvadorans living abroad become a visible, everyday part of an "imagined community" (Anderson 1991) of readers. In contrast, emigration practices during the 1980s acquired an extraordinary tone, as people were displaced violently, became refugees, and in many instances were forced to secretly leave El Salvador to escape the explicit violence and political terror of war.

"Departamento 15" and "En el camino" produce news of migration, where the movement of bodies is risky but necessary for a country defined by various degrees of violence, economic necessity, and dependence on remittances. It is "a country of desperate people," according to one of the online forum participants, where stories shock and become everyday news. The travel path is dangerous, and its violence is a test of the limits of society (Hall et al. 1978, 68). The networks that are used to make travel and reunification possible sometimes hint of illegality or criminality in news portrayals, and their existence also points to the necessity of the migrants who resort to these networks. Narratives of migration and violence are also constructed in the forum of "Departamento 15," virtual yet anchored in vivid memories of emigration. The complex transnational imaginary assembled in these sites seeks to engage all Salvadorans, regardless of location.

These spaces of circulation are mediated and representational, between El Salvador and Salvadorans abroad; as constructed by reporters, people at "home," and migrants, these are shared stories. A simple account of domination and hegemony would not fully capture this space or people's continuous participation in it: the view of globalization and movement that emerges is controlled in certain ways but still complex, where contradictions, the management of violence, portrayals of patriotism, and of who is worthy of being reclaimed to the nation are very much part of the story.

3

Vega's Disgust

Edgardo Vega's aversion and *asco* ("disgust") for El Salvador has only grown since he emigrated in the late 1970s and made his new home in Montreal, Canada, where he has cultivated a satisfying academic career in art history. It is clear that Vega—the protagonist of Horacio Castellanos Moya's 1997 novel *El asco: Thomas Bernhard en San Salvador*—never wanted to return to his birthplace. The idea of returning to El Salvador represented a bitter, ongoing battle and a source of deep tension between Vega and his mother while she was alive. She pleaded with him for years, yet he never gave in and never returned to visit her. But now it is the mid-1990s, Vega's mother has died, and he had promised her that he would return for her funeral and to fulfill the final wishes expressed in her will. When the novel begins he is sitting at "La Lumbre," a bar in San Salvador, sipping his first (or is it his third?) whisky while telling his friend Moya about what he has lived during the past two weeks. All this, because of that promise: "My mother won, Moya, she made me return, already deceased, of course, but she won: here I am after eighteen years, I returned only to confirm that I did very well by leaving," Vega ruefully admits (Castellanos Moya 1997, 19).

In this chapter I offer a close reading of *El asco* as an example of literary representations of emotion, disgust, and the relationship of the emigrant protagonist to postwar Salvadoran society. As in previous chapters, I address the ambivalences surrounding national belonging and connection to El Salvador, including the question of how different sites and situations present us with instances of connection accentuated by distance from El Salvador. *El asco* grapples with nostalgia, the commonly held notion that certain emblematic aspects of Salvadoran history, culture, and places—food, childhood home, and tourist attractions—along with ways of socializing are invariably productive of migrant sentimentality. Vega mocks this assumption of nostalgic feelings, actively differentiating himself from (and feeling superior to) those who ache for El Salvador and for memories of "better times" before emigration. Vega certainly remembers El Salvador and the time before his emigration to Canada. However, his memories are transgressive—that is, his idea that El Salvador evokes deep disgust offends many of his relatives (and maybe even some readers). "As if this country had anything valuable for which a person like me could feel nostalgia," Vega tells his friend and confidant Moya while at the bar (Castellanos Moya 1997, 60).

Vega is marked by a stark sense of himself as an estranged Salvadoran, someone who remains paradoxically connected to the Salvadoran nation by a very profound feeling of disenchantment and aversion toward the repulsive subjects that he criticizes. I develop the idea of Vega's transgressive nostalgia as I discuss the intertwined narratives of disgust, reluctant return, and sense of obligation (however deferred and ambivalent) to family and friends that are entangled thematics in *El asco.*

Moya and Vega

Vega does not have many friends left in El Salvador. Over the years, as he remade his life in Canada he intentionally lost contact with most of the people he knew during his childhood and teenage years. And now, in the reencounter at the bar that opens the novel, Vega has been waiting for Moya. Moya, a privileged interlocutor and rare friend of the protagonist, is a way to tell the story of *El asco.* Sitting at "La Lumbre," Moya is a character we meet at this bar and Vega's sounding board—the narrator and a literary device to connect the characters and interlocutors to the novel's real author, Horacio Castellanos Moya. We could interpret this as an effort to connect the San Salvador of this novel to a possible version of the postwar reality of the city and its inhabitants, lending a form of verisimilitude and immediacy to the narrative. Moya is also a writer of fiction, especially short stories. Like the real author, Moya was born in Honduras but moved to El Salvador when he was young. Like the real author, Moya spent most of the war years in Mexico but has returned to San Salvador in the postwar to try to make a living as a writer. We learn this much about Moya from what Vega says.

In the course of *El asco* Vega tells Moya about his two weeks in San Salvador. In itself, perhaps Vega's telling only takes two hours, or the time it takes him to drink several whiskies, or the time between late afternoon and dinner: five to seven, a liminal and even uneventful time-space between late afternoon and early evening. However, the recounted events exceed the temporal limits of the two hours at the bar and Vega's two weeks in the city, and exceed even the two decades that have passed since Vega lived in San Salvador or the years since Vega and Moya were classmates. Vega talks about the faults of politicians past and present, about his uncomfortable, fetid, and noisy airplane flight and arrival in the company of other Salvadorans (84–95), about the deplorable state of higher education in El Salvador, and about a recent and detestable trip with his brother and his family to a well-known Salvadoran beach. All of these events coexist in the same storytelling, and their common characteristic is that Vega considers them as disgusting and Salvadoran, as "the degradation of taste" (84). Vega's telling is a stream of accumulated impressions and memories. Some events appear to be more important or consequential than others, but that does not matter, they all exist in the same negative space. Throughout this conversation that spins to other places and times, there is no response from Moya, who does not make judgments and does not ask anything. Moya is present at the bar only so Vega can talk. Stylistically, Vega is a voice looking for a listener—a desperate, disgusted voice.

At the bar, it is entirely Vega's story—digressions, disgust, and everything else—to tell. It also becomes the story of Moya, as narrator, and of his own relationship to disgust as an emotion and an idea. Vega draws him in, thanking him for listening, complaining to him that over the years all their other classmates have given in to ordinary careers and inconsequential lives in El Salvador—and that the two are the only exceptions to this fate. Importantly, Vega asks Moya why he tries so hard to make a living as a writer in a country that does not even appreciate literature. Moya's choice to live and work in the disgusting situation or squalor (*asquerosidad*) of El Salvador is something that Vega cannot understand—why would anyone not born in El Salvador choose to return and stay, when Salvadorans have widely accepted emigration as a fact of life? On this, Vega questions his friend, "I do not understand what you are doing here, Moya, that is one of the things that I wanted to ask you . . . how someone who can go to live to another country, to a minimally decent place, prefers to stay in this asquerosidad. . . . You were born in Tegucigalpa, Moya, and you spent the ten years of the war in Mexico, that is why I do not understand what you are doing here . . ." (Castellanos Moya 1997, 21).

In the novel, Vega expresses outrage that literature and history do not exist in El Salvador as viable careers and academic fields. *How can a country exist without a department of literature in the National University?* Vega wonders. He thinks it is absurd that his former classmate Moya is trying to earn a living as a writer in this milieu: "nobody who is interested in literature can opt for a degenerate country like this one, a country where nobody reads literature . . . an incredible country, Moya, nobody can study history because there is no history career" (24–25, see also 77–80). Vega conveys his impression that every young Salvadoran in higher education is materialistic, career-minded in a very narrow way, and only wants to study business administration. His specific point that history and literature are sacrificed while business administration is the most popular program in universities speaks to Vega's growing unease and disgust at the prospects and career choices of young Salvadorans growing up and seeking jobs in the postwar years. While these may be individual choices made by students, they are also the product of lacking university resources and incentives, along with long-standing and quite real institutional limitations at the decision-making levels of the state: "El Salvador has suffered from a dearth of readers because of high rates of illiteracy, an almost nonexistent internal market for books and thus few publishing houses, censorship of written literature and the mass media, threats to writers who challenge the system, and the departure of most committed writers into exile. . . . It takes more than authorial desire to make a novel in El Salvador" (Craft 1997, 62). History also seems to be a rare pursuit, as Robin DeLugan notes: "Prior to 2000, El Salvador offered no formal academic opportunities to study history. That fact makes El Salvador unusual among modern nation-states" (2012, 47). Speaking in the mid-1990s, Vega laments the deteriorated state of the National University, a public institution that was greatly affected, even shut down, during the civil war—however, he is also disgusted at what he perceives as the continuous politicization of this institution's postwar mission and significance.

Vega does not receive a response from Moya on these questions of writing and living in El Salvador, and on other questions that emerge during their meeting at "La Lumbre." Moya becomes the trusted listener-writer-friend, and the phrase *me dijo Vega* ("Vega told me") interspersed throughout *El asco* implies closeness, confidence, and hints at this relationship between Vega and Moya. Vega does all the talking, while Moya, as the confidant, listens (but does not reply). Perhaps the narration of Vega's experience in San Salvador can extend, spiraling beyond this moment of the bar, be retold in another time and possibly another place, long after Vega has finished his story and his whisky. What we read in *El asco* is a reconstruction of their meeting: *these are Vega's complaints*, the novel seems to convey, *this is Vega's viewpoint from his disgusting two weeks in El Salvador*. It is as if Moya is now retelling the story of Vega, what "Vega told me," for all to read.

As a work of fiction, this telling and retelling has a porous relationship to Salvadoran national reality and is thus open to interpretations and critique. Authors and intellectuals might have posed the same questions in real life that Vega and Moya grapple with in the novel. Why remain in El Salvador? Why aspire to live as a writer in the midst of this postwar society? What to do with these feelings of disgust? In a June 2002 interview with Rafael Menjívar Ochoa published in *Vértice* (the literary supplement of *El Diario de Hoy*), Horacio Castellanos Moya discusses these questions of contemporary Salvadoran reality, and how they might be related to the structure and wide-ranging interpretations of his novels. Regarding the context of *El asco,* Castellanos Moya addresses the questions of how readerships and publics are formed and maintained as political and social communities. In his view this has ramifications for the reception of a work of fiction that, nevertheless, critiques many real problems and sectors of society. He tells *Vértice:* "Generally when a novel makes very strong critiques about political or cultural aspects, and when it is published in a world of readers more accustomed to the text of testimonio, which seeks historical truth, people do not react in a literary sense, do not conduct a literary reading." He continues: "With *El asco* the reader, in general, does not consider the literary aspects, of the construction of characters, of the plot . . . but rather concentrates on the aspects that [to the reader] seem most sensitive with regard to [his or her] way of seeing the world." Asked by Menjívar Ochoa if *El asco* intended to be provocative, or if there had been a "somewhat obvious" interpretation of the novel, Castellanos Moya said that it was "A bit of both things . . . When one enters the terrain of the essential values of the national, evidently one questions people's definite judgments around which their values are constructed."[1]

Advising his readers not to look for historical truth or evidence in his novels, not to look at this as a testimonio or confirmation of their deeply held values, ideologies, or patriotic beliefs, Castellanos Moya signals that it is indeed time to negotiate this line of truth and fiction in Salvadoran politics and culture.[2] This presents a complicated task of readership in the Salvadoran imaginary—the fictional world of *El asco* quickly rejects the possibility of humanistic inquiry, for it is a world of materialism where history and literature are always denigrated. Meanwhile, the reality of postwar El Salvador is hardly more appealing. The reader is left to negotiate, to read (and even try to accept) a novel that is fundamentally full of contempt for the idea or possibility of national unity. *El asco* rejects the idea of the nostalgic emigrant who can be successfully reclaimed to the current realities of the nation—it is a novel where the overarching sentiment is disgust and whose protagonist, Vega, is simply disgusted and annoyed about everything. In doing so, Castellanos Moya critiques and points to fundamental ruptures in issues of representation, veracity, and claims to truth in postwar El Salvador. Intertwined narratives of reluctant return, disgust, and an ambivalent sense of obligation to family and friends are central to my discussion of this novel and its context.

Much like Vega's feelings of estrangement in this work of postwar fiction, the trajectory of the novel and its author suggests a rupture and turn in Salvadoran literary and political culture. Beatriz Cortez discusses and defines *estética del cinismo* ("aesthetic of cynicism") in order to analyze this central characteristic of literary production in postwar El Salvador; "the cynicism that characterizes the postwar sensibility in Central America opens spaces to live and to explore passion. It also has its limitations: although it allows the subject to laugh at its own faults, at its own fears, at its own desires, finally cynicism takes the individual to its own destruction" (2010, 37–38).

When *El asco* was published in San Salvador in 1997, many readers and critics focused on how the novel questioned certain sensibilities of ideology and patriotism, and how it exposed the faults of the national project, as the author noted to *Vértice*. The polemic that ensued—the unflattering light cast on nationalist sentiments that often seem so unquestionable—took Horacio Castellanos Moya into "what has become a long, self-imposed exile; in the years since its publication, he has lived in Tokyo, Frankfurt, and, most recently, Pittsburgh."[3] It was not the first time Castellanos Moya had been in this state of exile—he spent most of the 1980s in Mexico. His 1989 novel *La diáspora* was widely interpreted as a critique of the Salvadoran left.[4] In a 2001 opinion column that appeared in *La Prensa Gráfica*, Juan José Dalton commented on the work and trajectory of Castellanos Moya: "From my point of view, the author could be called author of rupture: he breaks with everything and simultaneously suggests (without saying so, because that is how fiction is) the foundation of the new, which is not configured in paradises or in purities, but has to do with the honest and the real, the possible."[5]

Cynicism and rupture are elements of this body of work. Vega and the real "self-exiled" novelist echo each other in some ways, as they grapple with their connection to *El asco*'s version of El Salvador. Vega physically breaks with it by not returning to visit his country of birth, and further rejects it by refusing to associate with his compatriots who live in Canada (Castellanos Moya 1997, 17–18). Vega's account of how and why he has returned to San Salvador begins with him stating his own version of rupture, of why he emigrated. He must reiterate to Moya, his confidant, that he did not leave El Salvador eighteen years prior because of the war. Vega is adamant about maintaining this distinction, about establishing the context of his exit from El Salvador in a special temporal space within the nation's migrant imaginary: he left *before* the war, before others displaced by the war arrived in Montreal, Canada. He never wanted anything to do with these later arrivals, with refugees, with political exiles, setting himself apart by time of migration and other political and socioeconomic factors, including urban origin and level of education. Vega attended a private school in San Salvador and pursued higher education abroad. His reason for leaving El Salvador was his own disgust and dissatisfaction—he could never accept "destiny's macabre joke" (Castellanos Moya 1997, 17) that he was born a Salvadoran: "I had not returned to the country in eighteen years, eighteen years in which I did not miss any of this, because I left precisely fleeing this country, to me it seemed like the most cruel and inhumane thing that out of all the places in the planet I had to be born in this place, I could never accept that out of hundreds of countries I had to be born in the worst of all, in the most stupid, in the most criminal, I could never accept it, Moya, that is why I went to Montreal, long before the war began" (17).

Edgardo Vega may not realize or readily admit it, but he exhibits a "very Salvadoran" trait—the tendency to view emigration as a solution to El Salvador's social ills and personal issues alike. I must say more about Vega's version of his emigration. The circumstances of his departure are both privileged and tragic. His story forms part of the diversity of Salvadoran migrants in Canada, the United States, and other countries—a diversity that is sometimes clouded by stereotypes and not fully acknowledged or explored. In Vega's case, emigration is a status symbol. He was able to leave on his own before the war, before Salvadoran emigration to North America became marked as clandestine, motivated by war, poverty, and political oppression, and characterized by dangerous, even fatal, border crossings. In the postwar period this continues to be an important line to draw, and Vega remains conscious of this. Emigration is a symbol of his own capacity, agency, taste, and subjectivity; but it is also the result of his dissatisfaction and his feeling of misfortune that he was born in "the worst" country. In case people who meet Vega in Canada do not know about his unique circumstances, and assume that he is associated with the stories of migration of political refugees and impoverished peasants from war-torn El Salvador, he must demarcate, categorize, and insist on his decision to leave as an individual one.

The insistence on this individuality highlights Vega's strong refusal to accept the fact that because he was born in El Salvador he must remain Salvadoran—being Salvadoran by birth may be a joke of destiny, but Vega changed this fate by leaving for Canada and eventually becoming a Canadian citizen. Furthermore, his decision separates and distinguishes him from the war, an important (yet tainted) period in contemporary Salvadoran history. This account of his departure also reveals Vega's mentality that to remain in El Salvador is to experience a form of social death, intellectual decay, and lack of opportunities, particularly because he is convinced that he might not have been able to fulfill his academic aspirations if he had conformed to the educational and career paths offered in the Salvadoran university system, at least as he describes it—a country full of people who study business administration and live in a climate of violence and materialism.

Vega is now an art history professor at a major Canadian university, an educational path and profession that would have been impossible (or at least highly unlikely) to pursue if he had stayed in San Salvador. Over the years his mother tried to update him about what some of his former classmates had become: doctors, engineers. But these tales of success do not convince him that he should return to Salvadoran society. He rejects this news of conformity, uninterested in the destinies and ordinary lives of his former peers. As we already know, Vega has returned because his mother died, and over the years she had insisted that he attend her funeral. Another important factor in his return is that he is now a Canadian citizen. Vega describes the emotional distress and chronic loss of sleep he suffered over his many years as a noncitizen migrant, over the possibility of returning to El Salvador, and finally his relief when he became a Canadian citizen. With his Canadian passport he judges that he is able to return, albeit reluctantly, with the knowledge that he does not have to stay in El Salvador. "My Canadian passport is my guarantee," he tells Moya (Castellanos Moya 1997, 18). It is his safe-conduct, especially now that the war has ended. Nothing, it seems, can force him to remain in El Salvador.

Postwar Disenchantment and the "Inner Cop"

Vega's motivation for sharing his experience with Moya is disgust, the deep and chronic emotion that defines his stay in El Salvador: "I have suffered disgust for fifteen days, it is the only thing that the people in this country produce in me, Moya, disgust, a terrible, horrible, and ghastly disgust" (Castellanos Moya 1997, 22). This visceral, bodily emotion is triggered by his return to El Salvador and by his interactions with Salvadorans going about their everyday lives. This story of disgust and repugnance takes the form, as many of Castellanos Moya's novels do, of an "unhinged first-person rant."[6]

It is clear that Vega does not return to a fertile literary environment when he visits the version of San Salvador presented in *El asco*. He does not find intellectually stimulating conversations in cafés, on the media, or even with his own relatives—his brother, sister-in-law, and nephews spend their free time watching television. For Vega, television programming is useless, and the newspapers are not worth reading, "precisely the best proof of the intellectual and spiritual misery of *este pueblo* [this nation, or people]"(58). The universities, especially academic programs in the humanities, are in disarray.

In the midst of this uninteresting, intellectually barren landscape, "La Lumbre" is the only place Vega likes in the city.[7] Since he discovered this bar, he sits there in the late afternoons, daily, for two hours from five to seven P.M., seeking tranquility and listening to jazz records and classical music in the company of a good bartender. Vega prefers to sit in the patio since it is too hot indoors at the bar. He drinks whisky before the rock band begins to play and it becomes impossible to sustain a meaningful conversation. It is during one of these short-lived moments of peace and refuge that Vega manages to recount his two weeks of disgust to Moya, a former classmate from their days at a private religious school in San Salvador. He is the only person Vega wants to meet. Moya arrives at "La Lumbre" punctually. This pleases Vega, who by this point in his stay in San Salvador has lowered his expectations of anyone keeping their word when they say they will meet socially. "How lucky that you came, Moya, I had my doubts that you would come, because not many people in this city like this place," the novel begins (11).

Vega, as the narrative makes clear, is deeply exasperated by the social norms and expectations that come with this trip: the stay with his brother and his family, the funeral service, the forced condolences, the tense discussion of his mother's will and what to do with her house. Vega wants to sell the house as soon as possible and take his share of the money back to Canada, while his brother is more sentimental and wants to keep the house they grew up in as family patrimony. Of course, Vega is not interested in living in a house in San Salvador, and views his brother's intentions with suspicion. So in more ways than one, his talk with Moya, and the drinks they share, become an opportunity to vent, to let loose, to say things to a trusted listener. Vega has obviously had enough, as he tells Moya with urgency, "I must speak with you before I leave, I have to tell you what I think of all this filth, there is not another person to whom I can tell my impressions, the horrible ideas that I have had while here" (13).

Disgust is a main theme in the novel, and in Castellanos Moya's oeuvre more generally. Since the 1990s, Salvadoran literature has been renovated by the official end of war yet marked by themes of disenchantment, the paradox of interpersonal violence as a primary social relationship, and cynicism. Salvadoran literature carries marks of war, even when it does not always refer directly to the armed conflict, making the "aesthetic of violence" an important component of the creative forces of this literary production (Villalta 2004, 6). In her interpretation of the compelling idea of "splendid hells," Nilda Villalta proposes that a new generation of Salvadoran postwar writers has indeed emerged from infernal conditions, to produce a transformative literature: "From death, destruction, body parts, the immigrant experience, these writers are collectively creating a new literary expression, a new aesthetic capable of narrating those violences" (Villalta 2004, 6). In addition, processes of globalization—for example, migration, foreign investment, and regional market integration—have affected the meanings and reach of national and isthmian identities, including interventions in national reality and cultural production. Scholars of Central American literature emphasize this view of rupture and continuity in their analyses of testimonio, politics, culture, and the disenchanted literary moment of the 1990s and beyond (Arias 2007; Beverley and Zimmerman 1990; Cortez 2010; Craft 1997; Rodríguez 2009). Beatriz Cortez traces these links and contrasts: "Fiction, with its disenchanted portrait of life in Central American urban spaces, seeks to accomplish something that testimonio also sought: to put into evidence the inexactitude of the official versions of Central American reality. In contrast to testimonio, fiction lacks the idealist spirit that characterized Central American literature linked to the context of civil wars" (2010, 27).

Given this complex context of literary production, it is not entirely surprising that postwar El Salvador jars Edgardo Vega's senses. The civil wars transformed the Central American isthmus in a paradoxical manner—while socioeconomic conditions did not change for the majority, these countries had somehow moved toward "peace," transitioning to democracy and macroeconomic stability. This transformation has been especially important for the Central American structure of feeling and for the role of literature in projects and configurations of national identity. The end of the civil war in El Salvador marked a significant moment in literary and cultural production: a movement from the revolutionary poetry and testimonial literature analyzed by John Beverley and Marc Zimmerman (1990) and Linda Craft (1997) to a new form of critique, a literature of *desencanto.* While Central American literature was part of conflicts and change, viewed "as an ideological practice of national liberation struggle" (Beverley and Zimmerman 1990, ix) the study of postwar literary production must be involved in "a critical exploration of El Salvador's new neoliberal reality" (Padilla 2008, 136). Arturo Arias describes this shift in terms of pleasure descending into physical discomfort: "when we rethink contemporary Central American narrative, we can see in its most recent examples how a certain past intoxication with revolutionary utopias has given way to a heavy hangover" (2007, 22).

Writers such as Horacio Castellanos Moya, Jacinta Escudos, and others have thus stepped onto the postwar Salvadoran literary landscape as producers of fiction and pointed journalistic commentary that questions traditional, dominant notions of Salvadoran identity. For instance, Escudos's short story "La noche de los escritores asesinos," included in *Cuentos sucios* (1997), questions traditional gender roles, signaling that something has shifted in these relationships (and their portrayal) in the postwar. The collective voice of the testimonial has given way to an individual, self-destructive narrative of the "assassin writers" of this title. In "La noche de los escritores asesinos," competition between the protagonists, two writers, is not only along ideological positions but also along gendered axes. The male writer is intensely jealous of the female writer's success; "both former guerillas, they meet years later in a corrupt and crime-ridden postwar San Salvador when they go to work for the same newspaper" (Padilla 2008, 141). Their rivalry becomes deadly.

Fiction resonates with the "newly respun corporatism" (Rockwell and Janus 2003, 30), which is a strong feature of this changing media landscape. Whether these changes are considered to be deep or merely cosmetic, in the postwar media institutions described in other sections of this book and by other media scholars, this shift has real effects in perceptions of market appeal and readership. In fiction and in reality, the "former guerrillas" join media institutions in San Salvador in the postwar, as it is presumed that all past resentments and competitiveness are set aside while solidarity lives on in the national imaginary. However, it is clear—as Yajaira Padilla's analysis of gender and neoliberalism in postwar fiction demonstrates—that it is not that simple: "Although at heart 'La noche de los escritores asesinos' is a story about writing and creation, it is a story about writing in a postwar era and redefining a woman's place within a patriarchal society that continually negates her by appropriating her words" (2008, 143).

In light of these new political realities, urban spaces, and transnational markets, literature is a productive site where multiple meanings of these global transformations and connections are constituted and examined in light of national identities and events, as Arturo Arias and Silvia L. López note. Arias frankly points out the changes in perceived (and globally exotic) market appeal since the neoliberal 1990s, changes that affect the character and thematic angles of postwar literature: "Undoubtedly, Central American literary discourse has been disempowered politically while, paradoxically, being empowered as a commodity by globalizing trends" (2007, 25). Meanwhile, López considers the postwar moment of the 1990s as continuously radical-political, one that remains concerned with the paradoxes of the national: "Literature speaks of its time. Postwar literature, in all its diversity, shares some common narrative features. Contradiction, both political and personal, structures most of the plots. While many of the plots rework historical events or figures, the storytelling is imbricated in a complex presentation of the everyday and the personal. . . . This may sound not very radical. People are picking up a book or a paper, not a gun. But the true radical nature of that simple event is that a population once afraid and terrorized now feels confident to say, write, and read what it thinks about its own history" (2004, 86).

The varied interpretations of the meaning of postwar literary discourse—as radical, or as commercially appealing—resonate in ways that become significant to the Salvadoran context and to wider discussions of Central American literature in the isthmus and beyond. Works of fiction, including novels, constitute a new (and renewed) cultural and political reality. This reality reaches beyond official, state-sanctioned versions of the economic development and democratic transition of Central America that followed the decades of dictatorship and war in the region.

In *El asco*, the protagonist, Vega, is openly critical of the lack of sustained support for intellectual pursuits, literature, and cultural institutions and practices (for instance, those discussed by López). El Salvador is disgusting to Vega's

sensibilities because it offends his tastes, his level of education and appreciation for art, and his social and intellectual aspirations. In addition to Vega's
complaints about identity and the shortcomings of national culture, his observations about postwar violence reveal the disturbing legacies of the civil war—
the people of El Salvador "would like to be soldiers to be able to kill, that's what
it means to be Salvadoran, Moya, to want to resemble a soldier" (Castellanos
Moya 1997, 22). To be a member of this community, then, is to fundamentally
reject history and literature, and to identify with the "inner cop" within every
Salvadoran (94); to aspire to be a soldier with the rash inclination to commit
acts of violence with impunity, as if in an eternal civil war and state of exception. According to Vega, nothing has really changed since the war, and this in
part explains why Salvadorans continue to have very incompetent political leaders, "it does not matter if they are from the right or the left" (28).

Vega's comments refer to the continual fear and insecurity experienced
in Salvadoran society, where meanings and regimes of violence and death are
shifting in value. The desire to behave like a soldier is a grisly attempt at puri-
fication, the elimination of fear through impositions of order, authoritative-
ness, and lack of freedom—in some sense, a restoration of the remnants of
the war and its defined "enemies" in combat. This sort of order was marked,
enforced, and understood across Salvadoran society after decades of military
rule. In contrast, the perceived disorder of democratic transition gave rise to
a new regime of uncertainty around everyday crime. Notions of personal security became incoherent in the postwar. The enemy was no longer identifiable
as any particular armed group that represented a threat or subversion against
the nation. Salvadorans needed new words to spell a new kind of diffuse and
unknown risk, where "the nation is never in danger, just individuals" (Moodie
2010, 54).

Castellanos Moya explores this condition of diffuse, militarized danger in
his 2001 novel *El arma en el hombre*, where a former soldier known as "Robocop" is unable to function in civilian life after the signing of a peace accord
between opposing forces, the historic event that officially concludes a bitter
war and marks the end of Robocop's military career. Robocop is discharged
from the army. Rather than settling into a civilian life that he equates with
unemployment and loss of power, he turns to a life of crime in which the high-
est bidder can buy his skills—stealing cars, killing for hire, crossing borders as
the drug wars spread throughout the isthmus. Robocop is the eternal merce-
nary/soldier, the embodiment of the soldier Vega despises,[8] a representation
of a once patriotic but now ideologically tarnished Salvadoran fighter and war
veteran. Robocop is an orphan who feels out of place: "the Armed Forces had
been my father and the Acahuapa Battalion my mother. I could not imagine

myself converted overnight into a civilian, someone unemployed" (Castellanos Moya 2001, 12).

This attitude of militaristic violence has transcended the war years. It is ingrained in sectors of society that see themselves as still powerful. To behave like a soldier, to have this power to kill, to forcefully defend one's interests without consequences—this is the foremost aspiration in life for many of the inhabitants of San Salvador imagined in *El asco* and other novels. It also appears, ghostlike, in some current, postwar media portrayals. Luis Armando González conveys this idea in his analysis of how the founder of the right-wing party Alianza Republicana Nacionalista (ARENA) is remembered and portrayed in conservative media. González argues that some media institutions continue to represent, even unconsciously, an authoritarian reading of how to be Salvadoran, the construction of an "ideal" that refers us to decades of dictatorship: "It is a reading of the Salvadoran being, a throwback to the oligarchic and authoritarian cultural traditions of the twentieth century: firmness of character, fearlessness, without compassion toward enemies or rivals, masculine, of few words, willing to sacrifice, and of audacious decisions. It is about an ideal of the Salvadoran being. . . . A nation and a nationalism which, although the old oligarchies have disappeared and the military no longer control the power of the state, are always longed for by those who know themselves as its heirs" (González 2005, 539).

This vision of Salvadoran identity and values emphasizes qualities associated with patriarchy and war; visions of the nation that continue to privilege the memory of inequality. These memories are now framed in media as a longing for lost economic and political power, as "better times" of "order" and particular forms of patriotism. As González argues, these qualities live on in conservative media representations, as privileged memories that gain renewed circulation as hegemonic and "ideal" Salvadoran values. Meanwhile, other ideas—solidarity, mercy, empathy, care for history and culture—still have to fight to emerge, to gain currency, and to be accepted as viable elements of postwar society. It is useless and dangerous to imagine a return to an oppressive era of "order" and state of exception. The current moment of postwar is far messier, yet more challenging, interesting, and uncertain in its mix of potential failure and possibility.

On the one hand, *El asco* is a critique of this ideal of the "inner cop/soldier" and his authority in the national imaginary. On the other, the novel is a cynical, male-centered narrative. Vega, his trusted interlocutor Moya, and Vega's brother Ivo are protagonists, speakers, or narrators while women are invisible, serving as one-dimensional background: gossipy wives, domestic workers, prostitutes, or deceased (as is the case with Vega's mother). The male protagonists

are linked to El Salvador in various ways, exhibiting different degrees of conformity (or disdain) with Salvadoran society. Unlike the disgusted Vega, Vega's
brother, Ivo, is happy to live in El Salvador. Ivo has never felt the need to leave,
and has settled into a satisfactory routine of family life, watching television, job,
and Saturday nights drinking beer with friends. It is to this relationship between
brothers—or lack thereof—that I now turn.

Understanding Disgust: "Blood Does Not Mean Anything"

Disgust is usually understood as an aversive physical reaction, immediately visible in facial expressions and body language. However, it can be analyzed as a
far more complex emotion and in multiple dimensions, including the moral
and the ethical: "for all of its engagement of bodily responses, disgust is also an
emotion that is at work in creating and sustaining our social and cultural reality" (Korsmeyer and Smith in Kolnai 2004, 1). This emotion has been the subject
of rare and nuanced critiques by scholars in the humanities and social sciences
who seek to understand its affective, moral, material, and bodily dimensions.
William Ian Miller argues that disgust is an emotion with intensely political
significance. Emotions such as disgust and contempt "work to hierarchize our
political order: in some settings they do the work of maintaining hierarchy; in
other settings they constitute righteously presented claims for superiority; in
yet other settings they are themselves elicited as an indication of one's proper
placement in the social order. Disgust evaluates (negatively) what it touches,
proclaims the meanness and inferiority of its object" (Miller 1997, 8–9). Colin
McGinn perceptively recognizes the contradictory aspects of disgust, charac-
terizing it as "both an aversive *and* an attractive emotion. It repels us from its
object, and that is surely its primary character, but it can also draw us to that
object" (2011, 46; emphasis original).

Vega's situation of reluctant return and his reencounter with his brother
represents an example of this emotional paradox. His disgust is not a simple
feeling expressed lightly or in an accidental, offhand manner. Rather, disgust
in *El asco* is deeply rooted, felt, and brought on in reaction and relationship to
all aspects of Salvadoran culture, hierarchies, and political orders in their complexity and fascination. It is less socially acceptable to vent and convey moral
and visceral feelings of disgust than, say, nostalgic and patriotic expressions of
love of country. As my discussion in this chapter demonstrates, the disgust Vega
expresses is in part his own attempt to order this postwar culture and society,
along with his own ruptured, politically ambivalent place in it.

Alongside the political significance of disgust discussed by William Ian
Miller and other scholars, disgust is felt directly and intensely on the body
and the senses: "No other emotion, not even hatred, paints its object so

unflatteringly, because no other emotion forces such concrete sensual descriptions of its object. This, I suspect, is what we really mean when we describe disgust as more visceral than most other emotions" (Miller 1997, 9). Disgust might be the domain of deep secrets, of conflicting physical aversions and moral conundrums, a "hardwired reaction designed for protection against contamination" (Korsmeyer 2011, 9). Disgust is a deep and complicated relationship to something that may be concrete or abstract. The list of "elicitors of disgust" is long and includes rotting corpses, bodily substances and organs, disfigurements of the skin, some plants and animals, dirt, and certain behaviors (McGinn 2011, 13–39). "We are a disgust-obsessed species. Our psyche is saturated with disgust reactions at many levels," writes Colin McGinn (2011, 38). As Rachel Herz notes, "we could be disgusted by nearly anything, depending on how we think of it" (2012, 37).

As a Salvadoran emigrant and Canadian citizen, Vega makes every effort to set himself apart from this postwar society, from El Salvador's neoliberal social order that influences relationships at every level. Vega's interactions with his brother, Ivo, are symbolic of this estrangement. Over the years they have barely spoken to each other, and Vega has never missed his brother. "Each has been able to make his life without even having to remember the other, because we are complete strangers, we are the antipodes, proof that blood does not mean anything" (Castellanos Moya 1997, 36). The novel represents the disavowal and separation of the protagonist from his family and his country of origin. "Blood does not mean anything," Vega avers. Blood is disgusting. Vega's distance from his brother is not the result of hatred or wartime violence, but simply the acceptance of the way things are after a lifetime of separation—they inhabit different orbits, never intersecting. Vega describes his relationship with Ivo in these terms: "we do not even have hatred or rancor for each other, simply and plainly we are two planets on distinct orbits" (37).

Vega has made a different life for himself and never felt the need to connect materially or emotionally with his family. Ivo is four years younger than Vega, and never left the small orbit that is El Salvador. He is a small business owner, a locksmith (37–38). As a small entrepreneur, Ivo is part of an emerging capitalism in a climate of postwar insecurity, in a city of barbed wire and walls. In fact, Ivo's lock and key-making business, "El millón de llaves," is very successful and keeps growing. As perceptions of insecurity grow and the demand for locks and copies of keys increases, the more profitable Ivo's business becomes.

Vega cannot believe that he could have anything in common with someone like Ivo or his wife and children. Vega feels superior to his brother in terms of their profession—he, as someone with cultural capital, a professor of art history, while Ivo's work is less intellectual but perhaps more profitable in El Salvador.

Vega cannot identify with his brother's life and aspirations as a small business owner. He even expresses some sadness regarding his brother's lifestyle and occupation (37). However, it is a sadness combined with disgust.

Somehow Ivo convinces Vega to join him for a night of drinking. In the novel, Vega's night out with his brother and his brother's friend is portrayed as a typical men's night out in San Salvador. It revolves around drinking beer, dancing and sweating in a noisy, crowded club, and trying to pick up women (98). Vega is disgusted by this vulgar behavior. As someone who enjoys whisky and uninterrupted conversations, Vega feels that everyone in San Salvador is somewhat underdeveloped in their social relationships, tastes, and sensibilities. Vega has a strong aversion to Salvadoran beer—*how can this disgusting beer be a symbol of national pride,* he wonders.

Vega dislikes his brother's friend, and describes him in offensive terms. He refers to him as "el tal Juancho" (99), in this case, a pejoration of Juan as a "negroid" and as a noisy, imprudent man who talks too much: "A truly repulsive negroid, Moya" (100). Juancho, a marginal character, seems especially proud of his sexual exploits, which he describes loudly throughout the evening. Vega is disgusted and tired of hearing what to him are unbelievable and banal tales of nothing. He is annoyed to the point that he begins to imagine (fearfully, and somewhat perversely) that the four unfriendly looking men drinking at the next table are assassins, ready to throw a grenade at Vega, his brother, and especially Juancho, since he cannot stop talking and drawing attention to himself. Vega is bothered by his own growing paranoia and visions of carnage.

After several beers, Ivo and Juancho decide to visit prostitutes, and they take Vega along. Perhaps we may feel squeamish, even disgusted, in Castellanos Moya's description of "La oficina" ("The office") where Vega's brother and his friend want to end the night in the company of prostitutes (110–114). Vega is disgusted at the sight of these women who seem so willing to sell their bodies to disgusting men like Ivo and Juancho. He is disgusted at the soiled floors and the denigrated women—weak, immoral, unclean, and decaying female bodies. "Horrendous, Moya. I had never seen more lamentable women," he tells his confidant (112).

While he is at "La oficina" Vega vomits, overcome with nausea and disgust (113). Up to this point, the elicitors of his disgust have for the most part been moral, even ethical, but now his experience of this night out with Ivo and Juancho becomes physically unbearable as his senses are overwhelmed. In "La oficina" Vega was "in the vertigo of nausea, sitting on the edge of a chair" and careful about what he touched (112). As he sat there, *el rostro* ("the face") is *contraído* ("contracted") (112), an indication of the degree of disgust and displeasure that Vega is experiencing. He finds his way to the fetid restroom, and vomits. After this, Vega realizes, horrified, that he has lost his Canadian passport—his only guarantee that he can leave El Salvador and return to his orderly existence in Montreal. Vega panics, anguished as his mind races with possible scenarios of being stuck in El Salvador indefinitely, without his document. Where could his passport be; how did he lose it in the course of this horrible night out with his brother? How did his most valuable possession fall out of his pocket? How long would it take him to acquire a new document at the consulate?

Vega is desperate to leave "La oficina" and to retrace his steps to all the places that he has been to during this outing, even if it means reliving this night in San Salvador and once again experiencing the disgusting sensations of cheap beer, aimless conversation, and loud noises. At this moment, Vega is overcome with the panic of the loss of his valued and prestigious Canadian citizenship document. Despite his earlier disgust, Vega runs back to the fetid restroom and searches through the discarded toilet paper—maybe the passport had fallen out of his shirt pocket while he vomited (114–115). It is significant that Vega sets aside his earlier fears of contamination, at least during this moment of terror and concern for his Canadian citizenship. But his document was not in the restroom. He finds Ivo and his friend, and urges them to leave "La oficina" and to help him find his passport. At first they tell him not to worry, and do not take him seriously, but finally Ivo helps his brother. Ivo eventually finds the passport in the car. However, instead of expressing relief and gratitude, Vega is at this point even more contemptuous, mocking the effort of his brother: "And there it was, Moya, the hand of my brother extending my Canadian passport, the stupid smile of my brother behind the hand with my Canadian passport that had fallen without me noticing when I got in the car to flee the asphyxiating club" (117–118).

Vega experiences a heightened sense of disgust, nausea, and panic (almost terror) in the face of the loss of his prized document, and the possibility of staying in El Salvador for any period of time that he cannot control. It is this lack of control that is most disgusting. Vega experiences this evening with his brother bodily, vomiting. Amid his visions of violence, prostitutes, sickening food, and other disgusting things, he cannot express gratitude toward his Salvadoran brother—instead of reflecting on his own carelessness that resulted in the stressful loss of his passport, he grabs the document from his brother's hand and takes a taxi, leaving without saying a word (118).

Fear of pollution (and lack of control) is part of the overwhelming sensory and aversive experience of *El asco*. In the anthropological classic *Purity and Danger*, Mary Douglas takes a close look at "pollution-conscious cultures" and why individuals fear contamination. "It is not difficult to see how pollution beliefs can be used in a dialogue of claims and counter-claims to status. But as we examine pollution beliefs we find that the kind of contacts which are thought dangerous also carry a symbolic load," Douglas writes, emphasizing her argument "that some pollutions are used as analogies for expressing a general view of the social order" (1966, 3). These ideas are not only about dirt and contagion or even about the pollution of individual bodies, such as the female bodies in "La oficina" that so disgust Vega. These ideas might extend to actions and social standing—in other words, to relationships and to the body politic. More importantly, an emotion such as disgust has a significant role in the social and intellectual order, including sociological views of what is considered "dirty work" (Hughes 1994).

Vega's ideas and concerns with disgust and society are related to the complex totality of El Salvador. He experiences a mix of moral and physical disgust. For him, El Salvador is polluted, essentially dirty—a country tainted by brutal war, endless violence, intellectual laziness, political corruption, underdevelopment, and the lack of ambition and drive of its backward people, "a rotten race" (Castellanos Moya 1997, 21). He denounces this collectively by calling it disgusting. In the novel, a character like Edgardo Vega can express what for some would be taboo, irrational or even offensive opinions, and judge practices that inspire disgust and fear of pollution. These coexist with his self-identification and image as an intellectual, tasteful, and reasonable person. In fact, the maintenance of these distinctions between his reason and what he sees as the messy irrationality of El Salvador is essential to his own sense of someone who is clearly *not* of El Salvador any longer, adding to the significance of the people and culture that he finds disgusting and repulsive. After all, the blood he shares with his own brother *does not mean anything,* no matter what Ivo does. Fearing that he might catch the disgusting habits of Salvadorans, Vega is counting the days—fifteen so far—that he has been in contact with this disruptive and polluted world, one that is so inconsistent with the orderly life he has made for himself as an educated, hardworking citizen of Canada.

Conclusion

Vega's narrative of his stay in San Salvador presents us with a provocative notion—that disgust is foundational to certain literary and artistic expressions, to critiques of patriotism, and to extensive collective feelings within the Salvadoran national imaginary. Saying that something is "truly disgusting" is a way for Vega to repeatedly express his cynicism and ambivalence around national belonging and attachment, including the questions of how different places and situations in El Salvador mark his physical and emotional distance. These critical moments of rupture finally drive Vega to desperately seek Moya at the bar, to share this experience of return.

Vega's distanced eye allows us a glimpse into the spectrum of markers of Salvadoran society that he has grown to hate: from food to popular culture to sports to politics, there is not a facet of contemporary Salvadoran identity and culture that Vega does not hold up to scrutiny and find lacking. As their meeting at "La Lumbre" comes to an end, Vega reveals to Moya (and to the readers) that he changed his name when he became a Canadian citizen.

His name, Edgardo Vega, brought back to him the bad memory of being mugged in a San Salvador neighborhood of the same name, Barrio La Vega, when he was a teenager. This early memory of crime and being a victim is key. As one of the few things we learn about Vega's life before he emigrated, the violation of his sense of personal security tainted his own name. He has worked hard at scrubbing away these reminders of his identity and personal history from his new citizenship. In the official history that he now presents with his Canadian passport, he has renamed himself after Austrian writer Thomas Bernhard, a figure he "admires and that surely neither you nor the other simulators of this infamous province know" he tells Moya (Castellanos Moya 1997, 119). With these final comments, Vega/Bernhard manages to connect Moya to the provincial, ignorant "simulators" of San Salvador—they cannot appreciate Austrian literature and Bernhard's narrative style (and, in a possible extension, the style of *El asco: Thomas Bernhard en San Salvador*).

As "simulators," the citizens of *El asco*'s San Salvador fake their way through life: they are people who languish in ignorance and darkness, unable to appreciate literature, art, and anything that could be called peacetime culture. In this sense El Salvador remains as an uncultivated backwater, a ruined and rotting soil. As he speaks, Vega/Bernhard emphasizes his refusal to reconnect with his country of birth, and the ease with which he left at age twenty and never looked back. He can criticize this place deeply, in its most meaningful expressions and idiosyncrasies—perhaps because these are idiosyncrasies that he knows very well, that he has not forgotten—without establishing any significant investment or connection with the country. The only fact of "connection" to El Salvador that he cannot erase is the line printed on his Canadian passport that reads "place of birth." San Salvador, thirty-eight years ago.[9] As he sits in the taxi after leaving his brother Ivo behind, and opens the pages to verify his identity, Vega/Bernhard once again laments the indelible presence of this line.

Salvadoran transnational imaginaries and narratives that seem to "make sense" are produced, circulated, and mediated in everyday life by the interaction and constant contestation between people and institutions. In this renewed literary moment of the postwar, the people who inhabit El Salvador are witnesses to disenchantment, to cynicism, to the death of solidarity, and to the failure of various projects that promised revolution, change, and the solution to social inequalities in El Salvador and the rest of Central America.

The disgust of Vega/Bernhard is also disenchanted and disapproving. There is no love or appreciation for El Salvador, yet there is knowledge of the problems that beset its society. Vega/Bernhard has not forgotten how desperate (and to him, intellectually meaningless) life in El Salvador can be. His eye, in many ways now a stranger's eye after eighteen years abroad, is even more perceptive and raw, even more attuned to the objects and practices that seem "normal" and everyday to his brother, his family, and most of his former classmates and other people of San Salvador. But to Vega/Bernhard, this is not normal, this is no way to live—this is disgusting. Thus he is desperate to talk to someone, to produce his narrative, to confront his overwhelming sense of disgust with whiskies and the only person in San Salvador who might understand him—a writer, and hints of an author who would soon continue on his own long exile.

4

Exporting Voices

Aspirations and Fluency in the Call Center

Carla was in her twenties when I met her. She had graduated from a bilingual high school in San Salvador, and currently worked at a call center. I contacted her through a mutual friend, someone who was also her coworker, and we arranged an interview. On an August afternoon in 2006, Carla and I sat at a café in Multiplaza, a shopping mall, talking about her job, about what working at a customer service center for a software company involved. Unlike many others who talked with customers and answered questions on the phone, Carla's job required very good (even excellent) composition skills, since she answered questions in writing and via e-mail as leader of the technical support team. Carla had suggested that we meet at this mall at the end of her workday. This was a convenient midpoint in her daily commute between the call center job and home, located in one of many emerging residential developments in the new limits of San Salvador and Antiguo Cuscatlán. As is usual at this time of the day, the area near this comfortable café at the mall was lively with conversations, the sounds of meals, snacks consumed, and the clinking of coffee cups and spoonfuls of sugar. Looking around, this seemed to me like a fitting place to conduct our interview. The background noises, crowded corridors, and department stores, mostly conducive to face-to-face interactions between shoppers and cashiers, contrasted with the faceless telephone calls and e-mails Carla described as part of her daily workday ritual: troubleshooting, resolving questions, and providing information for customers.

In 2004, when I began researching bilingual (English-Spanish) and monolingual Spanish call centers in San Salvador, two major North American and European companies had recently established their call center operations in-country and were becoming places of employment for a specific sector of Salvadorans—especially the young and fluent in English, like Carla. These two companies were not the first or the only call centers in San Salvador. Laura and

Elizabeth, former neighbors in San Salvador, worked at a Spanish-language call center for a company that had started operating in El Salvador in 1998 and established its call center by 1999. The Spanish-language call center of this multinational corporation was an early operation; a few years later it would continue to be one important component of an ambitious investment promotion project that marketed Salvadoran Spanish as "neutral" in pronunciation and speech patterns. This marketing of "neutral Spanish" and bilingual workers carries interesting, critical implications of flexibility—in the sense that workers are expected to have schedule availability, and also in the sense of high labor turnover and even disposability of the worker in this sector—along with notions of national image-building. When I approached Laura and Elizabeth in 2004 with a basic question, asking for their thoughts about these new bilingual call centers, they replied that Gabriela, a third neighbor, was going to work in the human resources office of one of the newly established centers. I had the opportunity to interview all of them in 2005 and to follow up with Gabriela in late 2006. They were important contacts when I began my research, and were instrumental in putting me in touch with other interviewees as the project progressed.

By 2009, call centers were a significant industry in El Salvador, a country of approximately 6 million people with an economically active population of 2.8 million. Analysts of this industry note that "despite the size of the country, and the small percentage of the economically active population working in the outsourcing business, the economic spillover of the outsourcing industry was calculated around $75.8 million [in 2009] making it an important job and income-generating business for local people."[1]

The call centers emerge in this imaginary of postwar labor as strategically located worksites for mobile capital and local qualified employees. San Salvador becomes a city where complex transnational connections converge, collide, and mesh into common understandings of Salvadoran society. The tangible presence of this transnational worksite in the everyday life of a small yet significant group of mostly young and urban Salvadoran employees raises questions related to social class, mobility, and aspirations. How does this group of Salvadorans enter call center work? What are the expectations attached to this job? What views and opinions do call center agents and managers express about this occupation? This chapter considers these questions, and examines the hiring and training processes involved in call center employment in San Salvador. I examine call centers, or customer service centers, as important and complex sites where narratives and ideas of Salvadoran laborers and a "Salvadoran brand" are constructed and contested nationally and in relation to transnational labor. This is a space of opportunity, but also of meaningful constraints and contradictions. In the context of El Salvador's postwar social and economic transformations, the branding of this country as attractive for foreign direct investment is intertwined with formations of language ability and outsourced service work.

Call centers are not unique to El Salvador, but I argue that they are connected to the Salvadoran transnational imaginary in unique ways. Currently, India and the Philippines are countries with a strong presence and global reputation in this industry. Their industries not only draw on the convenience of global connections, but also become intensely local, highlighting certain traits or perceptions, such as hospitality, location, or familiarity with English to build their reputations as suitable places for companies to establish their centers. For instance, the widely held notion that call center agents in India are more proficient with computers and information technology may be stereotypical, yet it feeds into customer sentiments of reliability and technical knowledge. The Philippines dominates the call center sector globally, with 400,000 agents employed by the end of 2011.[2]

As outsourcing matures and the idea of globally available workers becomes more ingrained as a practice of consumption, customer preference for American English (among other accents) and other specific advantages outweigh the industry's traditional focus on cost reduction: "executives say they are now increasingly identifying places best suited for specific tasks."[3] El Salvador's call center sector is relatively small, not near the scale or volume of Great Britain's during the 1990s, where an estimated 247,000 to 400,000 agents were employed (Ball 2003, 203). In India, approximately 350,000 agents were employed in 2011, according to industry figures.[4] According to Reena Patel, call centers have been a part of the growing business process outsourcing sector in India since the 1990s, and currently this sector continues to be significant, employing an estimated 470,000 people (Patel 2010, 2). India and the Philippines are countries where English-language education is integral to the school system; they are nations intertwined with historical and colonial links to England and the United States for generations. Clearly, I am drawing a contrast to countries where this sector seems to be large-scale and visible. In this chapter I am discussing a relatively new and small sector concentrated in a small capital city where approximately five thousand people worked as agents in 2005–2006, when I conducted interviews with employees of five different call centers located in San Salvador. By 2012, the number of employees had nearly doubled, to 9,400 agents, "in forty-five local and foreign companies."[5]

Along with interviews with call center employees, my analysis combines informal conversations with everyday, common Salvadorans and textual analysis of various printed materials. I analyze advertisements and job descriptions that appeared in the employment section of Salvadoran newspapers, and the human resources training handbooks from one call center. I conducted most interviews during 2005 and 2006, primarily with human resources staff at different call centers in San Salvador, and with other people interested and involved in this sector.[6] These interviews and other material about language learning, training, and foreign investment helped me understand the context, and to some extent to gain insight into the institutional lens of call center promotion and the growth of this sector. In later trips to El Salvador, I spoke with people who work at more recently established call centers, and during my time in San Salvador I discussed call centers with some previous interviewees and in informal conversations.

On the one hand, in this chapter I interpret and discuss a snapshot of call center work, situated in a specific time and place: San Salvador during the first decade of the twenty-first century. A second aspect of the chapter is more symbolic, and more broadly inclined to my discussion of the ways in which the call centers represent connectedness, rapid social change, and the Salvadoran transnational imaginary. The call center is part of a transnational agenda, and an example of the ongoing process of deep transformations in the ways Salvadorans relate to work, to globalization, to perceptions of class and educational level, and to new understandings of individual risk and various forms of capital.

The call centers become part of an ensemble of institutions and practices enmeshed in the particularities of contemporary, transnational, neoliberal El Salvador. PROESA (Agencia de Promoción de Exportaciones e Inversiones de El Salvador, the Salvadoran investment promotion agency) and other institutions express interest in attracting companies to employ Salvadoran labor and create jobs that require fluency in English and familiarity with global consumer products and services. The discussion of call centers, then, involves the formation of ideas of Salvadoran laborers and their circulation of linguistic and mobility capital. What I mean by this is that the call centers in great measure exist thanks to globalizing processes that include media technologies and the ethnoscapes (Appadurai 1996, 33–34) produced by the movements of people—in particular, the mobilities of labor and corporate needs, along with the capital of the laborers. In addition, these worksites are also grounded in critical local conditions and opportunities such as the ones investment promotion agencies want to develop.

Since the 1990s, transnational circuits of labor and migration have become vital in discussions of Salvadoran postwar macroeconomic stability. These portrayals and practices—from media representations (such as those found in employment ads) to English-language learning and work opportunities—construct a complex imaginary of citizenship, the nation, migration, and ideas of modernity and institutional affiliations. During the 1990s, the Salvadoran government pursued a strategy of privatization of public services and utilities, including ANTEL (the national telecommunications institution) and the banking/financial services sectors. These projects of privatization and investment promotion in part laid the groundwork for what is now the call center sector. They made it legally and logistically possible for transnational telecommunications corporations (for instance, companies from France and Spain) to acquire significant ownership of the landline and wireless sectors. Foreign investors could establish their operations within newly created Salvadoran legal frameworks, especially after the passing of the "Ley de Zonas Francas," a law to regulate export-processing zones, commercialization, and other concerns related to outsourcing.

Legislative decree 405, "Ley de Zonas Francas Industriales y de Comercialización," is a legal instrument signed and passed into law by the Salvadoran Legislative Assembly in September 1998 and subsequently reformed in 1998, 2003, and 2005. This decree establishes the importance of the government of El Salvador in developing various capacities to attract foreign direct investment. The first part of the decree's text reads:

"The Legislative Assembly of the Republic of El Salvador, Considering:

I.   That in accordance with the Constitution of the Republic it is the function of the state to establish the necessary legal instruments to propitiate national and foreign investment;

II. That as part of the efforts that the present government is undertaking, so that our economy will be inserted in the process of worldwide globalization, the modernization and actualization of the legal and regulatory framework which promotes the establishment and development of export-processing zones in our country is necessary;

III. That consequently to the former, and given the strategic importance of the regimes of export-processing zones for the national economy, in the generation of productive employment and generation of capital [foreign currency], it is necessary to create optimal conditions of competitiveness in all the operations realized by the companies covered by this regime."[7]

The implications of these responsibilities and obligations are significant to the Salvadoran state: as was the case with the 1999 report, *Temas claves para el Plan de Nación: Consulta Especializada*, this law outlines a vision for the type of open investment climate encouraged and maintained by the government of El Salvador. In this legal document it is taken as a given that the establishment of export-processing zones is of strategic importance to the development, macroeconomic conditions, and modernization of El Salvador. As an instrument of governmentality, legislative decree 405 outlines dispositions and guidelines to modernize and update the legal and regulatory framework of these zones where foreign investors can take advantage of reduced tax rates and other incentives for their companies.

Beyond these noteworthy macroeconomic conditions and legislation, in this chapter I pay closer attention to another facet of the story of how call center work is possible in El Salvador. Common understandings of employees and managers take shape as they talk about their jobs, their skills, and their training. Individual job applicants present themselves with their voices and language fluency in this convergence of global and local opportunities. In the interviews I conducted, managers and some employees reveal various degrees of satisfaction with their work environment, while they also express concerns about the less attractive aspects of the job, such as the high levels of stress and their too-frequent interactions with rude or even irate customers.

In examining the country's call center sector, it is possible to evaluate the emergence of bilingual and transnational identities that converge with a nation-making agenda in postwar El Salvador. This labor site is one of many versions of the imaginary of El Salvador as a nation without borders. While a mobile and migrant people remain attached to Salvadoran identities even from afar, as represented in "Departmento 15" and other media, in the pages that follow I consider another possibility in which the connections between El Salvador and the United States are equally important and open to contradictions: we have the bilingual voice, situated in El Salvador yet quite knowledgeable of the United States, global culture, and its consumers. Thinking of globalization as a process with profound implications and transformations (Ong and Collier 2005) allows us to examine how the call center shapes and is shaped by transnational and local histories. Any account of development and globalization "is necessarily partial and selective, at best it can provide a focused illumination of a part of a complex whole" (Molyneux 2001, 273). Ideas of globalization are closely tied to specific and local ideas of development and modernization, even as they embody claims to universality.

For the most part, the call centers in El Salvador attend to customers calling from the United States. Thus I focus on the importance of English-language fluency, and especially on how recruiters and human resources managers at these call centers value the qualities of this skill. I discuss the screening, hiring, and training processes that enable call centers to produce and commercialize the characteristics that come to constitute a trained Salvadoran voice: fluency in English or, at times, a voice that conveys a "neutral" Spanish accent in a shared imaginary of global and mobile capital that, in turn, is useful for projects of national economic development. While my analysis of so-called "neutral" Spanish remains in the background in relation to my discussion of English fluency, I refer to it because it captures a central observation regarding class identifications and ideas of linguistic capital at some call centers. Moreover, to some extent the discussion of "neutral" Spanish is a possible entry point for thinking about racialization and inequality in wider Salvadoran society—that is, in social and cultural settings that extend beyond these specific worksites.

Exporting Voices

The call center is an example of a site where transnational imaginaries and linguistic capital are produced, generated, and commercialized via what Emily Martin calls "practicums," processes that "involve learning about new concepts of the ideal and fit person" (Martin 1994, 15). In San Salvador, a person who is fit to work at the call center is someone who in many cases is fluent in English, or at least can demonstrate the potential to become a competent speaker. Above all, it is someone who seeks this sort of work in the first place, who sees this as an opportunity.

Not surprisingly, banks, computer software companies, restaurant chains, telephone services, and airlines have call centers to support the global networks in which they are enmeshed. Nearly every business interested in maintaining contact with its customers has a call center. This has become part of certain brand and product identities: "All the marketing efforts, name-branding costs, and product offerings of a company are wasted efforts if an enterprise is not available to take a call or process an order" (Breakfield 2001, 267). The case of call centers in postwar El Salvador demonstrates how connections are shaped by economic development strategies and ideas about the linguistic and professional capacities of the Salvadoran workforce.

Researchers of the operations, design, and management of call centers attribute the worldwide growth of the sector since the 1980s and 1990s to advances in communication technology that "have enabled firms to sort incoming calls so that they can be routed to the appropriate departments within a firm" (Akşin and Harker 2001, 324; also see Ellis and Taylor 2006; Russell 2008). In addition to technological advances in the telecommunications field, other historical and social forces enable flexible global networks. Call centers and other forms of innovation are not simply neutral technological advances, but are "inflected by the values, cultures, power systems and institutional orders within which [they are] embedded" (Sassen 2004, 302–303). These values and changes in the economies and corporations of the United States and Europe—we can consider them as inflections of what is global—can thus be put into circulation in ways that affect transnational movements of capital.

Companies that decades ago might have maintained their entire operations in North America or Western Europe have split and moved segments of these to other parts of the world, including Central America, as a strategy to lower costs and access new markets and sources of labor. This practice and industry is known as business process outsourcing, or BPO. As processes are cut into blocks and established around the globe, once fully local practices of assembly lines and customer care become links in a transnational service sector: "the organization is a fleeting, fluid network of alliances, a highly decoupled and dynamic form with great organizational flexibility" (Martin 1994, 209). In the case of El Salvador and other countries of the region, call centers fulfill the BPO and customer service needs of many companies, in turn offering a range of services and products, including support for social networking sites, computer software, debt collection, and travel services such as hotel and airline reservations.

Call centers have become crucial to economic regimes of flexible accumulation (Harvey 1989). Corporations that aspire to build a successful, globally recognized brand need flexible bodies in their workforce; "the new workers that corporations desire: individuals—men and women—able to risk the unknown and tolerate fear, willing to explore unknown territories, but simultaneously able to accept their dependence on the help and support of their coworkers. In a word, *flexibility*" (Martin 1994, 214; emphasis original). While labor flexibility is an important concept, it is also pertinent to refer to practices of mobilities and immobilities. These emerging patterns of social organization affect the real and imagined movements through spaces in everyday life. In this regard, while we have large-scale movements of technology and information in the call centers, it is crucial to also examine "smaller" individual events and processes of talk, such as interviews and screenings with human resources staff.

El Salvador becomes a site of flexible labor and outsourcing, part of the "technologies of extraordinary speed [of capital and information circulation] and unprecedented immobility" of the worker (Aneesh 2001, 383). An immobile—and easily available—workforce becomes desirable and marketable in global, flexible labor regimes. As Aneesh notes, this immobile workforce facilitates the movement of financial transactions, purchases, and other areas of post-industrial service work. The quality of the voice, as a commodity for export, is part of the branding of El Salvador as transnational and global, as an ideal place for call centers. Skills such as listening comprehension and fluency in English are encouraged in the call center agent in order to increase productivity and efficiency. The use of a standard script makes a conversation predictable and controllable for the agent and the customer. Its purpose is to constrain and define the limits of the conversation. Deborah Cameron suggests that call centers are "communication factories" where workers follow a scripted conversation, a "regime" that tries to "regulate many aspects of talk" (Cameron 2000, 123). Winifred Poster explores the strategy of "national identity management" among call center workers in India, where practicing and using a script is a central aspect of the job and of managing the complex continuum of identity and language use, especially in cases where customers ask the agent in India where he or she is located (Poster 2007, 271–272).

Soon after the telecommunication sector privatizations of the 1990s, in 2001 El Salvador adopted the U.S. dollar as its official currency. By this time, the Salvadoran government pursued investment promotion as key to a national postwar development strategy. The media also played a role in the circulation of this discourse, especially in articles that highlighted the novelty of bilingual call centers and the role of PROESA in promoting investment in El Salvador.[8] A December 2003 article in the newspaper *La Prensa Gráfica*, titled "Call centers in search of Salvadoran voices: Two new centers in 2004,"[9] illustrates how the voices of Salvadorans are presented—in this case, by investment promoters and the journalists who report on these events—as a coveted export commodity, emphasizing the flexibility of the Salvadoran worker and the strategic location of El Salvador as an ideal place for investment. As the executive director of PROESA explained, with the new call centers, "We will export voices from El Salvador."[10] Representatives of this governmental investment promotion agency noted the advantages that in their view El Salvador offers for companies interested in establishing call center operations: "The modernization in telecommunications, the bilingual workforce, the [convenient] time zones, neutral accent and the distances between the country and North America have positioned El Salvador as one of the profitable nations for this business."[11]

The main requirement for employment, as the article notes, is "perfect English" because the call center employees "will wait on North American customers."[12] In addition to perfect English, Salvadoran call center employees should have what Salvadoran investment promotion executives routinely describe in their brochures, website, and other marketing materials as a "neutral" accent. Salvadoran Spanish is marketed and imagined by some business and government sectors in El Salvador as unmarked—in other words, almost invisible and not widely identifiable.

In relation to more recognizable Latin American ways of speaking Spanish, particularly those that have gained relevance in the Latino market in the United States (for example, Mexican and Puerto Rican accents common in the entertainment industry and marketing), the reasons for this characterization of Salvadoran Spanish as "neutral" Spanish seem somewhat obvious and strategic. A neutral accent promises correct usage, even "untainted language skills" (Dávila 2001, 35). While it would be difficult to locate in social, geographic, or linguistic space, and thus perfect for a dislocated call center with global appeal, it is paradoxical that it also must be identified as both a neutral and *Salvadoran* accent. In comparison, in this case "perfect English" in the call center is, of course, a North American accent that will be familiar to most callers. Through constructs of worker flexibility and language "neutrality," El

Salvador becomes part of a naturalized array of logics of hierarchical flows, where some histories and accents are made invisible while certain language skills and labor flexibility seem prestigious and thus especially valued and marketed to potential investors.

El Salvador Works

Rodolfo seems to be in his thirties. He is a recruitment manager at a call center that provides sales and technical support for a company based in the United States. I interviewed him in a small air-conditioned conference room, probably the same one where he routinely conducts candidate interviews and screenings. Although he is completely comfortable speaking in Spanish (he added that one of his parents is Central American), this was the only interview that I conducted entirely in English while in San Salvador. Rodolfo echoed many of the ideas about "exporting voices" as he spoke about what connects global media technologies, migration, the end of armed conflicts in the region, and the presence of call centers in El Salvador: "Since the war ended [in 1992] the country, the government, has tried to reach out to foreign countries to invest in El Salvador by having a series of plans, for example infrastructure. The telecommunications infrastructure in Central America, specifically El Salvador, is very, very modern, very advanced. I think there are three fiber-optic undersea lines that converge in El Salvador, and that makes it really advanced on a certain level." Rodolfo continued, "On the other hand, due to the massive emigration of Salvadorans to the [United] States and through the years and the cultural influence, culturally we are very, or up to a point similar to the [United States], and there is much affinity with U.S. culture and U.S. society because of so many expatriates being from this country there."[13]

Rodolfo places the call center and the Salvadoran investment climate within a complex historical-social-political frame. "Since the war ended" is a historical moment linked to events that have affected the Salvadoran population, both in El Salvador and in the United States. This ethnoscape of Salvadorans creates and sustains transnational practices and connections between El Salvador and the United States. Clearly, the sometimes uneasy and contradictory flows of people, commodities, cultural expressions, and discursive forms and practices have converged—like undersea fiber-optic lines—and become constitutive of postwar Salvadoran national and transnational identities. Cultural links are imagined, aided—and enmeshed in—new, real, and "advanced" infrastructure.[14] Salvadorans who live in the United States often continue to communicate and maintain ties with friends and family in El Salvador, shaping their perceptions and affinities to both countries. A familiar and marketable linguistic, cultural, and historical narrative emerges. Rodolfo readily adapts this market knowledge to his description of investment and the work of customer service—in addition to the crucial aspects of technology, Salvadoran agents in the call centers have a cultural edge that allows them to relate well to their North American customers.

The Salvadoran government also takes part in the formation of transnational business relationships through the establishment of institutions to attract investors. El Salvador becomes a brand, situated in strategic cultural, geographic, economic, and political spaces. As Rodolfo states, the government opened its markets to foreign investors partly through the privatization of the telecommunications sector in 1998 and the initial establishment of PROESA in June 2000.[15]

The agency's promotional material available on the Internet during these first years presents an impressive, ambitious list of possibilities for diversifying the Salvadoran economy.[16] "[PROESA] seeks to generate employment, transfer technology and aid the country's development process. The Agency's primary objective is to attract and assist foreign direct investment in industries such as: agro industry, textiles and apparel, contact centers, light manufacturing and electronics, logistics and distribution centers, software development, tourism and footwear. . . . PROESA has helped more than 138 multinational firms expand or establish operations in El Salvador. Successful companies have proved that El Salvador works for their business and that Salvadoran people work to make their firms even more productive and profitable."[17] The agency's brand logo and slogan, "El Salvador Works," represents a strategic link between labor, place, and bodies: "The slogan 'El Salvador Works' has a dual meaning: The people of El Salvador work hard, and El Salvador works for businesses. Warm colors were chosen for the logo. A circular shape that encloses three people united by the arms represents the human connection."[18]

Using the slogan "El Salvador Works" and a logo that "represents the human connection," at this time the government agency promoted and marketed El Salvador as a "brand that travels around the world," with an appealing set of characteristics represented in the warm colors—shades of beige, brown, and earth tones—of the logo. The people representing human connection are Salvadoran workers. Only arms, among the most important "links" in outsourcing operations and global labor, are shown. These body parts represent a new and even more flexible iteration of the Bracero Program, the mobile Mexican labor force recruited to the United States during the mid-twentieth century for agricultural work and so named because of the strength of their arms. This website also refers to Salvadoran labor at a regional and global level, about which the executive director states: "The human quality of our people makes our work force a very special one, so special that the Salvadoran labor force is recognized throughout the region and the world."[19] Readily available human capital, both within the country and outside El Salvador, is presented as one of the country's main assets.

The reference to Salvadoran narratives of work ethic is important on this website, which primarily promotes the capacities of Salvadorans within the country. It is particularly crucial in a context where labor migration is a common strategy for economic survival—historically, regionally, and globally. This acknowledgment of the millions of Salvadorans living and working abroad should further underline the extent to which El Salvador is connected to globalization processes and thus attractive to foreign investors. This tells us about the assumptions PROESA and other institutions might have about the mobility of many Salvadorans, and how this mobility might, paradoxically, inform investment promotion strategies that depend on a locally available, culturally informed, and skilled workforce in San Salvador.

Contradictions and Opportunities

Prospective call center employees in El Salvador undergo a series of interviews and assessments, including placement tests and language evaluations, to determine their competence in spoken English and listening comprehension. The managers described how this process unfolded in their human resources departments. Many of these activities and evaluations seem to be standardized across the bilingual call centers I researched in San Salvador and according to what the interviewees said about this topic.

In many cases the recruitment process might begin with an advertisement or job announcement. Often this ad is printed in English and published prominently in the employment section (and rarely in the small print of the classifieds) of one of the major Salvadoran newspapers. The ad might be posted as an announcement on the company's website. Word of mouth (personal referrals) and social media might also be involved. In other cases, commercials on English-language cable television channels make the pitch, depicting scenes of call center work as interactive and a good environment for young employees (and, it is more likely that these ads will reach English speakers in San Salvador). Sometimes job fairs are organized by a call center and held at shopping malls.

Many advertisements for call center employment published around the time I was conducting interviews in 2005 and 2006 focus on basic requirements: English language ability (mostly spoken, and sometimes written, English), schedule flexibility, and motivation. Some announcements were more specific, asking for travel services experience or knowledge of sales and computer hardware. "Upgrade your life: climb for success," one ad stated.[20] It went on to describe the job, providing technical support to consumers in the United States. The text of a 2006 advertisement for a call center reads:

How fast is your career growing?

. . . we offer an opportunity to start a high speed career as a sales or technical support representative. Apply today and be part of the best computer company in the world.

Requirements to apply: High school graduate, Be at least eighteen years of age, one hundred percent fluent in English, Computer knowledge

We offer: Competitive Salary, Opportunity to grow,

Teamwork environment, Benefits above the law

Call us for a job

Or send us your resumé[21]

This advertisement takes up one fourth of a newspaper's page, and is published prominently in the employment section of *La Prensa Gráfica*. It alludes to high speed and appeals to an audience interested in career growth, and with knowledge of English, sales, technology, e-mail, and social networking. It evokes ideas about the speed of globalization and connections, addressing the potential call center agent: someone who is comfortable with computers, at ease on the telephone, and perhaps with some idea—realistic or otherwise—of U.S. consumer cultures.

The ad may also appeal to high school graduates or young university students seeking to build their resumés with a first job in a globally known company linked to technology. Gabriela, for instance, emphasized this point several times during our discussion of her experiences at the call center where she works as a human resources manager. She also seemed to understand why young people are drawn to the call center, and in some cases why, after earning some money to treat themselves to new shoes or a trip to a longed-for vacation site, they might not continue on the job. Given this, the eighteen-to-twenty-four-year age group predominates in this sector, but it is not the only one employed as call center agents—or, I venture, the only and ideal long-term employee profile primarily targeted by this advertisement. Employees must be at least eighteen, since that is the legal age in El Salvador, but in most call center employment advertisements there is no stated age limit.[22] However, an age range in the early twenties is the most common and "corresponds not so much to a physical type as to a presumed social type with predictable consumer patterns" (Schudson 1984, 212), and thus seems like a desirable demographic for this advertising-employment image. Scholars of advertising and visual culture have argued that ads do not sell a product—rather, they persuade, selling ideas and a lifestyle associated with the represented product, arguing that "advertising functions in a much more indirect way to sell lifestyle and identification with brand names and corporate logos" (Sturken and Cartwright 2001, 198).

What are these advertisements for call center employment selling? They advertise the possibility of a job, the opportunity to be associated with a brand identity, in some cases as a bilingual employee of the "best computer company," or as someone with relevant travel experience, as someone who is fluent in English, motivated, and wants a competitive edge. The ads usually provide information that might make these aspirations a reality—for example, an e-mail address or telephone number that is easy to remember, asking the reader of the ad to "call us for a job" and make the most of the opportunity. In this sense, the employment ad exists in a particular time and place, and with the specific, real purpose of call center agent recruitment. However, the timeliness of these employment announcements also carries timeless elements related to the abstract, "high concept," and indirect approach of advertising—the set of aesthetic conventions that Michael Schudson refers to as capitalist realism: "abstraction is essential to the aesthetic and intention of contemporary national consumer-goods advertising. It does not represent reality nor does it build a fully fictive world. It exists, instead, on its own plane of reality, a plane I will call capitalist realism. By this term, I mean to label a set of aesthetic conventions, but I mean also to link them to the political economy whose values they celebrate and promote" (Schudson 1984, 214).

Beyond the possibility of employment, the ad for sales and technical support representatives is clearly an advertisement for the company's computers and related products—*the best ones,* even if the ad shows no actual images of the product or its users. The brand logo serves as sufficient identification globally, and we (presumably, the sophisticated consumers) should understand this symbol if we see it. We have seen their computers before, and will continue to see them. In the meantime, all we need is a subtle reminder of their existence—unlike the more urgent "call us" instructions. Furthermore, the abstract marketing and branding efforts are incomplete if this company is unable to provide efficient and friendly customer service. These ideas and signs—the timely job announcement plus the timeless brand appeal—coexist and make sense in post-war, capitalist El Salvador.

The timely arrangement of the text in the advertisement speaks to the skills and career aspirations of some Salvadorans who may be looking for a job that offers a comparatively good salary by the country's standards. Salaries in many call centers range from $450 to $600 per month (nearly three times the Salvadoran minimum wage in 2006, the publication time of the advertisements) and in some cases reach $1,500 per month,[23] including relatively good benefits. In addition to greater salary and better material conditions, the ad announces and becomes part of the perception of a novel, dynamic opportunity in this economy. It offers a new employment option, promising a break from stagnant or less exciting jobs. In the "How fast is your career growing?" advertisement, the phrase "benefits above the law" is perhaps not the most accurate translation of "beneficios sobre la ley"—that is, benefits according to the law in order to comply with what is required by the Salvadoran labor code in terms of medical insurance, access to pension and retirement planning, and working hours. In the use of these phrases, we get hints as to how the ad for this transnational corporation is in tune with local Salvadoran laws and related aspects of political economy. Interestingly (and somewhat ironically) the inaccurate translation in this specific text might distract from the stated requirement that applicants be "one hundred percent fluent in English" to work at the call center. This instance of being lost in translation seemed unusual (I did not see this phrase in similar ads for this same company or other call centers), and usually the phrase "competitive salary and benefits" was used by other call centers.

Gabriela was enthusiastic and emphatic about her hiring goals during our interview. "We don't want even the second-best, we want the best talent of El Salvador. That is our goal, to become the first employment option, so everyone will want to work with us, [and] we need people who speak English."[24] Advertising is only one element of this process. Once people respond to an ad such as "How fast is your career growing?" a lengthy process begins in the call center's offices in San Salvador. In some cases, about six weeks of interviews, tests, and paid training workshops pass between the first interview and the first actual day of work. Not everybody who is initially screened ends up employed and with a headset. At the call center where Rodolfo works, what he called the "take rate" or "staffing yield" is that only about 8.2 percent of the applicants who show up for the initial screening are eventually hired. To give me an idea of what this process entails, Gabriela explained the procedures of her workplace in detail:

GABRIELA: First we receive all the candidates interested in participating in the process. This [advertising] can be through the Internet, or advertisements in the newspapers, or directly [applicants bring their resumés to the call center in person]. We also have other programs, where employees can refer acquaintances or even relatives. The first thing that is done is a telephone screening, to know the level of English. If they can maintain a conversation over the phone, that is the most basic thing, and there we ask them certain questions to know more about the candidate's level of English. After this, if the person fulfills the requirements, we invite him/her to take a computerized test to measure their skills, technical as well as in personality, which he or she must have according to the profile we need for the position. If the person passes—and this is something very interesting—because if the person passes this test, the next step is an interview with the managers, who are fully bilingual. But if they do not pass, we invite them to take a course to improve, depending on how much they need it, and we give them a second chance, so they can retake the test.

CECILIA: And why is this, because there aren't enough bilingual people?

GABRIELA: No, the truth is that [*pauses, and briefly switches from Spanish to English*] *the lack of skills in terms of language* is so large that we need to invest in the people, so they can master the language. First the language, and then improve the accent.[25]

Gabriela's explanation, and her brief code-switching from Spanish to English, highlights an important point. Even as the process tries to be selective—involving aptitude tests and several interviews on the phone and in person—the demand for employees is high enough that when not enough applicants are fully qualified for specific accounts (as evidenced by the "take rate"), the call center has to produce *exactly* the competent and fluent English speaker, the Salvadoran employee with an improved accent of its imaginary. Spoken English needs to be processed; the employer has to "invest in the people" to actually take advantage of the decision to invest its capital in El Salvador and fulfill the aspiration to be the "number one" employer. In other words, the ideal, bilingual Salvadoran call center agent does not exist naturally as an immediately available workforce. This subject is shaped and produced by the very technologies of service and language it ultimately serves.[26] As prospective call center employees take language tests, employers are conducting surveillance and training in an effort to construct and evaluate competence and the linguistic capital represented by English language fluency.

Fluent, punctual, and trustworthy call center agents are vital for these companies, which are new investors in the country, while the employees themselves are also new to the industry and this type of job. In some ways, this is a complementary relationship—and also a contradictory one. "The quality of our work depends on the people we are able to hire," Sara, a human resources manager I interviewed in 2006, explained. It seems to me that this is among the most interesting and concise descriptions of the challenges of call center operations in this location, an insight that further illuminates the contradictory aspects of English-language fluency in Salvadoran call center hiring.

Sara had previous employment experience with nongovernmental organizations before joining the human resources department of a Canadian-European company where the agents handle mail-in rebates and collection of late bill payments, among other services, for North American companies that have outsourced these business operations. At the time of my interview with Sara, this company had been present in the Central American region for nearly a decade, first in Guatemala, and had very recently established call center operations in El Salvador. They had plans to eventually branch out to Nicaragua and Panama. Clearly, they were in a very active expansion and hiring mode regionally. Everything was new—even the recently installed security system in Sara's building. I interviewed Sara within her first three weeks of employment, which she described as extremely busy. New groups of approximately twenty-five agents were beginning their training every week. Impressively, Sara had hired fifty-three people so far, while she was in the process of negotiating with clients for possible new accounts and interviewing candidates for several positions in other areas of the company besides customer service/call center agents. She had recently processed the employment paperwork for an accountant and receptionists. Sara was already steeped in her work, and enthusiastically recounted some of her experiences with language evaluation, screening, and interviewing prospective employees.

As we discussed these topics, Sara turned to her computer screen and shared a slide presentation with me, detailing the vision, history, and corporate strategy of the company. This lengthy slideshow was in all likelihood used to pitch the contact center/call center services to clients in other markets and countries, and now to potential new clients in El Salvador. It listed the many regional partners and markets with which the company was associated, implying that the clients who decided to use the BPO/call center services of this company could join this special group of recognizable brands. The themes of this slideshow were "sun" and "shore," creative representations of the ideas that the sun never sets in this company's call centers and that strategically located Central America is not just one more off-shoring site—it is indeed the ideal place for these operations. The background image of most of the slides was a picture of a sun rising over clouds and the waters of an ocean. The design of this presentation is part of the company's advertising, deliberate signals it sends to the world of potential clients in this imaginary of postwar, investment-ready Central America. The brand elements it displays—round-the-clock hard work and accessibility—add to the discourses of other call centers, competing BPO operations, investment promoters, and the timely, appealing qualities of call center operations in the isthmus: "When your sun is rising, ours is too. And when your day is over, ours keeps on going round-the-clock," Sara reads from the presentation. She proceeded with the slideshow. "The time has come to outsource your business processing needs to the Best Shore, a new Central America where you'll find a friendly business environment, modern telecommunications, and an eager, highly-skilled workforce that speaks both English and Spanish."[27]

The initial screening and hiring process at Sara's workplace is similar to what Gabriela described: applicants present their resumés, interview with the managers, and take an English language test to determine their eligibility. After this, the personnel managers decide if they, as Sara explained, "feel comfortable with this accent or not, if we think the accent is too thick." If the "accent" is acceptable and the candidate passes the evaluations, the company then asks for references and a police record. Sara explained why: "In this world, if you ask for a native speaker of the language, someone who speaks English [fluently], you can get just about anything. Many of the applicants we receive are either deported or are people who maybe had legal problems."[28] She continued to tell me about the case of one applicant who seemed to fulfill the language requirements, but turned out to have a serious drug addiction (and during the job interview had lied about his efforts to quit), and about another case in which, after checking references, she found out the applicant had been fired from another call center for sexual harassment. Understandably, Sara takes these issues seriously. "Their English might be perfect. So the screening we do now is thorough. We ask for prison record, police record . . . precisely this is not about finding out the bad things about people before knowing them. But [it is about] having standards that are more or less acceptable." She elaborated, "In this case we also must take care. We are hiring people to have interpersonal relationships with others. And maybe they are not responsible."[29]

I asked her if the specific fact of being a deportee from the United States meant that an applicant could not be hired. For Sara, this is not the primary element of the applicant's file that determines employment eligibility in El Salvador. Instead, she considers the circumstances of deportation along with other relevant factors associated with each applicant's particular case. Some people have overstayed their tourist visas, while others have been deported after serving criminal sentences in the United States. She explains, "If they have been deported for any criminal act, there is nothing we can do. All of us need a second chance, and we have the will to help. But we cannot expose our other employees, or trust the agent with expensive equipment."[30]

The possible association of criminality with a fluent or native speaker of English—even when most Salvadoran deportees are not criminals or gang members—reveals another facet of the history of migration, bringing the relationship between the United States and El Salvador to the call center. The presence of deportees in this workplace highlights the increased significance of migration to the Salvadoran national imaginary and to notions such as the brand "El Salvador Works." Deportation and the social categories and subjects it produces become part of this reality. These social categories are not neat, and they create spaces of doubt and exclusion. Removal from the United States has far-reaching effects on the deportee's life in El Salvador: "The alienation and stigmatization that makes officials doubt deportees' Salvadoranness can also exclude deportees from other domains of social life" (Coutin 2010a, 363).

Where the applicant learned English marks the asymmetry between countries and the transnational inequalities between Salvadorans. The prospective employee who learned English at a bilingual school or after-school language academy in San Salvador has a legible, local explanation for her/his linguistic capital. This local bilingual person does not have a possibly misread (or in some cases, suspect) migration history to explain during the interview, in contrast to the deportee. In some sense, the deportee is still living a migratory process and

explaining her/his displacement. Speaking English "like a native," often perceived as a sign of integration into mainstream society in the United States,
becomes entangled with a history of deportation from the United States. It also
highlights the socioeconomic diversity of call center employees in El Salvador,
something that in my view should be greatly acknowledged by employers and
human resources managers. English-language fluency in call centers is mostly
discussed as a category and skill that requires management and standardization (for example, with "improving the accent" of the agent). Thus the origin
of the accent might be somehow leveled, equalized, or even erased by working
in the call center. Employers know that applicants learn English under different circumstances, but that does not change their idea that the call center is
an essentially equal workplace where language is an equalizer and an eraser of
other differences and understandings of status. The following exchange illustrates this aspect of call center work. I cite the transcript at some length because
of the range of topics discussed during the conversation. I asked Gabriela an
open-ended question about what she thinks are the most important and new
things she has learned by working at the call center. She replied that learning
about managing a workplace where employees bring varied levels of life experience has been personally and professionally fulfilling, as well as challenging:

GABRIELA: You learn that because of the culture . . . I should probably tell you
that there exist very evident extremes about people who speak English well.
In El Salvador, you either come from bilingual schools or you come from
the United States. For example, there are people who come from gangs, and
have rehabilitated. We have people like that in the call center. They have
been sent back from the United States.

CECILIA: Deportees?

GABRIELA: Deportees, correct. There are people like that. But they are people
who in the end are like you and like me. And there are people who you
know are from the best families of El Salvador [meaning, wealthy or well-
known] and who work because they like to work, not by necessity. Maybe
one of the nicest things is that there [at the call center] we are all equal.
We celebrate equally; we help each other out equally. So, there all the social
strata are torn down, economically-socially. *Es super nice.*

CECILIA: Because everyone is in the same room, speaking English?

GABRIELA: Yes! We are all equal. We eat in the same cafeteria, use the same
restrooms, everything is the same. Not even the general manager has
more privileges than other people. It is a philosophy; it is a culture very
much like *todos en la cama o todos en el suelo*, very even-handed. Among the
other things I have learned is that you never know enough when it comes
to language. It is incredible! And maybe it even involves the family, because
my husband sends me daily the word of the day in English; I mean he wants

me to learn more, so I can be a successful person in my work. So, there is always, always, *always* a better way or a more elegant way, a more professional way of communicating. And that is the challenge, I feel, for Salvadorans. Even for people who learned English since they were children, studying in a bilingual school, or for the people who come from over there [the United States]. You can always improve. So, that's it in the case of the call center.[31]

The deportee, an embodiment of displacement and the effects of migration, is stigmatized upon forced return to El Salvador and when job-hunting in San Salvador's call centers. Although the number of deportees working at call centers seems modest, it draws attention from other agents and from the staff in charge of hiring and training. In informal conversations with call center agents while I was conducting research in El Salvador, if the subject came up and I asked about deportees, they would usually answer something like "Yes, of course we have entire teams made up of deportees," or even something to the effect that deportees were distinct due to discernible details in the way they dressed or talked to each other, or because they usually sat together in the cafeteria.[32]

Another interesting aspect of this dynamic of globalization and displacement is that although many women work at the call centers, in this case it is primarily young men who draw attention as deportees and call center workers, as the interviews with Sara and Gabriela reveal. Reena Patel argues that women in India have re-spatialized both the call centers where they work the night shift, and their routes to and from work. Due to time zone differences, women in Mumbai travel at night in streets that may often be hostile and challenging to their presence. Patel engages categories such as domesticity, exploitation, danger, and liberation in women's work "as *spaces* that individuals embody and experience, often in overlapping and conflicting ways" (2010, 11; emphasis original). In connection with this gendered angle on call centers and mobility— where Indian women predominate and face specific challenges in the industry and beyond—the narrative and themes of young male deportees who may or may not be trustworthy or dangerous embody the contradictions of call center employment and transnational displacement in San Salvador. These young men are simultaneously representative and challenging of globalization's ideas of promise, anxiety, and change.

During the time I was conducting this research, I noticed that there was another image, another way to appeal to the interests of Salvadorans who currently live in North America, and perhaps attract them to the call centers. The idealized call center workers of the Salvadoran imaginary might look like the young people in the "Meet Your Roots: Work in El Salvador" campaign. "Meet Your Roots" is a program organized by PROESA in 2006, and is specifically aimed at second-generation Salvadorans living in the United States and Canada who may want to learn about El Salvador. The main idea of this program was that young Salvadoran-Americans (or Canadians of Salvadoran descent, if that is the case) would come to El Salvador from these countries, and work at a call center for a determined period of time, usually one year. During that time, they could travel within El Salvador and learn about Salvadoran culture. "Meet Your Roots" is presented as an opportunity to reconnect with the country that parents (and grandparents) emigrated from, and to enhance the skills of this young diaspora for future professional growth after their year in El Salvador, as a March 2006 PROESA press release explained: "This would increase the possibilities for young people that participate in the program in North America since upon return they would be prepared to assume employment challenges that require bilingual personnel, opportunities that tend to increase owing to the growth of the Latin[o] community in the United States and Canada."[33]

An advertisement accompanies this press release (figure 2). "El Salvador's Government and the Call Center Industry in El Salvador invites you to rediscover a totally new country, ideal for living and working," the ad states.[34] Who would not want to employ the young people featured in this ad, in San Salvador's call centers and beyond? They are young, presumably fluent in English, and completely familiar with the United States—but not in a "dangerous" way, since they don't appear to be gang-affiliated deportees. They are friendly, ready with their headsets and a smile, and dressed in a professional yet relaxed manner. Most important, they *want* to live in El Salvador, to work, to reconnect with Salvadoran culture, and to have fun on their days off, as the smaller pictures of beaches and a bar suggest. The ad extends an invitation to the daughters and sons of Salvadorans in the diaspora (many of them of rural or urban working-class origins) to return to San Salvador, to be productive, and to become part of a new reality of labor that seems far removed from the "roots" of their parents. The ad itself represents the aspiration of ideal transnationalism, of young professionals who cross borders freely, who find possibilities in North America and in Central America.

Despite differences in life experience and contradictory opportunities that converge in the call center, managers work hard to nurture the perception that this organizational culture is overall not hierarchical. Unlike the perceived formality of Salvadoran workplaces and corporate culture, the atmosphere in call centers is generally viewed as less formal, for instance in some aspects of dress code and employee interactions. For example, one of the call centers organized a "pajama day" as a fun activity for the agents. Games and theme days may be fun, but it is important to remember that these are forms of indirect control and management, "the appearance of a relaxation of control through the introduction of aesthetic fun and games, but this is all in the name of improving performance. Call centres are highly performance-driven workplaces" (Alferoff

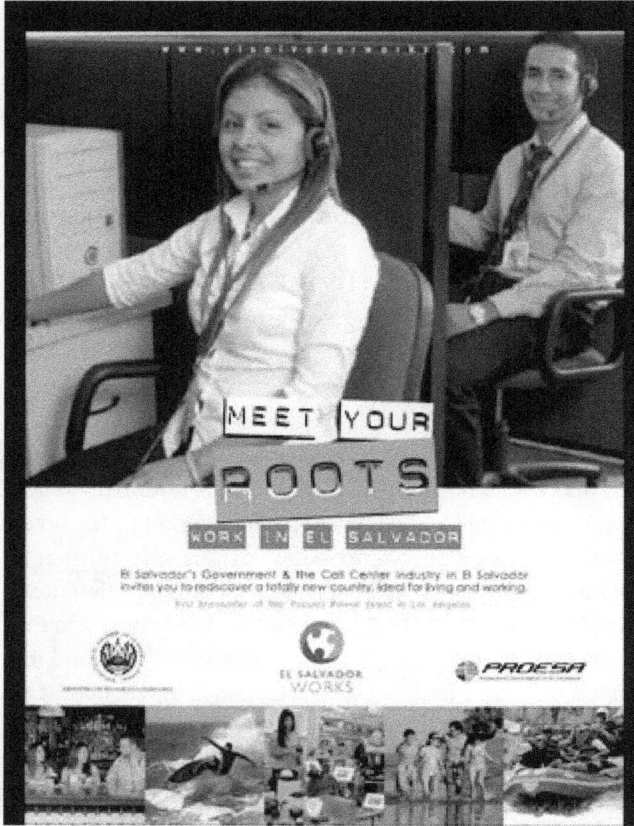

FIGURE 2. Meet your roots. Advertisement for "Meet Your Roots"
Program, PROESA, 18 March 2006.

and Knights 2003, 74). In fact, agents are held to strict schedules. To always be
on time, to stay on track with calls, and to follow a consistent script to ensure
a successful resolution of customer queries are crucial aspects of the job. But
a sense of openness, informality, motivational messages or games to achieve
these targets, and nonhierarchy is no small matter for employee morale, stress
management, and the idea that "everybody wins," as Gabriela described it: "It is
a culture of everybody wins . . . we are all winners, we can all enjoy our work . . .
it is a super motivating culture, full of positive energy."[35]

In this work culture, boosting employee morale and being positive about
work are key to motivating call center agents to stay on the job, decreasing
turnover. The investment promotion agency wants to "export voices" and market the "roots" and bilingualism of its national and transnational workforce.
Meanwhile, in call center human resources departments such as Sara's and

Gabriela's, transnational labor takes more complex forms—especially as these young managers face the real applicants, listen to the stories behind their English, try to fulfill the demands of hiring, and manage the everyday anxieties that surround the origins of the ideal, "native speaker" call center employee's much-desired linguistic capital.

Beyond hiring and language competency decisions, another facet of the stressful aspects of call center work and of service work in general involves handling interactions with frustrated, even irate and rude, customers. A human resources manager vividly described to me some aspects of these interactions that affect the work of call center agents in San Salvador. She began by saying that she thought the work which agents do every day is admirable, qualifying this statement by adding that when it comes to complaints, some agent positions seem less demanding than others. For instance, in the area of sales, since the interested customer is calling to buy a product, interactions are generally more cordial and successful. Predictably, areas of technical support are more stressful "because the first thing you hear is a complaint, people who are annoyed," the manager said. She elaborated on what these trouble-shooting interactions represent in the context of El Salvador. On one level, these are frustrations of any call center. She described unsuccessful calls: "I mean, really if we can solve it we will do whatever is possible to solve it so that the customer, when he hangs up, thanks us for the support that we have given. So, not all calls at the end of the day are successful. And the burden you have is heavy. Sometimes there are men [agents] crying from frustration. Because simply, there was someone at the other end of the line, hysterical, screaming, telling him, *'I am fed up that nobody solves my problem, and what are you going to do?'* Poor guys. Ah! It's horrible."[36]

The manager's description of call center work went beyond the interactions of the headset. She reflected on what the "horrible" feeling of frustration and rejection could mean for the employee, and what she as a manager could be responsible for after the call is over and the customer is no longer on the line. This situation has transformed (in this case at least) to empathy and insight into the lives and needs of agents in San Salvador. "Well, what do they [agents] need?" she said. "They need to learn to manage stress. Remember that we also live in a very violent society. The Salvadoran, by nature, we are like . . . yes! We are people who are very reactive to the moment. In some way, we have to help them [to make sure that] they do not take that problem home. . . . Everything they have received, they have to learn to let go of. Those are some of the most interesting, and the most draining, aspects [of the job] that we deal with. Because not solving a problem is also very frustrating for an agent, not receiving a 'thank you' from the customer is very frustrating. There are things you simply cannot do . . . !"[37] In the end, this manager somehow attempts to respond to the caller's earlier question—what are you going to do?

The agents can become frustrated due to ineffective communication. It is not simply a matter of understanding language (in this case, English) and of following instructions, but of effectively understanding the unfolding communicative event—that both agents and callers are communicating within a scripted and regulated system, where each agent has specific scripts (and, depending on the situation, some alternatives) to carry out particular requests such as sales, troubleshooting, mail-in rebate processing, and order confirmation. Here, it might seem like "talk" motivated by these requests is all that is happening—but, of course, the participants in this event bring something of their own experience to the interaction. This is made even more meaningful by the fact that the caller and the agent cannot see each other's gestures and facial expressions. The caller, for instance, only knows and consumes the brand or product and now has a question or even a complaint against it, motivating the call. The agent simply represents this brand (and its promise of service), at least for the duration of the company's contract with the call center. Since customer dissatisfaction with a product is at the root of many calls, building rapport is essential in the call center's customer service interactions. Rapport with callers—the conditions for relating to each other—is foundational, as one of the employee training manuals used in "Echoes," a call center in San Salvador, explains: "In business, rapport is needed to coordinate action and to exchange information. Rapport makes or breaks what you want." With self-explanatory chapter titles such as "Conveying Empathy to Customers," "Maintaining Call Control," and "Talking to Difficult Customers," it is evident that the training manuals of this and other call centers emphasize productive interactions and successful calls, a central concern during training and on the job.[38]

Furthermore, the violence of everyday life in postwar El Salvador is located beyond the communicative events of the call center operation. Some managers note that they are well aware of these circumstances, and how they might affect the attitude and well-being of employees, even to the point of identifying stress management for call center agents as one of the more challenging aspects of working in human resources. Maintaining the call center—continuously hiring and training people, fostering their language skills, and in turn attempting to minimize the frustration and turnover rates of the agents—becomes an operation that contradicts the global illusion of easily available, immediate services. In this context, workers might be (as one of the managers put it) "stressed" and even "reactive" to their surroundings inside and outside the workplace. Overall, the stressful work of hearing complaints day after day is a factor in the narrative of quick burnout and high turnover rates within the call center industry. For example, in the call center where Rodolfo works, about 70 percent of the agents quit before completing their first year of employment. They might move to other call centers looking for better work conditions or salary, or quit due to schedule constraints or because they start their university studies and cannot work full-time. Or they might simply find that the job is not satisfactory or what they expected. Good salaries, benefits, fun activities such as "pajama day," and an air-conditioned office in San Salvador contribute to a good working environment, but this is only part of the challenge of this operation.

Raquel's Story

The case of Raquel provides an example of the conflicts of call center hiring practices. At the time of our interview, Raquel was in her late forties, fluent in English, and had college-aged children. She went through the lengthy hiring process and workshops, and worked at a call center for only three days before quitting. Raquel said she had gone to six different appointments before she was hired. "I had to go many times. It took over a month. I had to wait for their calls, to take a drug test, to pick up my employee ID card, another time just to sign the contract. I don't know why they do not make [the process] simpler. Ah, and another time, for a typing exam."[39]

As she went through these appointments and the training process, Raquel felt uncertain about her abilities although she had scored very well in the spoken English test. "I do not feel that I have the agility to answer questions quickly, like a young person would. There were many young people at the training, high school age [most likely, recent high school graduates] or maybe in their first or second year of university."[40] Although according to Raquel she was told that she would have a choice when picking her schedule, later she figured that at some point, because of the rotation of employee shifts, she might eventually have to work evenings and weekends. This was an idea she rejected in favor of other obligations in her life. "My family is worth more than this," she said. Finally, she quit. "On the third day I did not go and I felt liberated," Raquel said. "It is not easy for women to combine everything, work, well-being. . . . That work was too much pressure. It ends up being like a *maquila*, working all weekend."[41]

Toward the end of our interview, Raquel noted that in her opinion women her age "do not have many opportunities." Career-wise, Raquel's experience is representative of many women of her generation (and level of education) in El Salvador. Before marrying in the early 1980s and becoming a housewife, she worked at an office. She described her job as a secretary in those days, where her training and fluency in English were an advantage. After marriage and raising her children, Raquel finds it difficult to return to a job that demands schedule flexibility and qualities that she labels as "agility"—thinking on your feet, feeling confident with technology. She concludes that the demands of call center work are not compatible with her lifestyle and family obligations. Despite her language skills and years of organizational experience, Raquel is not confident about her abilities to be a part of a transnational call center; she equates the strains of call center work to those in *maquiladoras*. In equating these, the skills of women in the global division of labor seem devalued and particularly exploitable. Melissa Wright has noted this representation in her discussion of the narratives of death, labor turnover, and women in the Mexican *maquiladora* industry, where "managers depict women as untrainable laborers; Mexican women represent the workers of declining value since their intrinsic value never appreciates into skill but instead dissipates over time. Their value is used up, not enhanced" (Wright 1999, 455). In addition, the assumptions of age and "agility" further naturalize the connection of technological know-how with youth. Although Raquel's age was not an impeding factor in the management's decision to hire her, she self-selected out of the call center job. *"At my age, how do you acquire flexibility?"* Raquel asked me during the interview.

Culture on the Telephone

Bilingualism and flexibility are important and commodified qualities for call center operations in San Salvador. The reach of English as the language of global corporations seeps into views of what is competitive and professional behavior. To attract global capital, the national investment promotion project depends on the presence and availability of a competent subject who can function in a bilingual environment—someone who speaks "neutral" Spanish and is fluent in English.

Call center work is represented as a desirable job option for English-speaking Salvadorans because it involves the use of linguistic and technical skills that are valuable in a global economy. Spanish/English bilingualism is an important asset for current and prospective employees in this sector, while training often emphasizes listening comprehension and the improvement of vocabulary, particularly what might be characterized as competent performance of an American English accent. Rodolfo described what this means for the hiring decisions that he is in charge of at the call center, where the focus is on sales and technical support:

CECILIA: How important is bilingualism, both written and spoken?
RODOLFO: Well, at least in a call center environment, especially this one that attends U.S. consumers, customers from all over the [United] States, it's really important because U.S. customers are very, very delicate when it comes to accent. . . . And vice versa. We get callers from different parts of the States that have very strong accents . . . like the South, for example, [or when] they speak really fast. So if we don't have agents with good

comprehension skills who understand the different accents, tone of voice, speech rate, if you don't understand the customer we will not give the service that we are required to give. If we do not communicate what we are doing, if we don't understand a customer's needs, we will fail at our jobs. So it's really important for people to have at least a native, 95 to 100 percent command of the language. The written part is not that important but the verbal understanding, comprehension, and speaking is the most important part.[42]

Rodolfo seems to recognize the difference between accents, and that there is not a single, "neutral" accent, particularly in the United States. Yet in his explanation—and as a supervisor—Rodolfo's awareness highlights the burden for the call center agents and the company. In this case, agents must somehow possess a clear, objective pronunciation, exceptional command of English, and listening comprehension skills. Otherwise, as Rodolfo said it, "we will fail at our jobs" and not communicate well with the customers.

Like their bilingual/English-speaking counterparts, Salvadoran agents in Spanish-only call centers are presented as speakers with objective "neutral accents" in PROESA's brochures and website. According to this claim, Salvadoran *Spanish* is not as defined or recognizable as the distinctive intonations from other parts of Latin America. This assumption of "neutrality"—whether speaking English or Spanish—is part of the brand presented in "El Salvador Works." The PROESA website claims, "Spanish spoken by Salvadorans is characterized by a neutral accent, another point in favor of the industry, opening up the possibility of answering calls from many different Spanish-speaking countries at one single place."[43]

However, Spanish is far from neutral. Anthropologist Pedro Geoffroy Rivas has argued that Salvadoran Spanish, what his 1978 linguistic study identifies as *lengua salvadoreña* ("Salvadoran tongue," or language) is the unique product of centuries of colonialism, followed by nearly two hundred years of independent life (see Geoffroy Rivas 1978). Salvadoran Spanish is a result of this regional and global history; of indigenous languages, colonization, conflict and coexistence with other Central American countries, immigration from different regions of Spain and other parts of the Spanish-speaking world, contact with the United States, and other changes that emerge from people's creative uses of language (see Geoffroy Rivas [1975] 1979). The language spoken by Salvadorans is unfixed, shifting, and innovative, and it is intertwined with social, political, and historical practices.

The idea of a neutrality of language in El Salvador's present glosses over the racial and class origins of many of its speakers. The idea of Spanish language neutrality in contemporary El Salvador echoes a long-standing idea of the cultural homogeneity of the Salvadoran population. The discourse of *mestizaje* as an unproblematic or harmonious mixture of people, essential to the coherent narrative of the modern nation, is often simplified in this way: El Salvador's indigenous population effectively "vanished," adopted the use of the Spanish language, and dropped its own Nahuatl language as well as the *refajo*—the traditionally hand-woven dress of women and girls—and other cultural norms (persuasive critiques of this view include Gould and Henríquez Consalvi 2002; Peterson 2007). This "vanishing" was due in part to the violence against indigenous populations, historically and especially after the 1932 *Matanza*, when up to thirty thousand people—indigenous inhabitants, peasants, and presumed participants in a labor uprising near the coffee plantations of western El Salvador—were killed over several weeks (Ching and Tilley 1998; Dunkerley 1991; Lindo-Fuentes, Ching, and Lara-Martínez 2007). Historians and other scholars of this event point to how the memories and narratives of 1932 have served as a foundation for various explanations of racial, political, and class attitudes, and for hegemonic understandings of El Salvador as a modern "mestizo nation" that does not pay much interest or attention to its indigenous roots.

A manager I interviewed in 2005 astutely noted that, while in El Salvador learning English was currently important for people who applied for jobs at the call centers, "How many people speak Nahuatl or are even interested in learning it? We're very strange in that way . . . El Salvador absorbs things from outside easily, but does not care about its own identity." Clearly, English and Spanish bilingualism is more valued and prioritized in the logic of the call centers and the postwar Salvadoran economy. As portrayed in PROESA's campaign, for young Salvadorans in the diaspora, meeting their "roots" means reconnecting to a modern, globally linked country and to call center employment (and not, in this case, to indigenous languages). John Lipski discusses the differences in language usage that arise from inequalities in Salvadoran society, especially in the area of access to education, observing "a sociolinguistic discontinuity between the speech of marginalized groups and that of the urban middle and professional class. The latter, increasingly, turns outward to Mexico, Spain, and the United States for advanced training, acquiring in the process a deregionalized language, while the socially marginalized sectors advance in their linguistic evolution at an ever greater rate. The discrepancy is immediately noticed upon listening to a Salvadorian, whose socioeconomic origins can be identified after only a few words" (Lipski 1994, 256).

The "neutral" Spanish and English (with an improved accent) which are supposedly spoken in call centers, then, aim to be global and more prestigious forms, "deregionalized" and professional languages that are readily marketable to the nation and the global consumer. In the context of language and commercialization, Arlene Dávila discusses the creation and portrayal "of a neutral or universal version of Hispanidad—the putatively neutral, 'non-accented' Spanish and 'generic' Latin look" (Dávila 2001, 93). She argues that the representation of Latinos in the United States by advertising agencies is overwhelmed by the codes and symbols of middle- or upper-class, fully bilingual, university-educated Latin Americans who arrive in the United States as adults to work as marketing creatives. The investment strategy involved in marketing and promoting the notion of linguistically deregionalized Salvadoran call center agents is part of postwar economic development projects, where Salvadoran business sectors and the government are able to present the linguistic abilities of Salvadoran workers as flexible and fit for a global market. The marginal, poor, or speaker of indigenous languages is not visible in this imaginary.

This focus on marketing "neutral Spanish" might lead one to believe that Spanish-language call centers attend exclusively to foreign callers from other Latin American countries or Spanish speakers calling from the United States. Yes, many of the calls are international. However, these call centers also serve Salvadoran companies and callers in need of local customer service. For the managers of these centers, it is crucial to maintain this local and regional perspective. "Each market is a different culture on the telephone," said Elizabeth, one of the managers of a Spanish-language call center.[44] What she meant by this is that for each client account (for example, an airline or telephone service), the call center workers had to get to know a brand well. In addition, agents should become familiar with slang or specific words depending on the countries and regions the calls are routed from—not because they will use this slang themselves during the conversation, but because it will be easier to understand the customers. Elizabeth and Laura (whom I interviewed together) are among the more experienced people in this area of Spanish-language call centers whom I had a chance to meet with early in my research. Elizabeth had worked at the same call center in San Salvador for almost five years, starting out as an agent and later promoted to planning analyst. She explained that her goal is to make sure that at least 85 percent of the incoming calls are answered within ten seconds, to avoid call abandonment or long wait times. To achieve this, she has to understand that some callers will wait longer than others, and that usually this depends on something as simple as whether the call is free (a toll-free number dialed from the United States, for instance) or not, as is currently the case for many local Salvadoran customer service numbers. For Elizabeth, it is important to make sure that all calls are resolved within a reasonable amount of time (an ideal time frame for successful call resolution is anywhere from two to five minutes maximum) and to maintain adequate call volume throughout the day. "If there are no calls, one gets bored," she added, recalling her own days as a customer service agent.[45] Not that this seems to be a problem; according to them this particular call center receives an average of thirty thousand calls per day. The number of calls also depends on the day-to-day operations of the corporate clients—for instance, if flights have been canceled or if there is a promotional airfare, this call center (which handles accounts for airlines among other clients) can expect a higher volume of calls.

This high volume of conversations is managed with the aid of a script. For those of us who are not in this type of work, a script with things to say and phrases to avoid may appear restrictive at times. However, it is also a tool for the agent to maintain rhythm and control over her/his work. There is a script for everything—to make a greeting and exit, to place people on hold, and to request appropriate personal information or extract additional details to assist the customer. "Sometimes we know that callers who are transferred to us are bored from hearing the same greeting or questions again and again. Some even say, 'Yes, I know, the other agent already said that, can you just help me.' *Hasta caemos mal de amables* ('we are polite to the point of annoying some callers')," Laura and Elizabeth commented.[46] They had several anecdotes about unusual calls they had received over the years. Laura remembered the specific case of a girl who called saying she was lost, and seemed to be in tears. Laura was concerned and kept her on the line, but in the end the girl said, "Ha! You fell for it!" Laura added, "We get prank calls, drunk people calling, but that happened more when the local calls were free."[47] Since those days this misuse of local telephone numbers has decreased somewhat, because these calls to the customer service centers of Salvadoran companies are now charged (some at eleven cents per call, in U.S. dollars). Also, the script dialogue sometimes helps the agent maintain the course of the call, to screen out and manage rude or prank callers.

For Laura and Elizabeth, this has been a job in which they have achieved considerable career growth as young women. During this time they have also completed their university degrees in engineering. "We feel like we have grown along with the company, and in our careers," Elizabeth said. "The work environment is really good, *bien chivo*," Laura added, "and yes, it is a young working environment, where we feel it is important to innovate, to not fall asleep!"[48]

Near the end of our interview, the three of us recalled a time during the 1980s when telephone service was limited. Infrastructure had not expanded to support widespread services in some areas of San Salvador, including the beautiful yet remote residential area outside the capital where we lived at the time. There, acquiring basic residential service from ANTEL often involved a lengthy wait (sometimes of months, and even years). And here were the sisters years later, spending so much time on the line, attending to calls from all over the Americas and traveling to Mexico and Panama to share their managerial experience with new call centers in the region.

We agreed that yes, overall their trajectory is sort of incredible.

Conclusion

Globalization processes enable and affect the call center in different ways, as Gabriela, Rodolfo, Sara, and other human resources managers noted in their extensive comments of who could be hired (and *trusted*) as a fluent speaker of English. The movement of capital (as a facilitator of foreign investment) and the availability of skilled employees are necessary factors in the development of this sector. The call center relies on migration and mobility and on some measure of immobility—on the hopes that tired and stressed employees do not suddenly abandon their jobs, and that foreign companies maintain their investment in El Salvador. This does not always happen: even in the time since I have been researching these sites, call centers have come and gone in San Salvador. Such is the rhythm of capital and investment. One of the large technical support call centers moved to another Central American country in 2008; some of the management followed this company's operations, relocating if they had the option. Meanwhile, perhaps some of the customer service agents continued to work for the next call center that soon occupied that large building, and maybe others found employment in other centers in San Salvador. Clearly, the mobility of workers is relative. Maintaining the call center by continuously hiring and training people becomes a local, challenging, and at times subjective exercise that contrasts with an uncritical illusion of easily available, immediate global services.

Investment promoters might assume and naturalize the importance of the bilingual call center as a link in the chain of production and consumption. Presented in this manner, bilingualism is indeed a hook for investment promotion, in that this is a relatively basic form of skilled labor that El Salvador can offer, and one that (at least on the surface) seems to cut across class and other signs of social status. My discussion of deportees in the call center indicates the awareness with which these hiring decisions are handled. The deportation of Salvadoran migrants from the United States and call center hiring/training are intertwined processes situated within the historical, political, and economic transformations of postwar El Salvador. As they are intertwined in this imaginary, they also seem to have clashing effects. That the call center industry in El Salvador can support contrasting ideas such as "Meet Your Roots" (and its multiple connotations of belonging and cultural origins) along with "neutral" Spanish (with the assumptions of erasure that I have already discussed) is not too surprising in neoliberal El Salvador.

The global reach of English seeps into views of competitive and professional behavior, as part of a project of global integration and labor flexibility that subsumes national inequalities. Speaking of the flexibility demanded as part of her daily duties, a call center human resources manager I talked to compared herself to a rubber band. She remarked, "It's like, 'stretch, stretch, people' . . . and then [snap] and they reward you." Changes in work culture encourage some call center employees to be "flexible" in the global division of labor. While young women like Gabriela, Elizabeth, and Laura have experienced career growth in this new workplace, other employees, such as Raquel, describe their situation in terms of constraints—as if she is unable to be flexible.

With practices such as the standardization of language and the use of scripts—prepared phrases which guide the customer service experience—call centers flatten the characteristics of difference among their agents in an effort to provide standard, consistent information and service to their callers. Standardization extends to the characteristics of the employees of customer service centers, in the shaping and surveillance of their voices and of how these voices become intelligible in a global conversation. The "exported voices" are brought into being by selected national histories, the words of corporate managers, foreign investors, and the institutions that help train their employees.

The call center, where voices are trained and commercialized for "export," is an example of the many reconfigurations of globalization as experienced by Salvadoran agents in these emerging workplaces and institutions. The search for an ideal, "neutral" accent involves a larger process of surveillance and regulation, as anxieties about the return of bodies from the United States conflict with the economic need to commercialize their language skills.

This work shapes and is shaped by the Salvadoran context, part of a moment in this imaginary, where personal aspirations for mobility are caught up in projects of national mobility—for instance, in the desire for prestigious foreign investment. There is tension in this imaginary: the creation of a brand such as "El Salvador Works" emphasizes the special characteristics of the *local* Salvadoran workforce, while also projecting itself as globally appealing. Migration is an important element of this brand and this imaginary, even to the point of trying to attract young Salvadoran-Americans in search of their roots.

Salvadoran call center agents are hired as bilingual, deterritorialized voices, but they might fashion themselves into something else. As the sector develops and changes, other issues might emerge: for example, the stress and high turnover rates commonly associated with call center work, and how this work may represent upward mobility for some and downward mobility for others. Production is segmented, outsourced, and divided dramatically between American consumer, in this case imagined as a monolingual English speaker, and bilingual Salvadoran agent. English proficiency is commercialized and tied to opportunities for career advancement, as portrayed by recruiters and in the advertisements. In this way, the voice as a commodity is exported and projected to the global.

5

"Heart of the City"

Life and Spaces of Consumption in San Salvador

The slogan of a famous shopping center in San Salvador is, "Metrocentro: El corazón de la ciudad y tú lo haces latir" ("the heart of the city and you make it beat"). Shopping malls seem ubiquitous—always a potential detour for everyday errands and the social interactions of many people in contemporary San Salvador. Growing up in San Salvador, I spent time in Metrocentro, and over the course of my research (especially since 2004) I have visited this and other malls frequently when I am in the city. The reasons vary—to meet friends, for errands, or to renew essential government identification documents. To spend time, observing, at different points in this project. To wait. I have also attended plays and other cultural functions in the evenings, since one of the malls has a theater. Relatives and friends would join me for lunch—we like each other's homes, but on some occasions the coffee shops and restaurants at the malls seemed more convenient. During my fieldwork and research, some respondents chose to meet with me at a mall for coffee and the interview. Of course, on certain afternoons my visits to the malls were simply to socialize, observe, and window-shop for a few hours.

I am certainly not alone in being a *flâneuse*—many people are walkers, leisurely wanderers of the malls of the San Salvador metropolitan area and its neighboring municipalities. The activities I have listed do not seem extraordinary in contemporary San Salvador or many other Latin American cities. The parking lots and corridors of the shopping malls look similar in their layout and are almost always full of people who are going about their everyday errands or shopping for a special occasion. The congestion of San Salvador's streets leads to the parking lots and mall corridors, where the crowds echo the street traffic—ever-changing, coming and going from the shops, food courts, kiosks, and movie theaters.

I trace the emergence, representation, and significance of the shopping mall in San Salvador, developing the idea of an imaginary of citizenship and consumption within the constraints of insecurity, common understandings of safety, poverty, and economic exclusion. Consumption, leisure, and socialization spaces have gained salience as new and recently remodeled shopping malls have altered San Salvador's physical and social landscape. The shopping mall is a creative space, one that can sustain certain, multiple practices that give the sometimes "too real" illusion of public space. This illusion is limited, however, since the use of the mall as a space for the public is shaped and created by tastes, status, economic opportunity, and fear of crime in actual public spaces. I specifically focus on this idea of created spaces of consumption, in the sense that these are private spaces made to stand for a public space—for example, the street. In a consideration of the sites of consumption, the shopping mall is situated as a space of imagination of the national and the global, where Salvadoran consumers are presented with a world of goods and choices that simultaneously constrain and liberate.

Consumption is a cultural, social, and economic practice, something that is part of a larger cycle of materials; it becomes concrete and meaningful in relation to how consumers are able to interact and participate in it (Conroy 1998; García Canclini 2001; Park 2005; Zukin 2004). The literature on consumption and commodities is extensive, a sign of the importance of this practice across cultures, borders, and disciplinary perspectives.[1] Consumption permeates everyday life and is intertwined with questions of social status, race, class, and taste, questions that have been pursued widely across academic disciplines. Consumption also raises questions of gender and socioeconomic status. Shopping—for groceries, for gifts, for clothes—seems like an ordinary activity in the everyday lives of women. It is both a repetitive chore and a welcome recreation. Sometimes shopping provokes anxiety and indecisiveness, while on other occasions it is viewed as an activity of considerable therapeutic value (Lears 1983). Shopping spaces are often linked to women and to feminized ideas of consumption and gender roles.

Many scholars critique the long-standing view of shopping as a frivolous or impulsive activity of women, a way for women to publicly display the wealth of their husbands or other male relatives. Noting this form of display in his analysis of the leisure class, economist and sociologist Thorstein Veblen wrote that "the dress of women goes even farther than that of men in the way of demonstrating the wearer's abstinence from productive employment" (Veblen [1899] 1992, 121). Veblen's discussion of economic forces and consumption patterns as the twentieth century approached identified the dimensions of consumer culture, gendered division of labor, and the shift from rural to urban, industrial life in the United States. He viewed the emerging accumulation of goods and the leisure class, along with "ownership of the women," as manifestations of class divisions and of women's dependence on the income of their husbands (33–34). In her analysis of the intersection of shopping and the growth of urban life in the United States during the late nineteenth century, Elaine Abelson argues that the growth of cities during a time of Victorian norms led to the medicalization of shoplifting. Respectable middle- or upperclass ladies were portrayed as ill and imbalanced, unable to control their urges to shoplift in the alluring, novel world of the department store. These ideas suggest that seemingly trivial acts of consumption and ways of dressing reveal the deep vulnerabilities of women—be it at the start of the twentieth century in the United States, or one hundred years later in El Salvador. Gendered consumption patterns unveil the stark conditions of a Salvadoran postwar culture of increased consumerism, enduring (and feminized) poverty, and "altered regimes of public value" (Moodie 2006, 63) in which some bodies have more meaning and symbolic weight than others.

The shopping mall embodies, sells, and produces a variety of needs, trends, and even modernity and cosmopolitan aspirations for the consumers who are drawn to it. Examining the specific case of El Salvador, it is evident that not everyone participates in these spaces equally. Every day, thousands of Salvadoran consumers circulate through these spaces, moving from the teeming parking lots or bus stops to the department stores to the smaller boutiques and shops, banks and other services, food courts, kiosks, and coffee shops strategically situated throughout this landscape.

My research in the malls combines observations and reflections on my own participation as a researcher and as a consumer, taking notes, visiting department stores, and engaging the field of consumption in the city. The analysis and observations that follow are based on my visits to several shopping malls in San Salvador; however, I primarily focus on three because of their location in the city, past and current name recognition, and other special characteristics: Metrocentro, La Gran Vía, and Multiplaza.[2] I also analyze the significance of downtown San Salvador and street vendors as key spaces that exist in contrast to the contained mall spaces, and as a reminder of the limits—geographic and in other ways—of the malls.

The relationship of acts of consumption to larger forces is key to an analysis of consumer cultures. Carrier (2006, 275) views consumption "less as an individual choice framed by meaning and more as a collective consequence, itself consequential, of political-economic forces." Karl Marx noted that a commodity is "a mysterious thing," a powerful object that satisfies human wants and actively shapes labor and social relations between people and things: "There is a definite social relation between men, that assumes, in their eyes, the fantastic form of a relation between things" (Marx [1867] 1978, 321). Appadurai (1986) argues that regimes of value and exchange shape the paths of commodities. Things, like persons, have complex social lives that do not end in the single moment when the commodity is bought or sold.

Néstor García Canclini proposes a "sociocultural theory of consumption" (2001, 38) to account for the complex processes that communicate and bring together multiple peoples and disciplinary perspectives. García Canclini, like other scholars, moves beyond questions of individuality, taste, and the isolated meaning of objects. He defines consumption as a politically important exercise intertwined with questions of citizenship, access to goods and institutions, and belonging; consumption is *"the ensemble of sociocultural processes in which the appropriation and use of products takes place"* (García Canclini 2001, 38; emphasis original). In his formulation, communication and consumption are no longer simply explained as processes of domination where consumers of media and commodities obediently receive messages. These processes are now interactive and thus they require creative engagements with the spaces of the city.

The study of spaces of consumption offers insights into the development of contradictory practices of inclusion, interaction, and exclusion. In U.S. popular culture, the shopping mall is often portrayed as a superficial, self-centered space of teenage alienation and mindless conformity, irrationality, or zombie-like consumption, a portrayal that has been critiqued (Friedberg 1993; Jacobs 1984, 97–102). The mall is associated with stereotypes of teenage boredom and immaturity—perhaps, even, with wastefulness and a less than complete understanding or appreciation of the value of objects. However, as Arlene Dávila (2012) notes in the case of Puerto Rico, malls are also spaces of socialization for retirees, people who after many years of work spend their leisure time at the mall with their peers. Based on my observations, on some weekdays this is the case in San Salvador as well. All age groups are part of this space. In San Salvador the growth and expansion of shopping malls presents an interesting and real contradiction in Salvadoran economic conditions. In a country where a great proportion of the population lives in conditions of poverty,[3] who, ideally and in reality, shops in the malls? How do these shops stay in business?

El Salvador's situation as a country with extreme social inequality compels us to address the ideas behind these questions; to consider the country's specificities and how commodities and space are central to social relations. Tracing these paths and interactions provides insights into the social structures and locations—such as the mall—that shape imaginaries of objects and consumers. As several of the scholars I have cited above note, when we research consumption, citizenship, labor, capitalism, and communication, we must critically analyze the (trans)formation of these processes and how they are connected. The study of spaces of consumption offers insights into the development of contradictory practices of inclusion, interaction, and exclusion.

Considering these complex contradictions, the rise of massive shopping spaces where Salvadorans spend money in the face of widespread poverty and debt cannot be simply explained as irrationality, or as a presumption of the inability of Salvadoran families to consume only according to expected, basic needs. New patterns of consumption cannot be characterized only as single-minded and wasteful attempts to emulate a leisure class. Furthermore, as Carlos Antonio Rodríguez argues, migrant remittances play an important role in the ability of many Salvadorans to consume. The relevance of these flows of money motivates discussions about their productive uses as savings, capital for small businesses, investments, and other policy proposals to be considered by government officials and agencies (Rodríguez 2004, 65–66). Over the past three decades, since the 1980s, migration has shaped many aspects of the lives of Salvadorans, including consumption patterns in fashion and food, which have gradually shifted for a majority. Speaking of this permeation of Salvadoran culture by the transculturation of Salvadorans in the United States, Waldemar Urquiza argues that this changing pattern of consumption has been primarily facilitated by the dedicated communication between split families, between migrants in U.S. cities and their families in the rural and urban areas of El Salvador: "This exchange perhaps was not intentional or conscious, it took place in linguistic expressions, in talking about what they did, what they learned, what they acquired, as they sent clothing, appliances, as they sent money" (Urquiza 2004, 93).

This gradual shift influenced Salvadorans, at least in their knowledge (and desire) of the consumer goods available in the United States. Flows of remittances affect a range of everyday consumption practices and cultural expressions in El Salvador. This financial support from abroad, especially from the United States, is a significant part of household income in some areas of El Salvador. This money, while not earned in El Salvador, has a significant impact on families and on what is bought and sold in the country. As Suzanne Kent notes, there are many ways to access the consumption system—and via "remittances and gifts, migrants fulfill familial obligations" (2010, 93). Ultimately, in some cases these dollars are more than "extra" income, since they represent nearly one-fifth of a typical Salvadoran transnational household's budget.

Since the numbers of emigrants increased in the 1980s, shifts in taste and patterns of consumption have become more apparent in urban as well as rural areas. For instance, different facets of the growing consumption of soft drinks, vitamin supplements, fast food, and electronics have attracted the interest of scholars (Urquiza 2004; Zilberg 2002). Clothing and other consumer products have become signs of the experience of Salvadoran migration and globalization. Sneakers, cell phones, and jeans connote a familiarity with the United States and its brands, and remittances are sometimes spent in many of the country's fast food franchises or in other forms of recreation. While transnational ties between migrants and their families are not the sole cause of the shifting consumption patterns found in postwar El Salvador, their importance in contemporary Salvadoran society lends predominance to this idea. Travel and mass media, for instance, also shape cultures of consumption—as have national economic and social policies. Spatial relations also shape consumption, as we will see in the next section.

The Shopping Mall and the City

Shopping malls in San Salvador are private spaces with a public character, where visitors can consume and often seek a brief respite from the nation's street violence. The potential of the shopping mall as a strange, novel place of study and theoretical inquiry is enhanced, paradoxically, by its characteristic hypervisibility and apparent superficiality. As a predictable (even familiar) building type, the mall has become prevalent in the landscape of North America and other parts of the world since the mid-twentieth century and in late capitalism (Friedberg 1993; Hardwick 2004; Harvey 1989; Jacobs 1984). While malls are designed to keep the consumer's attention on an array of desirable goods—and to make people circulate and buy—these sites also cultivate distinct characteristics to enhance their appeal and uniqueness. For example, in San Salvador the mall "La Gran Vía" intends to re-create the pedestrian streets of Europe; the shopper can walk outdoors, circulating at ease in this environment while avoiding the real city streets.

As cities grow, relatives, former neighbors, and childhood friends disperse throughout the city and its suburbs. In this dispersal the mall becomes a reference point, an accessible location that can replace the living room and the dining table as a space of interaction and hospitality. Moreover, as it has taken over the private space of the home, it has also overshadowed the downtown plaza, the street, and the public park: "people promenade less in the parks specific to each city and ever more in the shopping malls that mirror each other from one corner of the world to the other" (García Canclini 2001, 73). As the shopping mall substitutes these public and private spaces of social contact, it becomes even more attractive as a point of reference and simultaneously a theoretical "nonplace" (Augé in García Canclini 2001, 73), insofar as it can become whatever the privileged consumer wants it to be. Beatriz Sarlo characterizes malls as "spaces without qualities" and a place that is indifferent "to the city that surrounds it" (Sarlo in García Canclini 2001, 73). The mall is a socially and culturally produced space that shapes and enables experiences of mobility, access to goods, new habits, and other practices of the Salvadoran imaginary. In the context of El Salvador, the mall can be defined as "a privately owned commercial complex, conformed by independent establishments, which possesses a public character, own image, and interrelates commerce, services, cultural activities and entertainment. It is strategically designed to maximize the attendance and permanence of the public, as well as the good functioning of its activities, all under an environment of comfort and security" (Fuentes et al. 2005, 457).

From this perspective, the shopping mall is both private enterprise and public space, a mix of activities and intentions, a place that aims to please most or all sectors of the population—the mall, as a "nonplace," is whatever the consumer can imagine. The experience of consumption seems malleable, even as it is constrained by socioeconomic conditions. In all the characteristics listed above, we can see how the mall has come to substitute for public parks, downtown areas, and plazas as spaces of congregation, comfort, and imagination of community. The mall re-creates public spaces; it is appealing and attractive, like a theme park (Zukin 1991). In perceptions and in reality, it can supply a lifestyle—everything from secure parking and identification with brands, to "cultural activities and entertainment" in all its forms—for those who can afford to be its citizens.

What does this mean for the mall as a particular space for escaping violent national imaginaries and consuming transnational, idealized ones? The mall, as a space of new habits and lifestyles, is also a space of long-standing exclusion and inequalities. An architect I interviewed in San Salvador explained it to me in this way: "[The mall] is private but with a public character, there is an interest in making it look this way. There are invisible barriers. Yes, I would say it is an exclusive space. I mean, the mall is 'free,' but there is something that says 'no,' something that makes some people feel out of place."[4]

What is this *something* that the architect refers to? This is an important question in my analysis of postwar El Salvador and many privileged spaces of society, such as the mall, where exclusion and inclusion converge. Without engaging in a form of architectural determinism, we can say that architecture and spatial organization contribute to the development of new habits of circulation and new ways of relating to spaces. As new city centers where people come together to consume, the malls in San Salvador can provoke renewed perceptions of citizenship, modernity, and security—meanings increasingly attached to purchasing power, while they apply less to participation in San Salvador's public spaces and other areas of civic life. Edward Soja argues for a renewed attention to space and human geography in order to advance critiques of how these reproduce inequalities, and to "how space can be made to hide consequences from us, how relations of power and discipline are inscribed into the apparently innocent spatiality of social life, how human geographies become filled with politics and ideology" (Soja 1989, 6).

The mall can reproduce preexisting ideas of unequal access to goods, economic inequality, and "invisible barriers" of class (as the architect described it) even as it appears to be an innocent and novel—even classless—space. In his analysis of Brasília as a modernist city, James Holston writes that the architecture of Brazil's capital followed a central tenet of modernist planning, that "the creation of new forms of social experience would transform society, and [architects] viewed architectural innovation as precisely the opportunity to do this" (Holston 1989, 52). These ideas of proposed social transformation through spatial innovation are visible in specific shopping malls as realms of experience in San Salvador.

Some shopping malls in San Salvador are better known and draw more visitors, and in this manner are more successful and profitable than others. My research is not about describing or attempting to categorize all of them, or tracing every mall's life cycle from novelty to routine to decay. However, these are important components of our understanding of consumption practices and collective perceptions of these spaces. Each mall attempts to develop a distinct, even innovative, image. Real estate developers market and locate their malls with particular demographic and social segments in mind. J. T. Way observes this same dynamic, "the inexorable logic of class-based branding" (2012, 194), in Guatemala City's malls (it is known that some of the same mall developers who work in El Salvador also work in Guatemala and other countries of the isthmus). Three shopping malls in San Salvador, built decades apart, are examples of this logic and its influence in the imaginary: Metrocentro (inaugurated in 1971), Multiplaza (inaugurated in 2004), and La Gran Vía (inaugurated in 2004).

Metrocentro: Futuristic Visions

For many, the most popular shopping mall in San Salvador is Metrocentro. Better known by the familiar nickname, "Metro" has existed since the early 1970s and continues to expand in its infrastructure. With its twelve *etapas* ("stages" or "levels"), which have been built and remodeled over the course of decades, this mall is known as the largest in El Salvador, with hundreds of shops, a cinema, theater, food courts, and other services. When Metrocentro was under construction, this area of San Salvador was already a strategically located frontier, a direction in which the city was expanding and where urbanization would continue (see Herodier 1997, 327). Due to the city's growth, Metrocentro is now located in the geographic center of San Salvador, and as its slogan states, it is at "the heart" of the city. This is, of course, a matter of orientation. Placed in a symbolic center, the mall becomes even more significant in its accessible location and mass appeal to a broad socioeconomic segment. "Metrocentro is aimed at a middle-class market, and it pulls people from everywhere . . . some Salvadorans have never been to the beach, but they know Metrocentro."[5]

When Metrocentro opened its doors in October 1971, it was described in futuristic terms by its developers and on the media, highlighting its novelty. To understand how this new space was presented to the public(s), I visited the archives of *La Prensa Gráfica* and searched for news articles and advertisements related to the inauguration of Metrocentro. Reading the mall through the newspaper provides an insight into how these sites are connected in the imaginary of citizenship and consumption. For instance, both assume particular manners of circulation and participation—publics, readers, and shoppers sharing a space. Media consumption and window-shopping at the mall are intertwined, and each is connected to the Salvadoran imaginary as "a form of perception" (Buck-Morss 1989, 345).

The newspaper article "Hoy inauguran primera etapa Centro Comercial Metrocentro" ("First stage of Metrocentro Shopping Mall inaugurated today") described the shopping center as an innovative place that included a spacious, "American style" supermarket and a "soda fountain."[6] This October 1971 article makes a very specific reference to the size of the shopping mall, and to its imagined future expansion to a large, successful mall: "The first stage of the Metrocentro shopping center has a constructed area of 5,000 square meters. When the entire shopping center is completed, the constructed area will be approximately 20,000 square meters."[7]

In the same issue of this newspaper, I found what is probably Metrocentro's first slogan in an advertisement: "Ir al centro comercial de Metrocentro es gozar el placer de comprar" ("To visit the Metrocentro shopping center is to enjoy the pleasure of shopping").[8] It is interesting to note the repeated use of the phrase "Metrocentro shopping center" in this early advertisement and the news articles—apparently to link, inform, and explain the new concept of the mall to the potential shoppers, who in this case are also the readers of *La Prensa Gráfica*. Pleasure, leisure, shopping, and this novel built environment are connected ideas and activities, encapsulated in this ad and made memorable by this short phrase and the newly opened space associated with it. People are introduced to and encouraged to imagine Metrocentro, to develop an impression of the mall even before they visit it in person.

Another article, published on the day after the mall's inauguration, alludes to how the space of the shopping mall in 1971 represents a dream and vision of the future of San Salvador's growth as a city, of what could happen: "Metrocentro tiene proyección futurista dice el Sr. Poma" ("Metrocentro has futuristic projection says Mr. Poma").[9] The opening of this mall was a newsworthy event. President Fidel Sánchez Hernández, then in office, was in charge of the *corte de cinta* ("ribbon-cutting ceremony"), giving the inauguration of the mall an air of official Salvadoran state involvement, of a project of national development and infrastructural expansion that went beyond the interests of private enterprise. In 1971 Luis Poma, president of the real estate group that developed Metrocentro, projected that by 1981 the population of San Salvador would surpass one million inhabitants. He added, "The economic growth of the country requires the modernization of its service facilities. We do not work for today but for the San Salvador of tomorrow."[10] The growth of the city's population would go hand in hand with urbanization, modernity, growth of the service sector, consumption, and the demand for products and shopping spaces that Metrocentro would fulfill.

As the 1980s civil war displaced countless families from the rural areas to San Salvador, urban growth took another form. The city grew, along with a lack of infrastructure and public services—far from an ideal of orderly modernization. In a turn of the futuristic dream, it was war, not economic development, which in large part made the city's population grow rapidly. In the twenty-first century, San Salvador is a densely populated city, a conurbation of neighborhoods, municipalities, and districts that form what is presently known as the AMSS (Área Metropolitana de San Salvador, the Metropolitan Area of San Salvador). An area of approximately 650 square kilometers, currently the AMSS is home to nearly a third of El Salvador's population.[11]

In the news articles from 1971, Metrocentro was described as "an urban complex of multiple uses in an area of approximately thirty *manzanas*[12] of terrain, strategically located in the center of the metropolitan region of San Salvador."[13] This strategic, planned location became geographic and cultural reality. By 2007, about 30,000 people frequented Metrocentro every day—not only to purchase things, but to see movies, eat at the food courts, use the banking services, or simply walk and window-shop. The number of visitors increases to 55,000 on weekends, according to some estimates by an architect familiar with this mall, although the numbers may be higher.[14] During certain holiday seasons—particularly Christmas and the August holiday in honor of San Salvador's patron saint—live music and an amusement park with rides for children and adults entertain the crowds. The mall truly becomes a theme park, and part of the city's celebration.

As Fuentes et al. (2005) have argued, Metrocentro fulfills all the qualities of a successful shopping mall; because of its diversity of stores and "tenant mix," it attracts people from different parts of the city for diverse reasons. Its commercial image as a site of enjoyment, convenience, and shopping possibilities endures after several decades, it is a geographic reference point in the city, a required stop for many bus routes, a meeting point for tourist groups (it is located close to a well-known hotel, also a reference point). Metrocentro has expanded as "an architectural response to the social demand of each period during its thirty-plus years of existence" (Fuentes et al. 2005, 17) and become the "center" of the city's social life, ingrained in the minds of consumers. Its current slogan about being "the heart of the city" while its visitors "make it beat" connects Metrocentro to a system, a necessary relationship between people and space.[15] The mall and the consumer *together* create the "heartbeat" of a city and the vital circulation of commodities and ideas. Malling in Metrocentro is what William Kowinski (1985) refers to as "a chief cultural activity" that shapes memories and imaginaries of consumption, space, and belonging.

Advertisements for Metrocentro represent these enduring ideas of the mall as a space for social life and as a place to experience the pleasure of shopping. As part of the 2007 and 2008 campaigns (named "Metrocentro el Corazón de la Ciudad"), advertisements with this message of the heartbeat appeared in several formats on radio and television, and in colorful print, newspaper, and billboard images.[16] The ads portray everyday activities at the mall, activities that are normal but become special and memorable when Metrocentro is the place involved. The ads for Metrocentro sell a lifestyle associated with this mall, with friendship, with fun, and with fashion. The ads do not have to remind their viewers of the location of the mall—its brand elements already convey that Metrocentro is strategically located at the heart of the city, assuming the Salvadoran consumer's economic and emotional familiarity with this place.

These ads invite us, the shoppers, to imagine ourselves in familiar, happy situations associated with Metrocentro. Who has not enjoyed lunch or a snack with good friends at the food court, or searched for—and found—the perfect blouse? The consumers portrayed in this campaign feel this heartbeat too— Metrocentro, in short, is where people feel alive (for example, a young woman, credit card and "perfect blouse" in her hands, portrays this with her smile in one of the ads).[17] The young consumers in these advertisements are not making large purchases of expensive meals, wardrobe, or electronics—they are simply enjoying the small everyday moments that the social space of Metrocentro facilitates. It is a surprisingly simple yet multilayered message of belonging to San Salvador and habitually consuming in this mall.

In malls such as Metrocentro, sensory experience and personal memory are tied to stores, the everyday, and holidays. The mall can provide a sense of security during these times, but rarely a guarantee of safety outside its perimeter, as Ellen Moodie describes in an account of "Adventure Time in San Salvador," a carjacking and assault that "begins" in front of the mall at one in the afternoon of a seemingly ordinary day, and spirals to many other locations (2010, 113–138). Beyond personal security, many stores and products make up this memory of the senses—not only the visual and tactile, but also taste in its many connotations, as evidenced by several restaurants that were at first located in Metrocentro and have eventually spread to other parts of the country, influencing the food consumption habits of Salvadorans. For example, Mister Donut is a popular place to eat, not only in Metrocentro, but also in many other locations across San Salvador. It sells a variety of donuts and coffee, as well as traditional Salvadoran foods such as pupusas with cheese or other fillings, horchata (in El Salvador, this drink is made from the ground seeds of the *morro*, a type of gourd), and *desayunos típicos* ("typical breakfasts"—eggs, fried plantains, cheese, red beans, and tamales). While this donut franchise is becoming rare in the United States and Canada, Mister Donut has adapted to local tastes and grown in El Salvador (as it has in other parts of the world, particularly Asia).[18] Pollo Campero, a chain that originated in neighboring Guatemala, has become closely associated with Salvadorans and has been located in Metrocentro for decades. The fried and grilled chicken restaurant has opened several locations in the United States (from California to Virginia) and other countries beyond the Americas (Spain and Indonesia are some examples).[19] The Pollo Campero in El Salvador's Comalapa Airport, one of numerous locations in the country, is usually busy with customers. Travelers often buy boxes of chicken to take with them on the plane—a final purchase before leaving El Salvador—to carry and replicate the experience of the restaurant at their various destinations.

Why do people buy chicken to take with them on a flight to the United States, and why does a transnational donut franchise sell pupusas and tamales? In 1980s El Salvador, these places and foods were already present; they were part of the experience and the image of novelty of the shopping mall. Years would pass, and "time deepens definition and contrast, but the imprint of the image has been there from the start" (Buck-Morss 1989, 7). These tastes and environments were part of the lives of many Salvadoran consumers prior to their emigration—and somehow, they are integral to people's awareness and ways of experiencing transnational connections. For many emigrants, these recollections would later be part of meaningful exchanges with their relatives in San Salvador. In my case, my own memories and knowledge of the mall and the presence of the donut shop and the chicken restaurant only begin to sketch the complex picture of transnational circuits of brands, franchises, and the people who consume them in Metrocentro and beyond. Despite the remodeling and physical/infrastructural changes of recent years, walking through Metrocentro can be a specific experience in the Salvadoran imaginary, perhaps one that is distinct from walking through other malls. It might be because of the work of the memory and this "dreaming collective" (Buck-Morss 1989) of Salvadorans who visit that mall every weekend just to *walk*. The varied meanings of sites such as the mall, the donut shop, the department store window, the advertisements, and the restaurant are spread across the transnational imaginary of consumption as examples of the connections and the meaningful, contradictory, and multidirectional circuits of people and capital.

Multiplaza

Multiplaza is operated by the same real estate developers as Metrocentro. Multiplaza opened in 2004, and is remarkable in its architecture and use of bright colors. It is also maze-like, with its many corridors. The escalators that lead into the mall resemble a vault or a cavern, giving the impression of descent into a world where gazing and buying is the only escape. Mexican architect Ricardo Legorreta (1931–2011) became known for these design features evocative of Latin American culture. In contrast to other malls that seem generic and stereotypically "Americanized" in their architectural forms, Multiplaza is "Latinized" (see Davis 2001). The bright colors, for instance, bring to mind the exteriors of houses found in some Latin American villages and cities, Mexican folklore, and the eye-catching colors of tropical flora and fruits. Multiplaza was Legorreta's first shopping mall project in the Central American region. Most of his previous designs have been in hotels, universities, museums, factories, private homes, and other institutions (including the 1993 design for the Metropolitan Cathedral of Managua, Nicaragua), all part of a decades-long career since he founded his firm in 1964.[20] Legorreta's work is distinctive, with well-known features—"gigantic vaults, high flat surfaces finished with appealing colors, maximum use of light sources, and surprising turns. In Multiplaza, the visitor finds himself with all that and wanders along a corridor, without thinking that at its end he will encounter an aquatic illusion, or a waterfall whose end slides him to a coffee shop."[21]

Multiplaza invites the Salvadoran consumer to escape and wander, to simply follow the path, colors, and unexpected turns of the mall, to be led by the staircases, the soothing flow of the cascading water, the light from the windows, and to eventually stroll into a café or a department store. It invites the visitor to not think, to be surprised, to let the shape of this labyrinth—this combination of clean lines, colors, and serenity—dictate his or her circulation in it. Once the remaining phases of the project are completed, Multiplaza aims to be a city within itself.[22] Stores, supermarkets, restaurants, bars, coffee shops, and movie theaters are encompassed in this vast structure. Multiplaza suddenly emerges on the horizon, along a busy highway. In the 1990s, it was proposed that a former coffee estate near the San Salvador volcano could become a park and a protected ecological zone for trees and the dwindling parrot population of San Salvador and Antiguo Cuscatlán. Finca El Espino, a "lung" or forested area, has for decades been a contested zone between environmentalists, governments, urban developers, and others.[23] Public parks and similar spaces may still be under consideration and in the memories of many, but these projects have not yet been executed. Meanwhile, malls—as the existing spaces for social gatherings—definitely mark the expansion of the city and its population of consumers. Architecturally, the malls seem invasive in this area, as though these structures do not have to conform to their surroundings. In fact, they stand out, enhancing and altering the skyline.

As the visitor enters Multiplaza and parks in the large, multilevel underground parking lot, he or she (and I include myself) encounters one of the mall's most striking features—the use of vivid colors. The walls on different floors are painted in bright yellow, blue, pink, and orange. Color is supposed to evoke the *pueblos* of Latin America, a way of rescuing traces of the regional folklore. The orange and yellow walls, for example, might bring to mind the colors of mangos, papayas, and of the *árbol de fuego*, a tree with vivid orange-red flowers that look like flames, immortalized in the poetry of Alfredo Espino.[24]

In addition, the use of bright color in this building works within a capitalist logic—the autochthonous or traditional becomes the exotic, global culture with an ethnic touch. The use of traditional elements within a modern capitalist structure fulfills a powerful function of erasure, as Néstor García Canclini has noted in the case of the commodification of crafts in Mexico: "The picturesque, the primitive, can seduce the tourist because of their contrast to his/her everyday life, but it is even better if the folkloric-advertising discourse can convince him/her that poverty need not be eradicated" (García Canclini 1993, 42). Tradition lends social status; the local and folkloric lends legitimacy and coherence to a transnational project. This built environment, after all, is a luxury mall, an imaginary of wealth and good taste, designed by an internationally recognized architecture firm—not a tacky, kitschy rural home with bright (but peeling) fuchsia walls. In its scale, this and other malls seem to serve the function of monuments to the ideas of postwar, twenty-first-century consumption.

The appropriation of color and the local carries elements of high and low culture (and, as far as this divide might generally be perceived, it must also be questioned). As globalization and the complexities of contemporary urban culture make it increasingly problematic to claim a single "true" culture, Multiplaza can support contradictory discourses of tradition and modernity as they mix in the marketplace/mall, what Celeste Olalquiaga (1992, 38) calls a "synchronized difference" of objects and iconography. The circulation of things, images, and colors acquires new meanings, which are interesting as contestations to older forms and cultural boundaries.

Multiplaza is a single, enclosed structure that offers multiple meanings for its visitors, who will spatialize and experience the mall differently. Potentially (and critically) this unevenness and variety highlights certain economic choices and gaps in larger Salvadoran society, even within the unity of this building. While the style of Multiplaza is architecturally homogeneous, as a "whole" and enclosed mall, the stores within the building cultivate their own identity and image, in some ways like stores along a city street. They are, clearly, *multi-plazas*—multiple and individualistic spheres where people can democratically "choose" as they shop. The actual city street, which "embodies a principle of architectural order through which the public sphere of civic life is both represented and constituted" (Holston 1989, 103), almost becomes irrelevant, replaced by the mall's corridors and by the lifestyle that people can choose to purchase if they have the means. The actual public space of a city is forgotten in the mall, while idealized plazas or streets are created as points of connection between Salvadorans who can afford to be citizens of the mall—to escape in this maze—and the commodities they consume.

La Gran Vía, and Beyond

La Gran Vía—The Great Way—is a "cathedral of consumption" (Crossick and Jaumain 1999), a massive mall, sixty million dollars' worth of imported glass from Spain, French iron benches, polished stone and metallic surfaces, and elegantly painted walls.[25] The clear European glass shimmers against the warm tropical sky. The floor shines. Despite its fresh, modern, glimmering (and sometimes eclectic) look, La Gran Vía draws its inspiration mostly from nineteenth-century images. Architecturally, its main corridor is evocative of an arcade, a structure described in an 1852 illustrated guide to Paris and noted by Walter Benjamin: "These passages, a new discovery of industrial luxury, are glass-covered, marble-walled walkways through entire blocks of buildings, the owners of which have joined together to engage in such a venture. Lining both sides of these walkways which receive their light from above are the most elegant of commodity shops, so that such an arcade is a city, a world in miniature" (Benjamin in Buck-Morss 1989, 3).

How is the Parisian arcade, already a world in itself, recognizable as a shopping mall and "lifestyle center" in El Salvador? Clearly, La Gran Vía is tied to the imagining of European streets, complete with "outdoor" cafés, kiosks, and benches emulating the sidewalks and passages of Paris. La Gran Vía represents a nostalgic yet current "dreamworld" (Buck-Morss 1989) as a combination of the idealized space of nineteenth-century Europe and the modern, transformative aspirations of postwar Salvadoran transnational imaginaries, including the technologies of globalization and commerce that allow for the importation of products and materials to construct this site in El Salvador. La Gran Vía intends to feed the imagination, to provoke a movement in time and space, and "promises to transport its visitors to the ambiance of the classic European cities. Benches, garbage bins, and other implements have been imported from France, and the tempered glass that has been used is the same as in the terminal in Barajas, Spain."[26]

La Gran Vía re-creates some aspects of European streets and their "ambiance" as it might also evoke a sentimental, even selective, image of San Salvador's past—a time before the 1930s Great Depression, before the military coup of 1931, and before the violence against indigenous communities and poor peasants in 1932, "a moment of loss and of generation" (Peterson 2007, 60) that changed the political and economic landscape of the nation. In the visions of the late nineteenth century and the first decades of the twentieth century, San Salvador seems scenic and manageable. A city in an earthquake-prone region, it faced catastrophes yet "rose from its ruins" several times (Martin 1911, 257). "There are few more pleasant cities as a place of residence for all the year round than San Salvador. The climate is very agreeable, while the situation of the city, scenically speaking, is exceptionally beautiful," Percy F. Martin observes in *Salvador of the Twentieth Century* (1911, 256). He adds: "San Salvador is altogether a well-constructed and even a handsome city, with several notable public buildings which would grace any European capital" (Martin 1911, 257; also see Herodier 1997, 38–39).

The European arcades, or passages, "were the first international style of modern architecture" and became the "central image" of Benjamin's project (Buck-Morss 1989, 39). In the arcades, Benjamin observed the remains of a glittering culture of consumption—what he saw in the 1920s and 1930s was already in a form of decay, "commodity graveyards, containing the refuse of a discarded past" (Buck-Morss 1989, 37–38). Significantly, Benjamin's project "takes mass culture seriously" and modernity is not considered simply as "the demythification and disenchantment of the social world" (Buck-Morss 1989, 253). Instead, "Benjamin's central argument in the *Passagen-Werk* was that under conditions of capitalism, industrialization had brought about a *reen-chantment* of the social world" (Buck-Morss 1989, 253). Benjamin imagines alternatives in the arcades, and traces history in these nearly forgotten "dream worlds" once full of novelties and central to mass culture. By the late 1930s, many of the images Benjamin recorded "flash out in the present as urgent warnings, images far less of new political possibilities than of recurring political dangers" (Buck-Morss 1989, 304).

Benjamin's project explores the impact and relevance of the commodity on philosophical thought—it reveals the commodity's "contradictory 'faces': fetish and fossil; wish image and ruin" (Buck-Morss 1989, 211). With these critical angles on consumption and the commodity, the memory of the arcades opens an opportunity for connecting futures and pasts, the new and the old, and for collectively reviving and critiquing the historical and political potential of mass consumption. My reference to La Gran Vía links the ideas of fashion, "decay" of the European arcades, and the social worlds of El Salvador (and Europe) that shifted in the 1930s with this modern shopping mall of the twenty-first century. In this new arcade, the latest clothes and accessories may be recycled fashion dreams, futuristic garments, recirculations of older ideas, a "dream world of mass culture" (Buck-Morss 1989, 253) and—potentially—an opportunity for creativity, for rupture, and to "wake up from the world of our parents" (Benjamin in Buck-Morss 1989, 279).

This "dream world" reaches beyond La Gran Vía, existing in connection to other malls, practices, and spaces. I walked along the "street" of one of the malls and took a few pictures of the building and a fountain that adorns the entrance. These, of course, were interesting and attractive to me as part of the research. As I was finishing, a security guard approached me, maybe with some curiosity. He said that he had seen me take out my camera. In our strangely mistrustful world, shadowed by a history of violence, could taking pictures of buildings seem suspicious? What could be questionable about capturing (and consuming) the image of the photogenic fountain and Christmas lights, the graceful features of this building? Photography is not an uncommon activity during the holiday season. Visual consumption becomes a point of questions and critiques of commodification, looking, and taking a snapshot (Jameson 2000, 125).

I did not ask the mall security guard anything. Instead, since by then I had several photos in the picture card of my digital camera, I was done for the day and prepared to leave. This type of brief interaction with a mall security guard was unique in my time observing the malls in San Salvador. It only occurred once, but to me it highlighted the contradictory, paradoxical, public/private character of this "street," the shopping mall. In most cases, any security guard was someone helpful when I asked for, say, directions to the food court or a particular store. On this occasion, as I held my camera, he was a reminder that the mall, despite its advertised open character, could not readily accept situations that are not within its private and capitalist logic. While it poses as a public space of consumers' freedoms and choices, in actuality it also asserts its primary condition as private property, even in very subtle ways.

As many inhabitants of San Salvador aspire to become part of a community of consumers, those who cannot participate in this contested field are marginalized. In García Canclini's formulation, consumption is "a site that is good for thinking" because it potentially forms and reorganizes new understandings of identities and narratives, even opening access to goods and rights such as health and housing (García Canclini 2001, 5). In this regard, the state has a presence in these spaces of consumption, and in the idea of national identity. This is visible in that some Salvadoran government agencies maintain branches of their offices in different malls in San Salvador. These locations offer convenience, perhaps a more comfortable wait, parking, and the promise of security for important transactions—primarily, obtaining documents such as the Salvadoran national identification card or passport.

The presence of these offices (and, at various times of the day, the lines of people associated with bureaucracy) introduces interesting possibilities for relationships between shoppers and state institutions. The acquisition of important identification documents is now part of the shopping experience at the mall, one more errand. Salvadoran shoppers no longer have to make a special trip to a public, government building to obtain or renew their documents. Sometimes the lines at these mall locations are lengthy, while on other occasions the mall visitor/citizen does not have to wait more than one or two hours to obtain a new passport or identification card. If he or she brings all the appropriate documentation (for example, birth certificate and fee payment), this process can be relatively quick—unexpectedly smooth, some might even say. I experienced various wait times directly when I renewed my documents at two different malls. And yes, for the most part the location of these offices was convenient for me and, as I could observe, for many others around me. I should add that the document, for example a passport, must state the name and location of the issuing authority. Thus in the case of many Salvadoran passports the government office and the name of the mall are listed together. This is necessary information, of course, and also symbolic of the spaces of citizenship and consumption that many Salvadorans inhabit.

Javier Auyero's ethnography of the experiences of poor people, waiting, and state welfare institutions in Buenos Aires, Argentina, provides insights into the idea that "waiting is stratified, that there are variations in waiting time that are socially patterned and that respond to power differentials" (2011, 7). The people waiting for their passports in the mall are in many respects far more privileged than the patient subjects of Auyero's ethnography. However, they are connected by the idea that they must wait, that they must be patient, thus reproducing hierarchies of power that exist in the world beyond the mall in San Salvador and the welfare offices Auyero describes. Within a relatively privileged and practical situation, the bureaucratic apparatus of the state—the provider of legitimate and valuable documentation—has come to the mall and conveniently become a part of the consumer's habits.

While any city may offer an example of the production of spaces and imaginaries, specific projects of modernity and management of inequality encourage us to think about the contradictions of consumption, citizenship, and globalization as they appear in the mall. For many people of San Salvador, perceptions of belonging and connections become more about what one is able to consume (and where this activity takes place), and less about civic participation or everyday presence in public spaces. Brand loyalty contrasts with patriotism and identification with national civic symbols. The past meets the present in the world of commodities, and ultimately consumption marks the ways societies remember and live everyday life and culture, along with "a reorganization of public memory" and powerful sensory experiences (Seremetakis 1994, 3). La Gran Vía, Multiplaza, and other malls can create and provide a nostalgic, futuristic, convenient, or glamorous ambiance for their visitors. The existence of these sites is intertwined with a contemporary sensibility of belonging—while some mall visitors cannot always have the pleasure of capturing the images of their experience, others experience the pleasure of shopping. As I left the mall, this safe and enclosed space that can potentially support multiple discourses, I kept my digital camera in my bag and I continued to the parking lot, to the car, to return to the street.

Spheres of Life

Salvadorans who stroll and can afford to shop in Multiplaza, Metrocentro, and other malls rarely need to visit, consume, or socialize in the downtown markets or interact with the street vendors of San Salvador. For some socio-economic segments (middle-class seekers of sales, consumers of high-end or luxury goods), the various malls in San Salvador are a substitute for the city's downtown or pedestrian streets. The corridors, shop windows, and food courts of the malls offer an entertaining, sanitized version of San Salvador—and an escape from the traffic, pollution, crime, and congestion of the city's arteries. Who would habitually visit the Teatro Nacional in downtown San Salvador, where street parking is usually the only option, when the theater in Metrocentro, the restaurants in Multiplaza, or the cinemas at La Gran Vía offer an enhanced sense of security?

Even as the mall intends to reduce the consumer's need to confront the reality of the street, the street continues to be an important site where the social and political importance of consumption is realized for many Salvadorans who are economically excluded from shopping malls and the formal sector. While the malls are enclosed in their own worlds, framed by colorful concrete walls or under imported glass, most of the country is "a market under the open sky."[27] The entirety of El Salvador is a site of consumption, a world of goods and of competing forms of buying and selling. In 2004, the same year that Multiplaza and La Gran Vía opened, at least 772, 407 people—49.8 percent of the total economically active/working population of the country—were part of the informal sector, according to a national survey conducted by DIGESTYC, El Salvador's statistics and census bureau.[28] The nation's informal sector is concentrated in the country's capital city, especially in *ventas callejeras* (the spaces and kiosks of street vendors). The growth of the informal markets has been dramatic, and the ordering of the city streets has been a challenge for successive municipal administrations in San Salvador. According to the mayor's office, all of downtown San Salvador—an area of approximately sixty manzanas (mz), more extensive than any of the malls—is to some degree an open market: "The problem obviously grows in the last 25 manzanas of the historic center. The municipality estimates that in San Salvador alone there are between 17,000 and 27,000 informal vendors."[29]

This market can seem very disorderly, with limited sanitation and safety features. However, the vendors are organized. The removal or relocation of street vendors has posed a political challenge for every mayor of San Salvador in the past fifty years—from the first attempts at relocation by José Napoleón Duarte in 1964 to Héctor Silva in 2001 to Norman Quijano in 2012.[30] Through various policies, each mayor has attempted to regulate the space the vendors have claimed, but "they have returned like they have since the sixties, when they fought for the first time for that piece of public way which they defend like their property."[31]

On 25 November 2010, the mayor's office ordered the removal of 201 vendor posts from Calle Arce, a major street in the capital.[32] Two weeks later, in December 2010, nearly one hundred of these vendors collectively installed their merchandise on the sidewalks surrounding Metrocentro. The representative of their organization (Coordinadora Nacional de Vendedores, or CNV) informed the media, "Today we are inaugurating our shopping days in 'metrosuelo,' for the poor. Here we are not defying anybody, we are only trying to guarantee that our children will have their food assured for these days."[33] Installed on the streets and sidewalks—truly on the margins of the famous shopping mall—the vendors of metrosuelo place objects on public display in contrast to the private building. These "shopping days" did not last long and the vendors were removed from Metrocentro's vicinity, on this occasion without violent incidents.[34] While the shopping mall is presented as futuristic, orderly, secure, and in good taste, the market under the open sky is motivated—necessitated—by poverty. In addition, it contains products that may be "suspicious" and even illicit: bootleg DVDs, merchandise of indeterminate origin, or at the very least cheap imitations of well-known brands of jeans, sunglasses, perfumes, handbags, and sneakers.

The malls and their shops validate social status and a lifestyle legitimated by the loyal consumption of certain brands. Meanwhile, the space popularly referred to as metrosuelo in San Salvador is a site of *ropa pirateada* ("knockoff clothing") and ironic flows of the global imagination that represent subversions of trademarks and intellectual property rights. Brand recognition is brought to a new level in the capitalist informal sector: "Fake products are appropriated as tentative signs of social distinction" (Lin 2011, 55). The imitations bought and sold in these spaces of street vending are evidence of marginality within capitalism. Importantly, they also open a space of mimicry, and of making the trans/national influence and knowledge of brands and malls "strange," less naturalizable (Bhabha 1994, 87–89). Imitations, copies, and informality are forms of differential access and participation in the field of global and local consumption. Metrosuelo, of course, is a play on Metrocentro—and, while this appropriation of the recognizable name "mocks its power to be a model" (Bhabha 1994, 88) it also seeks proximity, recognition, opportunity, and (strategically) the possible clientele—the thousands who, as they leave the mall, might take a look at the less expensive products. Metrosuelo also refers to where the street vendors often display what they want to sell: *suelo*, the sidewalk, floor, or asphalt instead of the glass-enclosed shop windows and polished floors; it is a humble ground where we can gain a new perspective on objects. The public space of the street repeats or parodies the mall in its own creative way, while the mall re-creates an idealized version of the street.

Although in many ways alienated from each other, these spaces are involved in a dialogue about the processes and consequences of consumption in Salvadoran society. They communicate and link but also distinguish and differentiate. "If the members of a society did not share the meanings of commodities, if these were meaningful only for the elites or the minorities that use them, they would not serve the purposes of differentiation" (García Canclini 2001, 40). These objects and spaces are bridged in the sense that together they shape and legitimate certain meanings of wealth, aspirational access to goods, and security—or the lack thereof—in this imaginary. Without the marginal imitation or knockoff found in metrosuelo and similar sites, the expensive brand name presented at the mall is not considered as valuable. As this occurs, these spaces starkly represent political and economic gaps—the structuring and reproduction of inequalities between consumers in the "formal" and "informal" sectors of the economy.

The malls re-create the idealized city, reacting to (and even turning their back on) the city's reality, yet their importance as spaces of consumption is related to the existence of metrosuelo. The mall is a private "landscape of power" (Zukin 1991) and some sectors of society are constantly excluded from participation in it, due to limited purchasing power and other strong yet "invisible" barriers. Contemplating shopping malls such as Metrocentro, Multiplaza, and La Gran Vía as spaces where Salvadorans may escape violent imaginaries of the nation and consume transnational ones brings us to critically consider the contrasting portrayal of metrosuelo as an embattled, controversial space— for decades and for a few "shopping days for the poor" in San Salvador. Here, street vending becomes a site of critique, and raises significant questions of underemployment, poverty, and access to products within the constraints and necessities of capitalist logic. Newspaper portrayals of the malls as innovative and modern, together with the actual sensory experience of these spaces— Multiplaza's colorful walls, or the "ambiance" of La Gran Vía—project them as attractive and sophisticated worlds. In some of these portrayals, they appear as examples of an ideal version of modernization. An ideal past and future narrative of San Salvador can also be discerned in the existence of these monumental sites of consumption (be they considered as public, private, or deliberately ambiguous in character). It is important to ask how we think of innovative spaces of consumption if "the past haunts the present; but the latter denies it with good reason" (Buck-Morss 1989, 293). These histories made up of individual and collective memories are linked by commodities and the people who share, exchange, and find value in them.

Conclusion: Consuming Transnational Imaginaries

In her study of Salvadoran transnational practices, Patricia Landolt noted that during the early 1990s, as the civil war came to its final stages, there was a short-lived yet visible construction boom in San Miguel, located on the east of the country and near its most severely war-struck areas. Part of this boom involved the construction of a mall, Metrocentro San Miguel, and the establishment of department stores—a significant development that signaled the importance (and purchasing power) of this city. But Landolt, observing consumption and the possibility of uncertainty and failure, also noted at that time that "Metrocentro's store windows are empty" adding that consumption and dependence on remittances highlighted the precarious existence of the city's "totally fictitious economy, based solely on the circulation of money and credit" a situation that "forced a disregard for the simple postwar fact that San Miguel produces absolutely nothing" (Landolt 1997, n.p.).

Landolt's observations bring to life a changing social landscape punctuated by empty shop windows, the booms and bankruptcies of crops and construction, and purchased homes whose migrant owners live thousands of miles away. The production of "absolutely nothing" is, by necessity, aided by migrants' remittances, mainly from the United States. It is magnified by local conditions of poverty and the decline of the agricultural sector. The mall—at this time deserted, and in the context of the early postwar years—is a symbol of the unsuccessful attempts at creating a "productive" space of national socioeconomic development and consumption after war. However, there is more to this than a story of emptiness and uncertainty. Something *is* produced in San Miguel and anywhere in El Salvador's transnational space—powerful images, however abstract, of ideal Salvadoran consumers who are able to purchase, even beyond their means; an image of a transnational Salvadoran migrant and laborer whose earnings are to this day destined toward the consumption of food, her children's education, her mother's medicines, and much more, in his or her "home country." The remittances sent to San Miguel, San Salvador, and other parts of the country are not simply for the consumption of goods in the malls. They are destined for the basic survival and consumption needs of households split by war (and by postwar neoliberal realities) and economic inequality.[35]

The ties among consumption, images, and migration are significant in post–civil war El Salvador. Emigration is an accepted, well-known survival strategy—narratives of suffering and violence are crucial to the representation and production of uneven flows of people, commodities, and ideas in the national and transnational space. The material and emotional deprivation of emigrants portrayed in many of the stories of separated families and undocumented migrants in "Departamento 15" contrasts noticeably with the large sums of money they collectively remit and with the "excess" of malls in San Salvador. In turn, narratives of migrant success also "make sense" for this imaginary and the widely accepted idea that the available income from abroad has a significant effect on Salvadoran consumption patterns and Salvadoran macroeconomic stability.

Media institutions also play a role in this circuit of migration and consumption. A journalist of "Departamento 15" noted that initial interest in developing this migration section in *La Prensa Gráfica* stemmed directly from the observations that emigrants were not necessarily returning although the war had officially ended, and that as the 1990s passed, "people [in El Salvador] were dressing differently, eating differently" as a result of contact with their emigrant friends and relatives.[36] As "Departamento 15" claims the diaspora for the national, it is interesting to note that here the national is read as having been already shaped by transnational consumption, and this is a reason for having "Departamento 15." In the postwar Salvadoran imaginary, consumption and communication are closely linked to citizenship and ideas of Salvadoran modernity and presence in the global.

The shopping mall has become a significant site for consumers in contemporary Salvadoran society. As shopping malls have grown in number and size, the informal sector in San Salvador has also expanded, as has the country's dependence on remittances, migration, and other aspects of globalization. These conditions constitute each other in this transnational imaginary. Like migration, practices and sites of consumption have long histories rooted in prior contacts with spaces and countries where trends "originate," and in previous interactions with commodities, modernity, and cultural capital. Shopping in these spaces is not limited to the moment when a cashier scans product barcodes, or when money and purchases exchange hands. The commodity is central in the exchange and recirculation of materials in mass culture. In this "dream world" of objects, people who have access to shopping malls can gain relevant social status as consumers, and display this along with their economic power. Others, like San Salvador's street vendors in metrosuelo, are marginalized from formal, national economic life and the dominant construction of the global, sophisticated consumer. Their field of consumption is the informal sector, the sidewalks of the city, and a precarious experience that makes us rethink neoliberal regimes of value.

Metrosuelo contrasts with the private, enclosed space of the malls and their architectural façades as sanitized versions of the city's streets. To speak of adaptation and resourcefulness in metrosuelo is often to speak of marginality and necessity. This marginal space is not simply an inadequate reproduction of the modern, powerful model, Metrocentro (or any shopping mall). As an original space of the national imaginary, the city's historic center has experienced catastrophes, yet on many occasions has been "very pluckily rebuilt" (Martin 1911, 257) by its inhabitants, enduring into the twenty-first century. It continues to hold some power and possibility; its streets and sidewalks accept knockoffs, "illegitimate" products, traffic, protests, and controversies. Exclusion and consumption are elements of an imaginary portrayed in media narratives, advertisements, and the spatial and architectural features of shopping malls as "secure" spaces. The malls are part, and consequence, of a contradictory imaginary where Salvadorans participate and become transnational consumers (and part of larger political economies) through spaces where the everyday experience of consumption is often removed from explicit participation in citizenship and the complexity of the nation.

Conclusion

Renewing Narratives of Connection and Distance

I am at the Comalapa Airport in El Salvador. After checking in, I reach the area where travelers and their relatives assemble before the travelers say good-bye and proceed to airport security. The lobby is a farewell mini-mall for the already nostalgic traveler who, boarding pass in hand, prepares to leave El Salvador. A kiosk sells gum, cell phone accessories, and *La Prensa Gráfica* among other periodicals. Another sells traditional, artisanal Salvadoran candies, and another one sells coffee beans by the pound, and coffee liquor. The Pollo Campero restaurant is nearby, its tables occupied by people eating breakfast and ordering boxes of chicken to take on their flight. The smell of chicken will later waft through the airplane cabins.

The window of a crafts store—one of the bigger shops in the waiting area—displays colones, the former Salvadoran currency. Now the colones, colorful bills with pictures of Salvadoran monuments and historical figures, are for sale as souvenirs. Eight bills are pasted to a varnished wood board, in all the denominations that used to circulate: one, two, five, ten, twenty-five, fifty, one hundred, and two hundred colones. I add them. Based on the present currency conversion rate (one dollar equals eight colones and seventy-five cents), the bills would exchange for about forty-five dollars. But it is more difficult to calculate the actual value of this trophy of consumer nostalgia, a plaque to the triumph of global finance. Salvadoran money has become a commodity, a bizarre souvenir that can be purchased with a global currency. In a few decades, who will remember purchasing goods with these strange, varnished bills?

Moments later I pass the security check, an obligatory ritual in every airport. Once in the departure area I walk to the gate, passing the duty-free stores full of brand-name cosmetics, digital cameras, luggage, and other necessary luxuries for the cosmopolitan traveler. In the lounge, most people sit quietly, holding their passports and boarding passes, looking out through the glass panels at the airplanes on the runway or at the palm trees moving only slightly against what soon will be another hot morning on the Salvadoran littoral.

A few travelers softly ask each other, where are you going, what is your final destination? It seems to me that now the question is asked more cautiously—we are all flying to Houston, but who knows what the end of so many connecting flights might be.

A Narrative of Becoming Global

My intention in this final section is to further open the discussion of the primary argument that has been a thread throughout this book: that Salvadoran transnational imaginaries and narratives that seem to "make sense" are produced, circulated, consumed, and mediated in everyday life by the interaction and constant contestation between people and institutions. I have explored how media images of migration, transnational business practices, spaces of consumption, and literature constitute ways of "making sense" and inhabiting contemporary Salvadoran society, and how these sites represent instances of the production and commercialization of connection, location, and distance. I have argued that these sites coexist and form part of an imaginary of postwar El Salvador—where texts, voices, and other practices intersect and produce transnational subjects. The mall, the newspaper, and the call center bring together consumers, journalists, readers of newspapers, migrants, foreign investment promoters, bilingual call center employees and their customers, and other "ordinary" Salvadorans who inhabit the Salvadoran transnational imaginary.

Competing forms of citizenship and participation emerge and constitute each other on the pages of "Departamento 15," the interview rooms at the call centers, the "streets" of the shopping malls, and "La Lumbre," the bar portrayed in *El asco.* These are spaces of paradoxical freedom and interpellation; people participate in and occupy these spaces, but differentially and within certain discourses. Influential sectors, media and government institutions among them, can construct a narrative of El Salvador's place in globalizing processes, as a strategically located, even naturalized, location for flexible labor. Salvadorans already have "neutral" accents, perfect for the needs of foreign investors. Salvadorans already have a long history of migration; thus migrants can be conjured and marketed by investment promoters as evidence of the extent to which El Salvador is globalized, or claimed in media portrayals as exemplary citizens who care about their families and El Salvador's economy.

Changes in work culture encourage call center employees to become flexible in the global division of labor. While their voices are exported, for the most part workers remain relatively immobile within their workplace. The call center and investment promotion agencies shape expectations of linguistic ability and work ethic, even seeking potential workers who might want to return to El Salvador and meet their roots, and employing those who return involuntarily as well. This workplace trains and produces the ideal, bilingual employee of its own institutional imaginary of global capital and immediately available services—a friendly agent with perfect listening comprehension skills. As El Salvador becomes a brand that "works," it enters the terrain of global capital and the dogma of labor flexibility. The high quit rates of "frustrated" call center employees, who apparently can only fault themselves for not learning to adequately balance their lives, manage their own stress, and solve the problems of their callers, or for not having the right attitude in their work, are part of a discourse of individualism associated with neoliberalism.

Malls are spaces characterized as public, while they are also private and exclusive. They bring together and nurture the consuming communities that have already been invited to this part of the Salvadoran imaginary through a mix of economic decisions, interactions, and discriminations of class and taste that make up a "map of social space" (Taylor 2002, 107). Many are excluded for being poor or for looking suspicious. Other consuming communities come together in the informal sector, selling and buying ironic flows of "fake" brands and objects. The consumer is produced in connection to Metrocentro and metrosuelo, spaces that in the imaginary are projected, respectively, as futuristic and modern, or as controversial and dangerous. In the imaginary of citizenship and consumption, the individual consumer is sometimes imagined as a rational subject presented with a broad range of "choices" in the formal and informal sectors, an informed citizen who can be trusted to make the choices that are best for the market. She will somehow learn to avoid the "bad products" and the knockoffs.

The guard at the shopping mall (like the security staff at the airport) is part of a new normalized tale of heightened global terror and privatized security. It is okay to gaze at the mall in awe, to take family photographs in this "theme park," to escape the awful reality of the streets, and, of course, to spend whatever dollars are possible in the department stores and boutiques. The guard, however, stops visitors who photograph the mall in ways that seem out of place, visitors who engage this site in ways that do not conform to ideas of what is "safe." And what is safety? The mall visitors must learn to self-regulate and consume in the acceptable, established ways of global shopping culture.

The mediated narratives of people who have left the geographic space of the nation are also part of the Salvadoran imaginary. In "Departamento 15," Salvadorans abroad are portrayed as part of a "natural extension" of El Salvador's territory. The news articles written in El Salvador are aimed at Salvadoran migrants and readers around the world—preferably the patriotic and nostalgic ones who become ideal, responsive publics in these circuits of media and culture—making the newspaper one of the institutions that bring a "borderless" transnational imaginary into being. Salvadorans, addressed as a "social totality" (Warner 2002), are presented with stories of belonging, but also of wounded migrants, separated families, and unaccompanied children.

These stories are reminders of the real and violent consequences of poverty and forced emigration. In stories of repatriation, the power of the nation-state to reach across borders and reclaim the emigrants of its choosing is demonstrated. The violence of migration ceases to be extraordinary in the postwar period. Violence against migrants is absorbed as part of the discussion of who is "free" to occupy the space of the nation, and of who is worthy of being reclaimed. Some returnees are categorized as "undesirable," as people who cannot be fully trusted to be good citizens (or call center agents, or consumers). Narratives of suffering make the subject newsworthy in print and online; they also make the subject worthy of citizenship and belonging in the imaginary.

Tales of unwilling return to postwar Salvadoran society, such as Castellanos Moya's novel about Vega's return to El Salvador, compel us to examine contemporary cultural and literary sensibilities. What emerges is a narrative of disenchantment, of cynicism in the face of failed political and national projects. But even amid this feeling of disgust, Vega manages to express a potentially productive critique of contemporary San Salvador. What it reveals is a mutually constitutive narrative of disenchantment and reenchantment, one that must move beyond projects of revolution and El Salvador's current neoliberal reality.

A Narrative of Reenchantment

In this book I have asked questions about how the Salvadoran imaginary in the postwar period is enabled and co-constituted with practices of migration, consumption, work, and citizenship. El Salvador now has many years of postwar, longer than the armed conflict itself (1979–1992), and the Salvadoran imaginary is created and sustained by realities and common understandings of emigration as a survival strategy, of violence as an everyday occurrence, and of economic and political inequality. As this situation "makes sense," it has actual consequences for Salvadorans. And this is how the sites I have presented are especially important. They are part of the common understandings of who has the power and privilege to represent, exclude, and project itself to the global, and of who has the power to shape the national discourse on these issues, while others remain marginal and vulnerable.

We may feel disoriented. As many ask at the airport, *where are we going?* This question suggests meaningful spatial and temporal locations. The research sites relocate El Salvador in different ways, within economic, social, and cultural dimensions of globalization. As manifestations of unevenly experienced global-izing processes, these sites reproduce notions of whose narratives are dominant in the Salvadoran transnational imaginary.

If we could see beyond the predetermined discussion of how El Salvador becomes global, what might emerge is an equally limitless, but more *inclusive*, imaginary. The spaces I have explored in this project would give way to "new forms of social existence," to practices of social solidarity, and our surround-ings would become "fully reenchanted" (Buck-Morss 1989, 261 and 254). The sites I have researched are spaces of the imagination, but also have actual con-sequences as spaces of mobility, connectivity, and constraint. Their potential as linkages to a critical perspective on globalization lies in an expansion of the notion of what is legitimated in a narrative of becoming global, and in the pos-sibility of a reenchantment of the world.

NOTES

CHAPTER 1 TRACING THE BORDERLESS IN "DEPARTAMENTO 15"

1. The website for APES is: http://www.apes.org.sv/sitioapes/. Gabriel García Márquez, "El mejor oficio del mundo" (address to the 52nd General Assembly of the Inter American Press Association, Los Angeles, CA, 7 October 1996), is at http://www.fnpi.org/fileadmin/documentos/imagenes/Maestros/Textos_de_los_maestros/elmejor.pdf (accessed August 2010). The Inter American Press Association (IAPA, the English acronym for Sociedad Interamericana de Prensa, SIP) "is a nonprofit organization devoted to defending freedom of speech and freedom of the press in the Americas," as stated on the SIP/IAPA website, http://www.sipiapa.org/ (accessed August 2010 and 17 April 2013).

2. Gabriel García Márquez (in the October 1996 address cited earlier) made this comment about tape recorders and the use of voice-recording devices in journalism: "Antes de que ésta se inventara, el oficio se hacía bien con tres recursos de trabajo que en realidad eran uno sólo: la libreta de notas, una ética a toda prueba, y un par de oídos que los reporteros usábamos todavía para oír lo que nos decían. El manejo profesional y ético de la grabadora está por inventar." ("Before this was invented, the trade was carried out well with three work resources that were actually one: the notepad, solid ethics, and a pair of ears that the reporters still used to listen to what we were being told. The professional and ethical use of the tape recorder is yet to be invented.")

3. "Informes y Resoluciones: El Salvador," 65th General Assembly of the IAPA, 6–10 November 2009, Buenos Aires, Argentina, at http://www.sipiapa.com/v4/det_informe.php?asamblea=24&infoid=375&idioma=sp (accessed 17 April 2013).

4. The *Salvador* reporters share their name with the film directed by Oliver Stone (1986), and with Joan Didion's book *Salvador* (1983), both depictions of journalism and war.

5. Leticia Carías, "El nuevo rostro de *La Prensa Gráfica*," *La Prensa Gráfica*, 8 September 2006, 49. In contrast to the "cosmetic" shifts of the 1990s and early 2000s as described by Rockwell and Janus (2003), the changes in print and online design are offered as deeper, significant developments in *La Prensa Gráfica*'s history and philosophy, as presented in Leticia Carías, "El nuevo rostro de *La Prensa Gráfica*," *La Prensa Gráfica*, 8 September 2006, 48–49, and Reina María Aguilar, "*La Prensa Gráfica* revela su nuevo rostro," *La Prensa Gráfica*, 7 September 2006, 78–79.

6. "*La Prensa* mejora sus servicios," *La Prensa*, 8 October 1928. Reprinted in Dutriz 2002, 77.

7. "*La Prensa* se traslada a nuevo edificio," *La Prensa*, 19 August 1929. Reprinted in Dutriz 2002, 81–82.

8. Interview with "Departamento 15" journalists, 19 August 2005.

9. Interview with "Departamento 15" journalists, 19 August 2005.

10. Interview with "Departamento 15" journalists, 19 August 2005.

11. Advertisement for "Departamento 15," *La Prensa Gráfica*, 31 March 2000, 17.

12. Advertisement for "Departamento 15," *La Prensa Gráfica*, 31 March 2000, 17.

13. "Por el contacto cultural que han tenido en otros países, son fuente de inspiración y de experiencia científica, tecnológica, empresarial y cultural. Son mucho más que su valor en remesas, referencia casi única durante muchos años. Aquí queremos difundir las condiciones de vida de los salvadoreños en el exterior porque es importante sensibilizar y generar más opinión pública sobre el peso económico, social y cultural que tienen en la vida nacional" ("Buscando nuevos horizontes," *La Prensa Gráfica*, 3 April 2000, 50).

14. Ibid.

15. Ibid.

16. Ibid.

17. "La recompensa de ser pioneros," *La Prensa Gráfica*, 6 April 2000, 58.

18. "[Y]a es hora de reconocer el invaluable aporte que los salvadoreños hemos proveído a El Salvador a través de muchos años, y este sentimiento es compartido por muchos de mis compatriotas en el exterior. Ya estamos hartos de que sólo nos vean como fuente de divisas, pues sólo la salida de nuestro país fue suficientemente traumática para nosotros, ya no se diga haber dejado a nuestras familias, amigos, y recuerdos atrás, para llegar a lugares tan extraños. Gracias por esta sección" (ibid.).

19. Macarena Gómez-Barris writes about how the memories of Chilean exiles are (inevitably) framed by the 1973 military coup, trauma, and an uneasy sense of rupture. Even after the death of Augusto Pinochet, this unease persists in the search for redress: "transitional states of democracy, as in exclusionary nation-states, reinstate and often amplify historical inequalities rather than provide forms of social justice" (2009, 154).

20. "Buscando nuevos horizontes," *La Prensa Gráfica*, 3 April 2000, 50.

21. On a personal note regarding this research, and specifically this section of the chapter, I write this story of media and circulation with the memory of coming to California to begin my graduate studies during the same week in September 2002 that the newspaper announced this project of international outreach. The possibility of researching and tracing the circulation of a Salvadoran newspaper in the United States was one starting point for this project.

22. I find it interesting that the list of major cities for this circulation project did not at this point include Miami, a world city that for a long time has been a gateway and point of connection for Latin American business and banking (Brown, Catalano, and Taylor 2002) and a vacation and residence spot for many wealthy Salvadorans. Miami's absence at this time seems indicative of the newspaper's perception of where a good part of its migrant public/market/population is primarily (and strategically) located.

23. "[D]esde este lunes, nuestro periódico podrá llegar cotidianamente a las manos de los salvadoreños en las ciudades mencionadas, y con esa posibilidad nuestros compatriotas podrán sentirse más cerca de las realidades patrias, prácticamente como si estuvieran aquí. Este es un hecho que trasciende las políticas de mercado y los esfuerzos de logística: es la concreción de un acercamiento con el que venimos soñando desde hace ya tiempo, en la medida que las realidades y la interacción entre los salvadoreños de aquí y los salvadoreños de allá se han ido haciendo más fuertes y orgánicas" ("Una expansión histórica," Editorial, *La Prensa Gráfica*, 10 September 2002, 15).

24. Ibid.

25. In Althusserian terms, Salvadoran migrants become ideological subjects *and* consumers of this product: they are "interpellated . . . and often respond by seeing themselves as members of a national audience" (Sturken and Cartwright 2001, 177).

26. "Las necesidades de información crecen y cambian de manera acelerada, y el imperativo fundamental estriba en servir cada vez mejor y más oportuna y ampliamente a los ciudadanos, estén donde estuvieren" ("Una expansión histórica," Editorial, *La Prensa Gráfica*, 10 September 2002, 15).

27. Ibid.

28. "Poder tener a diario todo ese material informativo hará que los vínculos entre los connacionales y sus comunidades se mantengan más frescos y vigorosos. Nuestro país es, porcentualmente, el que mayor población tiene en Estados Unidos. Ese enorme contingente de salvadoreños que viven y trabajan en la sociedad más desarrollada de la tierra constituye una fuerza de extraordinario poder cultural y económico, que está incidiendo de manera decisiva en el destino patrio y en la configuración de la identidad moderna de nuestro conglomerado nacional" (ibid.).

29. Ibid.

30. "En el mundo hay ahora retos formidables para los países pequeños. La globalización provoca la creciente internacionalización de los procesos nacionales. . . . El Salvador tiene recursos para conectarse mejor al mundo. Al mismo tiempo, tiene condiciones para entrar a otra etapa de su historia. Durante el siglo XX nunca hubo tantos aspectos favorables para iniciar la erradicación de la pobreza y salir del atraso. Hay una experiencia humana sin par, la acumulada por los cientos de miles de mujeres y hombres radicados en el exterior que todavía mantienen vínculos con sus comunidades de origen" (Campos et al. 1999, 3).

31. In this article, Dutriz also explains that the newspaper acquired a license from the U.S. Department of Consumer and Regulatory Affairs Business Regulation Administration to distribute the newspaper in the United States, a process that required the formation of a new entity, "La Prensa Gráfica Incorporated." To expand the nation and its representations, the newspaper expands its corporate reach ("La objetividad no tiene fronteras," *La Prensa Gráfica*, 10 September 2002, 3). Other articles in *La Prensa Gráfica* that reported on this circulation project include "Desde El Salvador hasta los Estados Unidos," 10 September 2002, 2; and "Ediciones especiales: *La Prensa Gráfica* en E.U.A.," 11 September 2002, 10–11.

32. Carlos Dada, "*La Prensa Gráfica* llega a Nueva York," *La Prensa Gráfica*, 17 September 2002, 14.

33. "Felicito al grupo Dutriz por tan buen proyecto, me siento orgulloso de ser tan salvadoreño como *La Prensa Gráfica* y llevaré el nombre de mi país en alto, así como *La Prensa Gráfica* lo hace hoy" ("¡Felices con noticias de verdad!" *La Prensa Gráfica*, 13 September 2002, 11).

34. Ibid.

35. Ibid.

36. Interview with newspaper employee, 4 September 2006.

37. Interview with journalist, 22 December 2005.

38. Interview with journalist, 22 December 2005.

39. A similar turn to research has been documented by Arlene Dávila in relation to the emergence and consolidation of Hispanic/Latino marketing in the United States: "Defining Hispanics for marketing purposes thus depends today, as it always has, on

whatever audience is being targeted and which product is being sold: the definition arises from the right combination of research, generalizations, and clichés" (2001, 66).

40. Interview with journalist, 22 December 2005.

41. "Mensajes de nuestros lectores: Encuentre a sus seres queridos a través de Departamento 15," *La Prensa Gráfica*, 4 September 2003, 36; and "Mensajes de nuestros lectores: Encuentre a sus seres queridos a través del Departamento 15," *La Prensa Gráfica*, 2 October 2003, 42. Sometimes the title or subtitle varies, for example: "Mensajes de nuestros lectores: las familias y los amigos salvadoreños se reencuentran," *La Prensa Gráfica*, 6 November 2003, 40 ("Salvadoran families and friends meet again").

42. Interview with "Departamento 15" journalists, 19 August 2005.

43. Interview with journalist, 22 December 2005.

44. "Gracias por este gran paso," *La Prensa Gráfica*, 11 September 2002, 14.

45. "La recompensa de ser pioneros," *La Prensa Gráfica*, 6 April 2000, 58.

CHAPTER 2   THE DESPERATE IMAGES

1. Advertisement in *La Prensa Gráfica*, 19 June 2003, 22–23.

2. Paula Díaz, "Sacrificio y lágrimas de una madre emigrante: Salvadoreña pasará Día de la Madre sin sus hijos," *La Prensa Gráfica*, 10 May 2003, 38.

3. "Madre pagó $12 mil por reunirse con hijos: Salvadoreña cuenta su historia," *La Prensa Gráfica*, 13 December 2003, 46.

4. Ibid.

5. Ibid.

6. Ibid.

7. Ana Milena Varón, "Niño se reúne con su madre: Viajó indocumentado hasta la ciudad de Los Ángeles," *La Prensa Gráfica*, 8 December 2004, 53.

8. Ibid.

9. Ana Milena Varón, "Joven sobrevive peligros de viaje indocumentado: Se reunió con su madre en Los Ángeles," *La Prensa Gráfica*, 11 December 2004, 62.

10. Ibid.

11. Ibid.

12. Ibid.

13. Ibid.

14. "Joven madre narra su odisea para llegar a EUA: Viajó sin documentos más de un mes," *La Prensa Gráfica*, 16 December 2004, 78.

15. Gonzalo Egremy, "20 salvadoreños fallecidos en 2003: Murieron en tragedias ocurridas en el sureste de México," *La Prensa Gráfica*, 31 December 2003, 38.

16. Ibid.

17. Ibid.

18. Ibid.

19. At least 24,696 Salvadorans were repatriated/deported during 2003, according to figures provided by Mexican migration officials. From January to October 2003, a reported 151,697 Central American migrants were deported from Mexico (Adriana Valle and Gonzalo Egremy, "24 mil salvadoreños deportados en 2003: México reporta más heridos y accidentados," *La Prensa Gráfica*, 2 December 2003, 38). A Mexican migration official informed that during 2003, in addition to the nearly twenty-five thousand Salvadorans, detainees included sixty thousand Guatemalans, forty thousand Hondurans, three thousand Nicaraguans, and twelve thousand migrants of various other origins, including South America and Asia (Gonzalo Egremy, "México

deportó 25 mil salvadoreños en 2003: Número incrementó 25 por ciento en relación al año anterior," *La Prensa Gráfica*, 3 January 2004, 28). In total, during 2003 thirty-one thousand Salvadorans were deported, according to Salvadoran authorities. Most migrants returned to El Salvador after being detained during their transit through Mexico (as already stated); in addition 4,700 Salvadorans were deported from the United States (Amílcar Mejía, "31 mil salvadoreños fueron deportados: La mayoría procedía de México y los Estados Unidos," *La Prensa Gráfica*, 24 December 2003, 34).

20. It is important to note that the terms "repatriation" and "deportation" are sometimes used interchangeably in these news stories (and beyond) to refer to returns. As Cruz Monroy and Barrios Juárez Badillo explain in *Sur inicio de un camino*, the commonly used term "deportation" (meaning, "expelling a foreign person in an irregular situation from [Mexican] territory") has "acquired different official denominations" in recent years (2009, 140). Assessing these events depends on statistical data of reported cases made available by the INM (Instituto Nacional de Migración), and considering Mexican migration laws that allow migrants in transit to remain in Mexican territory for up to thirty days (Cruz Monroy and Barrios Juárez Badillo 2009, 138). In 2006, Mexico and Central American countries signed an agreement with the goal of making repatriations more orderly, safe, and secure, and since 2007 two categories—expulsions and voluntary repatriations—are used to refer to *devoluciones* ("returns"): "Expulsions, refer to returns of migrant persons to their country of origin with a previous administrative process of detention. Events of voluntary repatriation [refer to] return of migrant persons in which there is not necessarily a previous detention, although in many cases there is. Returns are, then, the sum of both events" (Cruz Monroy and Barrios Juárez Badillo 2009, 140).

21. Gonzalo Egremy, "Once pandilleros en la mira por asalto," *La Prensa Gráfica*, 31 December 2003, 38.

22. Gonzalo Egremy, "Salvadoreño herido de bala por mareros: Se recupera en hospital de Tapachula, Chiapas," *La Prensa Gráfica*, 17 November 2003, 54.

23. Gonzalo Egremy, "Salvadoreño herido expulsado de hospital: Fue asaltado por pandilleros en el tren," *La Prensa Gráfica*, 20 November 2003, 46.

24. Gonzalo Egremy, "Asaltan a cónsul y migrante," *La Prensa Gráfica*, 2 December 2003, 38.

25. "Siete mareros mueren a manos de rivales," *La Prensa Gráfica*, 15 September 2003, front page headline.

26. "Deseaba alistarse en el Ejército," *La Prensa Gráfica*, 15 March 2003, 17.

27. Ibid.

28. This was part of the reporting for the "En el camino" section of *El Faro*, first published online and later as a book (see Martínez 2010).

29. Gonzalo Egremy, "Compatriotas mueren en asalto," *La Prensa Gráfica*, 10 December 2003, 63.

30. Gonzalo Egremy, "Piden repatriación de dos fallecidas: Tres salvadoreños heridos en asalto en Chiapas, México," *La Prensa Gráfica*, 11 December 2003, 42.

31. Ibid.

32. "Detienen a 10 pandilleros," *La Prensa Gráfica*, 11 December 2003, 42.

33. Saúl Barrera, "Cadáveres de mujeres asesinadas en Chiapas serán repatriados: Ambas fueron muertas a balazos el martes pasado," *La Prensa Gráfica*, 12 December 2003, 106.

34. "Repatrían a dos heridos," *La Prensa Gráfica*, 18 December 2003, 48.

35. Saúl Barrera, "'Me daban machetazos . . .': Sobreviviente de tragedia relata la pesadilla que vivió," *La Prensa Gráfica*, 20 December 2003, 66.

36. Ibid.

37. Internet Forum on Violence and Emigration, www.laprensagrafica.com, 3 May 2005 (accessed 7 May 2005).

38. Interview with journalist, 22 December 2005.

39. Interview with journalist, 22 December 2005.

40. Internet Forum on Violence and Emigration, www.laprensagrafica.com, 3 May 2005 (accessed 7 May 2005).

41. Ibid.

42. Ibid.

43. Ibid.

44. Ibid.

CHAPTER 3   VEGA'S DISGUST

1. "Entrevista, Horacio Castellanos Moya: 'La violencia . . . es parte de la salvadoreñidad,'" by Rafael Menjívar Ochoa, *Vértice,* 16 June 2002, http://www.elsalvador.com/vertice/2002/06/16/entrevista.html (accessed 14 March 2012).

2. In his novel *Tyrant Memory,* Castellanos Moya further reflects on this question, and includes this note: "Let me be clear: in this book, history has been placed at the service of the novel, that is, I have taken liberties with it according to the needs of the fictional narrative. Do not, then, look for 'historical truth'" (Castellanos Moya 2011, 269).

3. Sheila Glaser, "The Salvadoran Exile Novelist," review of *Tyrant Memory,* by Horacio Castellanos Moya (translated by Katherine Silver), *New York Times,* 8 July 2011, *Sunday Book Review,* http://www.nytimes.com/2011/07/10/books/review/book-review-tyrant-memory-by-horacio-castellanos-moya.html?pagewanted=all&_r=0 (accessed 18 January 2012 and 10 April 2013).

4. Ibid. Also see Menjívar Ochoa, "Entrevista, Horacio Castellanos Moya."

5. Juan José Dalton, "El asco, la diabla y el arma," Opinión, *La Prensa Gráfica,* 17 June 2001, http://archive.laprensa.com.sv/20010617/opinion/opi4.asp (accessed 21 March 2012).

6. Glaser, "Salvadoran Exile Novelist." About the writing of this novel, Castellanos Moya has said: "I did not plan *El asco* very much. I wrote it in one month, and when I was on the second sheet I did not know where I was heading. It was a very compulsive text, not very planned. I think that is explicable. And it did not emerge from my personal case, but from a group, and many of that group do not live here anymore either" (Menjívar Ochoa, "Entrevista, Horacio Castellanos Moya"). The final page of *El asco* reads "San Pedro de los Pinos, Ciudad de México, 31-diciembre-1995/5-febrero-1996," an author's convention, and a hint of his location and time of writing (Castellanos Moya 1997, 119).

7. Elana Zilberg refers to a similar bar/live music club, "La Luna"—a place that exists in San Salvador and represents a form of "escape" from the stuffiness and noise of the city. In her ethnography of deported gang youth, Zilberg offers this description: "I'm astounded at the cultural fusion here. La Luna is a cultural café reminiscent of any number of places in, say, Coyoacán, Mexico, or Silver Lake in Los Angeles. For me, as a U.S.-based anthropologist, it is one of those places I would retreat to when I needed to escape the assault of being a foreign woman in a conservative society. So I'm curious that Weasel, self-described 'gangster' from Echo Park, seeks refuge there too. But there is a spatial logic at work here, which brings both Weasel and me into the same space—globalization" (Zilberg 2004, 768).

8. *El arma en el hombre* intersects with *El asco*—during his two weeks in El Salvador, Vega complains that his sister-in-law cannot stop talking about a crime in which a wealthy woman was assassinated in cold blood in front of her children. In *El asco,* the media covers this assassination incessantly, speculating on who might have committed it and why (Castellanos Moya 1997, 106–108). In *El arma en el hombre,* we learn that Robocop was the shooter, and we read about this from his point of view (Castellanos Moya 2001, 55). Yajaira Padilla (2008) discusses this same crime as portrayed in a third Castellanos Moya novel, *La diabla en el espejo,* an account of the crime and its circumstances narrated from the point of view of the victim's close friend.

9. Horacio Castellanos Moya was born in 1957—he was thirty-eight years old at the time *El asco* was reportedly written, in 1995–1996.

CHAPTER 4   EXPORTING VOICES: ASPIRATIONS
AND FLUENCY IN THE CALL CENTER

1. "El Salvador in Motion: From Call Center to BPO—What is the Salvadorian outsourcing industry doing to diversify in a competed Market?" Frost & Sullivan, 20 May 2010, available online at http://www.frost.com/sublib/display-market-insight-top.do?id=202261041 (accessed 16 August 2010 and 28 February 2013).

2. Vikas Bajaj, "A New Capital of Call Centers," *New York Times*, 26 November 2011, Business Day, B1 and B4.

3. Ibid., B4.

4. Ibid., B1.

5. Amanda Rodas, "Call center crean 1750 plazas a pesar de pobre oferta bilingüe," *El Diario de Hoy*, 3 November 2012, http://www.elsalvador.com/mwedh/nota/nota_completa.asp?idCat=47654&idArt=7399253 (accessed 18 April 2013).

6. As in other parts of this book, interviews with call center employees were conducted in confidentiality, and I refer to them in forms that are appropriate to this context.

7. The full text of this legislation (in its Spanish original) was at www.proesa.com.sv/downloads/ley_zonas_francas.pdf (accessed April 2012). The text of decree 405 is also available via the website of the Ministerio de Economía (Ministry of the Economy) at http://servicios.minec.gob.sv/leyes/zonafranca_es.htm (accessed 6 February 2013).

8. During 2003, PROESA facilitated the establishment of twenty-three foreign companies in various sectors, including textiles/clothing, electronics, tourism, and call centers. From 2000 (when PROESA was created) to 2003, 106 companies had invested in El Salvador, creating thirty thousand jobs. The clothing sector was predominant during these years, with 22,835 jobs created. At that time, 1,500 jobs were in call centers. (Luis Andrés Marroquín, "El año viejo deja 23 nuevas empresas: PROESA logra inversión con la marca El Salvador Works," *La Prensa Gráfica*, 23 December 2003, 72.)

9. "'Call centers' en busca de voces salvadoreñas: dos nuevos centros en el 2004," *La Prensa Gráfica*, 4 December 2003, 41.

10. Ibid.

11. Ibid.

12. Ibid.

13. Interview with Rodolfo, 6 September 2005.

14. During 2005 and 2006, approximately 475 kilometers of fiber-optic network were installed in El Salvador, to link it to other countries of the region. (Alexander Torres, "Navega.com invertirá $20 mill [million] en red fibra óptica," *La Prensa Gráfica*, 5 May 2006, 64–65.)

15. PROESA was initially created in that year, 2000. However, by executive decree, on 17 May 2011, the agency was created as Agencia de Promoción de Exportaciones e Inversiones de El Salvador, with the following objects: "promotion of exports of goods and services produced in El Salvador," "promotion and attraction of foreign investment," and "promotion and strategic direction of the collaborative frameworks of investment between the public sector and the private sector." ("Decreto No. 59 Creación de la Agencia de Promoción de Exportaciones e Inversiones de El Salvador," *Diario Oficial* (San Salvador, El Salvador) 391, no. 90, 17 May 2011, 8–11.)

16. The PROESA web pages I refer to in this chapter include the following, initially consulted in 2006 and 2007: "PROESA: Contact Centers," http://www.proesa.com.sv/industry/contact_centers.htm (accessed 29 October 2006); "PROESA: El Salvador Works: A Brand That Travels Around the World," http://www.proesa.com.sv/about/brand.htm (accessed 3 April 2007); "PROESA: Strategic Locations," http://www.proesa.com.sv/why/strategic_location.htm (accessed 30 October 2006); and "PROESA: Telecommunications," http://www.proesa.com.sv/infrastructure/telecommunications.htm (accessed 31 October 2006). The website for this agency has changed in format and modified content over the years and under different administrations, but consistently has sections that provide information similar to that on the sites I initially consulted, detailing El Salvador's investment climate, past and current foreign investors, and other economic indicators. Currently PROESA's web pages include http://inversiones.proesa.gob.sv/ (accessed 6 February 2013) and http://www.proesa.gob.sv/ (accessed 18 June 2013).

17. "PROESA: Who We Are," http://www.proesa.com.sv (accessed 3 April 2007).

18. "PROESA: El Salvador Works: A Brand That Travels Around the World," http://www.proesa.com.sv/about/brand.htm (accessed 3 April 2007).

19. "PROESA: Strategic Locations," http://www.proesa.com.sv/why/strategic_location.htm (accessed 30 October 2006).

20. Employment advertisement, *La Prensa Gráfica*, 11 September 2006, Oferta Empleos, 11.

21. Employment advertisement, *La Prensa Gráfica*, 8 May 2006, Oferta Empleos, 13.

22. I point this out because in many employment announcements in El Salvador it is common to see a stated age range and gender as part of the requisites, for example: "multinational company seeks a plant manager, male, age between thirty and fifty years old, results oriented, strong leadership" (employment advertisement, *La Prensa Gráfica*, 24 July 2006, Oferta Empleos, n.p.). For someone to be in charge of a sales floor for a well-known Salvadoran company, the ad states: "sexo femenino, excelente presentación, totalmente extrovertida, amable y enérgica, buenos conocimientos de manejo de personal, edad entre los veinticinco y cuarenta y cinco años." In this case, this company is seeking someone who is female, with "excellent presentation" (this phrase may have many meanings, ranging from appearance and comportment to choice of clothing and accessories); the candidate should also be "totally extroverted," and with "good knowledge of personnel management," and—finally—she should be "between twenty-five and forty-five years old" (employment advertisement, *La Prensa Gráfica*, 28 August 2006, Oferta Empleos, 7).

23. Christian Zappone, "U.S. workers need work? Go to El Salvador," http://money.cnn.com/2006/07/27/news/international/salvador/index.htm, 27 July 2006 (accessed 27 February 2009 and 16 September 2010).

24. Interview with Gabriela, 23 August 2005.

25. Interview with Gabriela, 23 August 2005.

26. Along with these processes that were taking place at the call centers, various Salvadoran institutions recognized the importance of and demand for English speakers in this job and investment landscape. The National English Center (NEC) was formed during this time, to address the demands for qualified candidates for call center employment. The NEC emerged from the collaboration between the Salvadoran Ministry of Education, PROESA, and other organizations. In 2006, the NEC was administered by ITCA (an educational/technological institute) and FEPADE (an educational development foundation). The NEC offered "specialized English courses for the call centers field" (advertisement for NEC, *La Prensa Gráfica*, 8 May 2006, Oferta Empleos, 13). The first group of NEC graduates completed their ten-week course in July and August 2006 (Reina María Aguilar, "Primera promoción del Centro Nacional de Inglés," *La Prensa Gráfica*, 3 August 2006, 54; and Clara Villatoro, "Nuevos jóvenes bilingües para 'call centers,'" *La Prensa Gráfica*, 22 July 2006, 24).

27. Interview with Sara, 15 August 2006.

28. Interview with Sara, 15 August 2006.

29. Interview with Sara, 15 August 2006.

30. Interview with Sara, 15 August 2006.

31. Interview with Gabriela, 23 August 2005.

32. Similar cases of deportees working in call centers have been reported in Mexico City and Monterrey—in Mexico they are sometimes called *the homies of the call center*. Their migration, return, difficult reintegration into Mexican society, and work in English-language call centers has received some media attention, for example: Julio I. Godínez Hernández, "En 3 meses, 2 mil 364 deportados: Los 'homies' del 'call center,'" *Milenio* (Mexico), 20 January 2013, http://www.milenio.com/cdb/doc/noticias2011/c18dc9bda9c61ce5104ab704e9b1aafe (accessed 22 January 2013 and 18 August 2013), and Jason Buch, "Pew report: More people now moving from U.S. to Mexico," *Houston Chronicle*, 6 October 2012, http://www.chron.com/default/article/Pew-report-More-people-now-moving-from-U-S-to-3925393.php (accessed 27 March 2013 and 17 August 2013).

33. PROESA, "Meet Your Roots Is Launched in Dallas," press release, 18 March 2006, http://www.proesa.com.sv/news/2006/press270306_1.htm (accessed 2 April 2007).

34. Ibid.

35. Interview with Gabriela, 23 August 2005.

36. Interview with call center manager, 23 August 2005.

37. Interview with call center manager, 23 August 2005.

38. The training manual and employee handbook quoted here are produced and used by "Echoes," a company that provides customer service to a wide range of corporations based in the United States, especially in the areas of information technology and computer software support. I have changed the name of the company to preserve confidentiality and the anonymity of those who shared these instructional materials with me.

39. Interview with Raquel, 5 September 2005.

40. Interview with Raquel, 5 September 2005.

41. Interview with Raquel, 5 September 2005.

42. Interview with Rodolfo, 6 September 2005.

43. "PROESA: Contact Centers," http://www.proesa.com.sv/industry/contact_centers.htm (accessed 29 October 2006).

44. Interview with Laura and Elizabeth, 16 August 2005.

45. Interview with Laura and Elizabeth, 16 August 2005.

46. Interview with Laura and Elizabeth, 16 August 2005.
47. Interview with Laura and Elizabeth, 16 August 2005.
48. Interview with Laura and Elizabeth, 16 August 2005.

CHAPTER 5 "HEART OF THE CITY": LIFE AND SPACES
OF CONSUMPTION IN SAN SALVADOR

1. Scholars of consumption have focused on many aspects of this practice, including the nature and significance of the gift, reciprocity, and responsibility (a foundational example of this anthropological understanding of exchange is Mauss 1950), and on the meaning and value of certain objects and rituals (for example, Appadurai 1986; Baudrillard 1981; Otnes and Lowrey 2004), in addition to how consumption and material culture relate to larger socioeconomic processes.

2. I use the actual names of the malls in this book. I find that these names hold special significance as part of the Salvadoran landscape. The malls would be easily identifiable to anyone familiar with San Salvador. Moodie (2010) and Kent (2010) use actual names in their research as well.

3. Data from a 2010 household survey indicated that nationally, 36.5 percent of Salvadoran households were in conditions of poverty; in urban areas the figure was 33 percent, and in rural areas 43.2 percent of households lived in conditions of poverty. Source: Ministerio de Economía, Gerencia de Comunicaciones y Relaciones Públicas, "DIGESTYC da a conocer resultados de Encuesta de Hogares de Propósitos Múltiples (EHPM) 2010," news release, 19 August 2011, http://www.minec.gob.sv/index .php?option=com_content&view=article&catid=1:noticias-ciudadano&id=1567 :encuesta&Itemid=77 (accessed 12 April 2013).

4. Interview with architect, 5 September 2006.

5. Interview with architect, 5 September 2006.

6. "Hoy inauguran primera etapa Centro Comercial Metrocentro," *La Prensa Gráfica*, 25 October 1971, 3, 32.

7. Ibid., 32.

8. Advertisement for Metrocentro, *La Prensa Gráfica*, 25 October 1971, 55.

9. "Metrocentro tiene proyección futurista dice el Sr. Poma," *La Prensa Gráfica*, 26 October 1971, 3, 22.

10. Ibid., 3.

11. Gabriela Melara, con reportes de German Rivas, "Subregión AMSS alberga 32% de la población salvadoreña," *La Prensa Gráfica*, 31 October 2012, http://www.laprensagrafica .com/Subregion-AMSS-alberga-32-de-la-poblacion-salvadorena (accessed 12 April 2013).

12. A *manzana* (mz) is a unit of land measurement equivalent to .6989 hectares or 6,989 square meters; 30 mz equals 20.967 hectares.

13. "Metrocentro tiene proyección futurista dice el Sr. Poma," *La Prensa Gráfica*, 26 October 1971, 3, 22.

14. Interview with architect, 5 September 2006. Figures reported on the media in 2011 are higher: "Every month, 1.8 million people visit Metrocentro San Salvador, and [during holiday months] the number increases to 2.4–2.5 million people." Keny López, "Grupo Roble remodela octava etapa de Metrocentro," *La Prensa Gráfica*, 1 July 2011, http://www.laprensagrafica.com/economia/nacional/202261-grupo-roble-remodela -80-etapa-de-metrocentro (accessed 8 March 2013). The website for Metrocentro San Salvador also reports that 1.8 million people visit the mall monthly. "Metrocentro

El Salvador, Metrocentro San Salvador," http://www.metrocentro.com/inicio-SS (accessed 9 June 2013).

15. This idea of a city and its heart resonates with the work of Austrian architect Victor Gruen, "the so-called philosopher and father of the shopping center" (Hardwick 2004, 2). Although a significant part of Gruen's architectural career in the United States involved the creation of suburban retail environments that promised community, his 1964 book *The Heart of Our Cities* was a critique of the state of cities—"In a strange twist, his argument for American cities became a jeremiad against them" (Hardwick 2004, 207).

16. "Effie Plata: Categoría Éxito Sostenido, Metrocentro el Corazón de la Ciudad," http://www.effie.com.sv/ganadores/2007/metrocentro.html (accessed 23 July 2012).

17. Ibid.

18. The website for Mister Donut in El Salvador is http://www.misterdonut.com.sv/ (accessed 11 August 2013).

19. In 2013, the website for Pollo Campero lists restaurant locations in many parts of the world; it is http://www.campero.com/international.aspx (accessed 11 August 2013).

20. See "Catedral Metropolitana de Managua," http://legorretalegorreta.com/catedral-metropolitana-de-managua/ (accessed 19 August 2013), "Ricardo Legorreta Biography," http://legorretalegorreta.com/en/perfil/experiencia-ricardo/ (accessed 19 August 2013), and "Historia," http://legorretalegorreta.com/historia-firma/ (accessed 19 August 2013).

21. Guadalupe Trigueros, "La magia de los Legorreta," *El Diario de Hoy*, 10 December 2004, http://www.elsalvador.com/noticias/2004/12/10/negocios/neg11.asp# (accessed 7 February 2013).

22. "Legorreta+Legorreta" architecture firm website; the firm's page for the Multiplaza project is http://legorretalegorreta.com/multiplaza-panamericana/ (accessed 28 February 2013).

23. Enrique Miranda, "Discordia: Finca El Espino, más de dos décadas en la incertidumbre," *El Diario de Hoy*, 1 October 2006, http://www.elsalvador.com/noticias/2006/10/01/nacional/nac1.asp (accessed 9 June 2013).

24. Alfredo Espino's poem "Árbol de fuego" is included in his posthumous book *Jícaras tristes* (1936).

25. "La Gran Vía costará $60 millones," *La Prensa Gráfica*, 7 December 2004, 56–57.

26. Ibid., 56.

27. "El Salvador un mercado a cielo abierto," *La Prensa Gráfica*, 20 April 2007, http://www.laprensagrafica.com/eleconomista/753751.asp (accessed 24 April 2007).

28. Ibid.

29. Ibid.

30. Ronald Portillo, "Los inamovibles," *La Prensa Gráfica*, 3 March 2013, http://www.laprensagrafica.com/Los-inamovibles (accessed 8 March 2013). This article estimates that approximately thirty thousand Salvadorans worked as vendors in the streets of the capital at the time of the October–November 2012 removals.

31. Ibid.

32. Yanira Aparicio, "Vendedores se instalan en las aceras de Metrocentro," *Diario Co-Latino*, 9 December 2010, http://www.diariocolatino.com/es/20101209/municipalismo/87267/Vendedores-se-instalan-en-las-aceras-de-Metrocentro.htm?tpl=71 (accessed 28 February 2013).

33. Ibid.

34. Evelyn Machuca, Franklin Zelaya, and Liseth Alas, "Vendedores informales retiran mercadería de Metrocentro," *El Diario de Hoy*, 8 December 2010, http://www.elsalvador

.com/mwedh/nota/nota_completa.asp?idCat=6375&idArt=5384892 (accessed 28 February 2013). While this 2010 removal reportedly took place without excessive force, on multiple occasions the removal of street vendors and their merchandise has turned violent. In October 2012, the mayor of San Salvador ordered the removal of hundreds of vendor sites in the Calle Arce area. These sites were dismantled, merchandise was confiscated, people were injured, and thousands of vendors once again protested their displacement. These incidents highlight the ongoing need to address this issue realistically and humanely in any proposed plan for the downtown area of San Salvador. Media reports of these removals also point to the recurrent, even cyclical, nature of this issue, and the relationship between the municipal police and the street vendors. An ice cream vendor in the streets of San Salvador affirms: "Their job is to remove us, and ours is to come back," as reported in Ronald Portillo, "Los inamovibles," *La Prensa Gráfica*, 3 March 2013, http://www.laprensagrafica.com/Los-inamovibles (accessed 8 March 2013).

35. Sancho (2004), Rodríguez (2004), Pedersen (2002), and Zilberg (2002) analyze various aspects of these postwar economic and social/cultural conditions. This scholarship focuses on migration, remittances, and other forms of transnational exchange and value that affect urban and rural areas of El Salvador.

36. Interview with journalist, 22 December 2005.

BIBLIOGRAPHY

Abelson, Elaine S. 1989. *When Ladies Go A-Thieving: Middle-Class Shoplifters in the Victorian Department Store*. New York: Oxford University Press.

Aguayo, Fernando, and Lourdes Roca, coordinators. 2005. *Imágenes e investigación social*. Mexico City: Instituto Mora.

Akşin, O. Zeynep, and Patrick T. Harker. 2001. "Modeling a Phone Center: Analysis of a Multichannel, Multiresource Processor Shared Loss System." *Management Science* 47 (2): 324–336.

Alferoff, Catrina, and David Knights. 2003. "We're All Partying Here: Target and Games, or Targets as Games in Call Centre Management." In *Art and Aesthetics at Work*, edited by Adrian Carr and Philip Hancock, 70–92. Houndmills, UK: Palgrave Macmillan.

Alisky, Marvin. 1981. *Latin American Media: Guidance and Censorship*. Ames: Iowa State University Press.

Anderson, Benedict. 1991. *Imagined Communities: Reflections on the Origin and Spread of Nationalism*. Rev. ed. London: Verso.

Aneesh, Aneesh. 2001. "Skill Saturation: Rationalization and Post-industrial Work." *Theory and Society* 30: 363–396.

Appadurai, Arjun. 1986. "Introduction: Commodities and the Politics of Value." In *The Social Life of Things: Commodities in Cultural Perspective*, edited by Arjun Appadurai, 3–63. Cambridge: Cambridge University Press.

———. 1996. *Modernity at Large: Cultural Dimensions of Globalization*. Minneapolis: University of Minnesota Press.

Arias, Arturo. 2007. *Taking Their Word: Literature and the Signs of Central America*. Minneapolis: University of Minnesota Press.

Ashplant, T. G., Graham Dawson, and Michael Roper, eds. 2000. *The Politics of War Memory and Commemoration*. London: Routledge.

Auyero, Javier. 2011. "Patients of the State: An Ethnographic Account of Poor People's Waiting." *Latin American Research Review* 46 (1): 5–29.

Baker-Cristales, Beth. 1999. "El Hermano Lejano: The Transnational Space of Salvadoran Migration to the United States." PhD diss., University of New Mexico (Albuquerque).

———. 2004. *Salvadoran Migration to Southern California: Redefining El Hermano Lejano*. Gainesville: University Press of Florida.

Bakhtin, M. M. 1981. "Forms of Time and of the Chronotope in the Novel: Notes toward a Historical Poetics." In *The Dialogic Imagination: Four Essays*, edited by Michael Holquist; translated by Caryl Emerson and Michael Holquist, 84–258. Austin: University of Texas Press.

Ball, Kirstie. 2003. "Categorizing the Workers: Electronic Surveillance and Social Ordering in the Call Center." In *Surveillance as Social Sorting: Privacy, Risk, and Digital Discrimination*, edited by David Lyon, 201–225. London: Routledge.

Baudrillard, Jean. 1981. *For a Critique of the Political Economy of the Sign*. Translated and with an introduction by Charles Levin. St. Louis: Telos Press.

Beverley, John, and Marc Zimmerman. 1990. *Literature and Politics in the Central American Revolutions*. Austin: University of Texas Press.

Bhabha, Homi K. 1994. *The Location of Culture*. London: Routledge.

Binford, Leigh. 1999. "Hegemony in the Interior of the Salvadoran Revolution: The ERP in Northern Morazán." *Journal of Latin American Anthropology* 4 (1): 2–45.

Boczkowski, Pablo J. 2004. *Digitizing the News: Innovation in Online Newspapers*. Cambridge, MA: MIT Press.

Booth, John A., Christine J. Wade, and Thomas W. Walker. 2006. *Understanding Central America: Global Forces, Rebellion, and Change*. 4th ed. Boulder, CO: Westview.

Bourdieu, Pierre. 1984. *Distinction: A Social Critique of the Judgement of Taste*. Translated by Richard Nice. Cambridge, MA: Harvard University Press.

Breakfield, Charles V. 2001. "Failover, Redundancy, and High-Availability Applications in the Call Center Environment." In *Designing a Total Data Solution: Technology, Implementation, and Deployment*, edited by Roxanne E. Burkey and Charles V. Breakfield, 257–267. Boca Raton: CRC Press.

Brown, Ed, Gilda Catalano, and Peter J. Taylor. 2002. "Beyond World Cities: Central America in a Global Space of Flows." *Area* 34 (2): 139–148.

Buck-Morss, Susan. 1989. *The Dialectics of Seeing: Walter Benjamin and the Arcades Project*. Cambridge, MA: MIT Press.

Buff, Rachel. 2001. *Immigration and the Political Economy of Home: West Indian Brooklyn and American Indian Minneapolis, 1945–1992*. Berkeley: University of California Press.

Calderón Chelius, Leticia, coordinator. 2004. *Votar en la distancia: La extensión de los derechos políticos a migrantes, experiencias comparadas*. 2nd ed. Mexico City: Instituto Mora / Coordinación General para la Atención al Migrante Michoacano.

Cameron, Deborah. 2000. *Good to Talk? Living and Working in a Communication Culture*. London: Sage.

Campos, Napoleón, Roberto Meza, William Pleitez, Sigfrido Reyes, David Rivas, Cecilia Rodas, Carlos Mauricio Rosales, and Roberto Turcios. 1999. "Sociedad sin fronteras." In *Temas claves para el Plan de Nación: Consulta Especializada*, by Comisión Nacional de Desarrollo, 3–15. San Salvador: Talleres Gráficos UCA.

Carrier, James G. 2006. "The Limits of Culture: Political Economy and the Anthropology of Consumption." In *The Making of the Consumer: Knowledge, Power and Identity in the Modern World*, edited by Frank Trentmann, 271–289. Oxford: Berg.

Castellanos Moya, Horacio. 1997. *El asco: Thomas Bernhard en San Salvador*. San Salvador: Editorial Arcoiris.

———. 2001. *El arma en el hombre*. Barcelona: Tusquets Editores.

———. 2011. *Tyrant Memory*. Translated by Katherine Silver. New York: New Directions.

Ching, Erik, and Virginia Tilley. 1998. "Indians, the Military and the Rebellion of 1932 in El Salvador." *Journal of Latin American Studies* 30 (1): 121–156.

Conroy, Marianne. 1998. "Discount Dreams: Factory Outlet Malls, Consumption, and the Performance of Middle-Class Identity." *Social Text* 54, 16 (1): 63–83.

Cortez, Beatriz. 2010. *Estética del cinismo: Pasión y desencanto en la literatura centroamericana de posguerra*. Guatemala: F&G Editores.

Coutin, Susan Bibler. 2000. *Legalizing Moves: Salvadoran Immigrants' Struggle for U.S. Residency*. Ann Arbor: University of Michigan Press.

——. 2007. *Nations of Emigrants: Shifting Boundaries of Citizenship in El Salvador and the United States*. Ithaca, NY: Cornell University Press.

——. 2010a. "Exiled by Law: Deportation and the Inviability of Life." In *The Deportation Regime: Sovereignty, Space, and the Freedom of Movement*, edited by Nicholas De Genova and Nathalie Peutz, 351–370. Durham, NC: Duke University Press.

——. 2010b. "Originary Destinations: Re/membered Communities and Salvadoran Diasporas," in "Salvadoran Migration to the United States," special issue, *Urban Anthropology and Studies of Cultural Systems and World Economic Development* 39 (1–2): 47–72.

Craft, Linda J. 1997. *Novels of Testimony and Resistance from Central America*. Gainesville: University Press of Florida.

Crossick, Geoffrey, and Serge Jaumain, eds. 1999. *Cathedrals of Consumption: The European Department Store, 1850–1939*. Aldershot, UK: Ashgate.

Cruz Monroy, Dafne Isis, and Ana Elena Barrios Juárez Badillo. 2009. *Sur inicio de un camino: Una mirada global de los Derechos Humanos en la Frontera Sur de México en su triple condición de origen-retorno, tránsito y destino de trabajadoras y trabajadores migrantes*, coordinated by Miguel Ángel Paz Carrasco. Mexico City: Asociación Latinoamericana de Organizaciones de Promoción al Desarrollo, A. C. ALOP / ENLACE, Comunicación y Capacitación, A. C.

Cruz Salazar, Tania. 2011. "Transitando la vida: Migración, juventud y vulnerabilidad en la Frontera Sur." In *Chiapas: Territorio, fronteras, migraciones, desarrollo; Visiones interculturales multidisciplinarias*, coordinated by Andrés Fábregas Puig, 231–262. San Cristóbal de las Casas: Universidad Intercultural de Chiapas.

Das, Veena. 2007. *Life and Words: Violence and the Descent into the Ordinary*. Berkeley: University of California Press.

Dávila, Arlene. 2001. *Latinos, Inc.: The Marketing and Making of a People*. Berkeley: University of California Press.

——. 2008. *Latino Spin: Public Image and the Whitewashing of Race*. New York: New York University Press.

——. 2012. *Culture Works: Space, Value, and Mobility across the Neoliberal Americas*. New York: New York University Press.

Davis, Mike. 2001. *Magical Urbanism: Latinos Reinvent the US City*. Rev. ed. London: Verso.

Dean, Jodi. 2001. "Cybersalons and Civil Society: Rethinking the Public Sphere in Transnational Technoculture." *Public Culture* 13 (2): 243–265.

DeLugan, Robin Maria. 2012. *Reimagining National Belonging: Post–Civil War El Salvador in a Global Context*. Tucson: University of Arizona Press.

Didion, Joan. 1983. *Salvador*. New York: Washington Square Press.

Douglas, Mary. 1966. *Purity and Danger: An Analysis of Concepts of Pollution and Taboo*. London: Routledge & Kegan Paul.

Dreby, Joanna. 2006. "Honor and Virtue: Mexican Parenting in the Transnational Context." *Gender & Society* 20 (1): 32–59.

Dunkerley, James. 1991. "El Salvador since 1930." In *Central America since Independence*, edited by Leslie Bethell, 159–190. Cambridge: Cambridge University Press.

——. 1994. *The Pacification of Central America: Political Change in the Isthmus, 1987–1993*. London: Verso.

Dunn, Timothy J. 1996. *The Militarization of the U.S.-Mexico Border, 1978–1992: Low- Intensity Conflict Doctrine Comes Home*. Austin: CMAS Books, The Center for Mexican American Studies, The University of Texas at Austin. Distributed by arrangement with University of Texas Press.

Dutriz, José. 2002. *José Dutriz y el diario "La Prensa," 1915–1934*. San Salvador: Dirección de Publicaciones e Impresos, Consejo Nacional para la Cultura y el Arte.

Ellis, Vaughan, and Phil Taylor. 2006. "'You don't know what you've got till it's gone': Recontextualising the Origins, Development, and Impact of the Call Centre." *New Technology, Work, and Employment* 21 (2): 107–122.

Escobar, Cristina. 2007. "Extraterritorial Political Rights and Dual Citizenship in Latin America." *Latin American Research Review* 42 (3): 43–75.

Escudos, Jacinta. 1997. "La noche de los escritores asesinos." In *Cuentos sucios*, 83-123. San Salvador: Dirección de Publicaciones e Impresos, Consejo Nacional para la Cultura y el Arte.

Espiritu, Yen Le. 2003. *Home Bound: Filipino American Lives across Cultures, Communities, and Countries*. Berkeley: University of California Press.

Flores, Juan. 2009. *The Diaspora Strikes Back: Caribeño Tales of Learning and Turning*. New York: Routledge.

Friedberg, Anne. 1993. *Window Shopping: Cinema and the Postmodern*. Berkeley: University of California Press.

Fuentes, Pedro, Christian Lama, Guillermo Mata, and Johanna Vazquez. 2005. "La Arquitectura de los centros comerciales en El Salvador y Metrocentro como caso de estudio." Thesis, Universidad Albert Einstein, San Salvador, El Salvador.

García Canclini, Néstor. 1993. *Transforming Modernity: Popular Culture in Mexico*. Translated by Lidia Lozano. Austin: University of Texas Press.

———. 2001. *Consumers and Citizens: Globalization and Multicultural Conflicts*. Translated and with an introduction by George Yúdice. Minneapolis: University of Minnesota Press.

Geoffroy Rivas, Pedro. 1978. *La lengua salvadoreña*. San Salvador: Ministerio de Educación, Dirección de Publicaciones.

———. 1979. *El español que hablamos en El Salvador*. 4th ed. San Salvador: Ministerio de Educación, Dirección de Publicaciones.

Gilman, Sander L. 1988. *Disease and Representation: Images of Illness from Madness to AIDS*. Ithaca, NY: Cornell University Press.

Goffman, Erving. 1963. *Stigma: Notes on the Management of Spoiled Identity*. Englewood Cliffs, NJ: Prentice-Hall.

Gómez-Barris, Macarena. 2009. *Where Memory Dwells: Culture and State Violence in Chile*. Berkeley: University of California Press.

González, Luis Armando. 2005. "La globalización y la afirmación de las identidades locales: La mitificación de Roberto D'Aubuisson." *ECA Estudios Centroamericanos* 679–680 (May-June): 534–539.

Gordon, Avery F. 1997. *Ghostly Matters: Haunting and the Sociological Imagination*. Minneapolis: University of Minnesota Press.

Gosse, Van. 1996. "'El Salvador is Spanish for Vietnam': A New Immigrant Left and the Politics of Solidarity." In *The Immigrant Left in the United States*, edited by Paul Buhle and Dan Georgakas, 302–329. Albany: State University of New York Press.

Gottdiener, Mark. 2000. "Approaches to Consumption: Classical and Contemporary Perspectives." In *New Forms of Consumption: Consumers, Culture, and Commodification*, edited by Mark Gottdiener, 3–31. Lanham, MD: Rowman & Littlefield.

Gould, Jeffrey L., and Carlos Henríquez Consalvi, directors. 2002. *1932, cicatriz de la memoria* [1932: Scars of Memory]. 53 min. Museo de la Palabra y la Imagen, San Salvador, El Salvador.

Hall, Stuart, ed. 1997. *Representation: Cultural Representations and Signifying Practices*. London: Sage/The Open University.

Hall, Stuart, Chas Critcher, Tony Jefferson, John Clarke, and Brian Roberts. 1978. *Policing the Crisis: Mugging, the State, and Law and Order*. London: Macmillan.

Hallin, Daniel C. 1994. *We Keep America on Top of the World: Television Journalism and the Public Sphere*. London: Routledge.

Hardwick, M. Jeffrey. 2004. *Mall Maker: Victor Gruen, Architect of an American Dream*. Philadelphia: University of Pennsylvania Press.

Harvey, David. 1989. *The Condition of Postmodernity: An Enquiry into the Origins of Cultural Change*. Cambridge, MA: Blackwell.

Herodier, Gustavo. 1997. *San Salvador: El esplendor de una ciudad, 1880–1930*. San Salvador: ASESUISA / Fundación María Escalón de Núñez.

Herz, Rachel. 2012. *That's Disgusting: Unraveling the Mysteries of Repulsion*. New York: W. W. Norton.

Hobsbawm, Eric, and Terence Ranger, eds. 1992. *The Invention of Tradition*. Canto ed. Cambridge: Cambridge University Press.

Holston, James. 1989. *The Modernist City: An Anthropological Critique of Brasília*. Chicago: University of Chicago Press.

Hondagneu-Sotelo, Pierrette, and Ernestine Avila. 1997. "'I'm Here, But I'm There': The Meanings of Latina Transnational Motherhood." *Gender & Society* 11 (5): 548–571.

Horton, Sarah. 2009. "A Mother's Heart is Weighed Down with Stones: A Phenomenological Approach to the Experience of Transnational Motherhood." *Culture, Medicine and Psychiatry* 33 (1): 21–40.

Hughes, Everett C. 1994. *On Work, Race, and the Sociological Imagination*. Edited and with an introduction by Lewis A. Coser. Chicago: University of Chicago Press.

Hume, Mo. 2009. *The Politics of Violence: Gender, Conflict and Community in El Salvador*. Malden, MA: Wiley-Blackwell.

Ignacio, Emily Noelle. 2005. *Building Diaspora: Filipino Community Formation on the Internet*. New Brunswick, NJ: Rutgers University Press.

Jacobs, Jerry. 1984. *The Mall: An Attempted Escape from Everyday Life*. Prospect Heights, IL: Waveland Press.

Jameson, Fredric. 1991. *Postmodernism, or, The Cultural Logic of Late Capitalism*. Durham, NC: Duke University Press.

———. 2000. "Reification and Utopia in Mass Culture." In *The Jameson Reader*, edited by Michael Hardt and Kathi Weeks, 123–148. Oxford: Blackwell.

Kent, Suzanne. 2010. "Symbols of Love: Consumption, Transnational Migration, and the Family in San Salvador, El Salvador," in "Salvadoran Migration to the United States," special issue, *Urban Anthropology and Studies of Cultural Systems and World Economic Development* 39 (1–2): 73–108.

Kolnai, Aurel. 2004. *On Disgust*. Edited and with an introduction by Barry Smith and Carolyn Korsmeyer. Chicago: Open Court.

Korsmeyer, Carolyn. 2011. *Savoring Disgust: The Foul and the Fair in Aesthetics*. New York: Oxford University Press.

Kowinski, William Severini. 1985. *The Malling of America: An Inside Look at the Great Consumer Paradise*. New York: William Morrow.

LaFeber, Walter. 1993. *Inevitable Revolutions: The United States in Central America*. 2nd ed. New York: W. W. Norton.

Landolt, Patricia. 1997. "Salvadoran Transnationalism: Towards the Redefinition of the National Community." Working Paper #18, Program in Comparative International Development Working Paper Series, The Johns Hopkins University (Baltimore). http://www.jhu.edu/~soc/pcid/papers/18.htm (accessed 5 February 2001).

Lauria-Santiago, Aldo A. 1995. "Historical Research and Sources on El Salvador." *Latin American Research Review* 30 (2): 151–176.

Lears, T. J. Jackson. 1983. "From Salvation to Self-Realization: Advertising and the Therapeutic Roots of the Consumer Culture, 1880–1930." In *The Culture of Consumption: Critical Essays in American History, 1880–1980*, edited by Richard Wightman Fox and T. J. Jackson Lears, 1–38. New York: Pantheon Books.

Levine, Barry B., ed. 1992. *El desafío neoliberal: El fin del tercermundismo en América Latina*. Bogota: Grupo Editorial Norma.

Lin, Yi-Chieh Jessica. 2011. *Fake Stuff: China and the Rise of Counterfeit Goods*. New York: Routledge.

Lindo-Fuentes, Héctor, Erik Ching, and Rafael A. Lara-Martínez. 2007. *Remembering a Massacre in El Salvador: The Insurrection of 1932, Roque Dalton, and the Politics of Historical Memory*. Albuquerque: University of New Mexico Press.

Lipski, John M. 1994. *Latin American Spanish*. London: Longman.

López, Silvia L. 2004. "National Culture, Globalization and the Case of Post-War El Salvador." *Comparative Literature Studies* 41 (1): 80–100.

López Vigil, José Ignacio. 1994. *Rebel Radio: The Story of El Salvador's Radio Venceremos*. Translated by Mark Fried. Willimantic, CT: Curbstone Press.

Machuca, Milton R. 2010. "In Search of Salvadorans in the United States: Contextualizing the Ethnographic Record." "Salvadoran Migration to the United States," special issue, *Urban Anthropology and Studies of Cultural Systems and World Economic Development* 39 (1–2): 1–45.

Martel Trigueros, Roxana. 2007. "Las maras salvadoreñas: Nuevas formas de espanto y control social." In *Las maras: Identidades juveniles al límite*, coordinated by José Manuel Valenzuela Arce, Alfredo Nateras Domínguez, and Rossana Reguillo Cruz, 83–125. Mexico City: Universidad Autónoma Metropolitana (Unidad Iztapalapa) / El Colegio de la Frontera Norte / Casa Juan Pablos.

Martin, Emily. 1994. *Flexible Bodies: Tracking Immunity in American Culture—From the Days of Polio to the Age of AIDS*. Boston: Beacon Press.

Martin, Percy F. 1911. *Salvador of the Twentieth Century*. London: Edward Arnold. http://hdl.handle.net/2027/mdp.39015005318285 (accessed 24 August 2013).

Martín-Barbero, Jesús. 1993. *Communication, Culture and Hegemony: From the Media to Mediations*. Translated by Elizabeth Fox and Robert A. White. With an introduction by Philip Schlesinger. London: Sage Publications.

Martínez, Óscar. 2010. *Los migrantes que no importan: En el camino con los centroamericanos indocumentados en México*. Barcelona: Icaria Editorial.

Marx, Karl. (1867) 1978. "Capital, Volume One, Part I. Commodities and Money, Chapter I. Commodities." In *The Marx-Engels Reader*, 2nd ed., edited by Robert C. Tucker, 302–329. New York: W. W. Norton.

Mauss, Marcel. 1950. *The Gift: The Form and Reason for Exchange in Archaic Societies*. Translated by W. D. Halls. With a foreword by Mary Douglas. New York: W. W. Norton.

McGinn, Colin. 2011. *The Meaning of Disgust*. Oxford: Oxford University Press.

Menjívar, Cecilia. 2000. *Fragmented Ties: Salvadoran Immigrant Networks in America*. Berkeley: University of California Press.

———. 2011. *Enduring Violence: Ladina Women's Lives in Guatemala*. Berkeley: University of California Press.

Miller, Nicola. 2006. "The Historiography of Nationalism and National Identity in Latin America." *Nations and Nationalism* 12 (2): 201–221.

Miller, Susan B. 2004. *Disgust: The Gatekeeper Emotion*. Hillsdale, NJ: Analytic Press.

Miller, William Ian. 1997. *The Anatomy of Disgust*. Cambridge, MA: Harvard University Press.

Molyneux, Maxine. 2001. "Ethnography and Global Processes." *Ethnography* 2 (2): 273–282.

Montes, Segundo. 1987. *El Salvador 1987: Salvadoreños refugiados en los Estados Unidos*. San Salvador: IDHUCA.

Moodie, Ellen. 2006. "Microbus Crashes and Coca-Cola Cash: The Value of Death in 'Free-Market' El Salvador." *American Ethnologist* 33 (1): 63–80.

———. 2010. *El Salvador in the Aftermath of Peace: Crime, Uncertainty, and the Transition to Democracy*. Philadelphia: University of Pennsylvania Press.

Morán-Taylor, Michelle, and Cecilia Menjívar. 2005. "Unpacking Longings to Return: Guatemalans and Salvadorans in Phoenix, Arizona." *International Migration* 43 (4): 91–121.

Morello, Gustavo. 2007. "Charles Taylor's 'Imaginary' and 'Best Account' in Latin America." *Philosophy & Social Criticism* 33 (5): 617–639.

Nakamura, Lisa. 2002. *Cybertypes: Race, Ethnicity, and Identity on the Internet*. New York: Routledge.

Newcomb, Horace M. 1984. "On the Dialogic Aspects of Mass Communication." *Critical Studies in Mass Communication* 1 (1): 34–50.

Olalquiaga, Celeste. 1992. *Megalopolis: Contemporary Cultural Sensibilities*. Minneapolis: University of Minnesota Press.

Ong, Aihwa, and Stephen J. Collier, eds. 2005. *Global Assemblages: Technology, Politics, and Ethics as Anthropological Problems*. Malden, MA: Blackwell.

Otnes, Cele C., and Tina M. Lowrey, eds. 2004. *Contemporary Consumption Rituals: A Research Anthology*. Mahwah, NJ: Lawrence Erlbaum Associates.

Padilla, Yajaira M. 2008. "Setting *La diabla* Free: Women, Violence, and the Struggle for Representation in Postwar El Salvador." *Latin American Perspectives* 35 (5): 133–145.

Park, Lisa Sun-Hee. 2005. *Consuming Citizenship: Children of Asian Immigrant Entrepreneurs*. Stanford, CA: Stanford University Press.

Patel, Reena. 2010. *Working the Night Shift: Women in India's Call Center Industry*. Stanford, CA: Stanford University Press.

Pedelty, Mark. 1995. *War Stories: The Culture of Foreign Correspondents*. New York: Routledge.

Pedersen, David. 2002. "The Storm We Call Dollars: Determining Value and Belief in El Salvador and the United States." *Cultural Anthropology* 17 (3): 431–459.

Perla, Héctor. 2008. "Si Nicaragua Venció, El Salvador Vencerá: Central American Agency in the Creation of the U.S.-Central American Peace and Solidarity Movement." *Latin American Research Review* 43 (2): 136–158.

Peterson, Brandt G. 2007. "Remains Out of Place: Race, Trauma, and Nationalism in El Salvador." *Anthropological Theory* 7 (1): 59–77.

Ponces, Edu, Toni Arnau, and Eduardo Soteras. 2010. *En el camino: México, la ruta de los migrantes que no importan*. Barcelona: Blume.

Poster, Winifred R. 2007. "Who's On the Line? Indian Call Center Agents Pose as Americans for U.S.-Outsourced Firms." *Industrial Relations* 46 (2): 271–304.

Rockwell, Rick, and Noreene Janus. 2003. *Media Power in Central America*. Urbana: University of Illinois Press.

Rodríguez, Ana Patricia. 2005. "'Departamento 15': Cultural Narratives of Salvadoran Transnational Migration." *Latino Studies* 3: 19–41.

———. 2009. *Dividing the Isthmus: Central American Transnational Histories, Literatures, and Cultures*. Austin: University of Texas Press.

Rodríguez, Carlos Antonio. 2004. "Estudio práctico sobre el análisis del flujo de remesas." *Cuaderno de Investigación: Emigración* 1 (1): 45–66.

Rotker, Susana, ed. 2002. *Citizens of Fear: Urban Violence in Latin America*. Edited in collaboration with Katherine Goldman. With an introduction by Jorge Balán. New Brunswick, NJ: Rutgers University Press.

Rowe, William, and Vivian Schelling. 1991. *Memory and Modernity: Popular Culture in Latin America*. London: Verso.

Russell, Bob. 2008. "Call Centres: A Decade of Research." *International Journal of Management Reviews* 10 (3): 195–219.

Sancho, Eduardo. 2004. "Hacia un nuevo enfoque de la migración globalizada." *Cuaderno de Investigación: Emigración* 1(1): 7–44.

Santa Ana, Otto. 2002. *Brown Tide Rising: Metaphors of Latinos in Contemporary American Public Discourse*. Austin: University of Texas Press.

Sassen, Saskia. 2004. "Sited Materialities with Global Span." In *Society Online: The Internet in Context*, edited by Philip N. Howard and Steve Jones, 295–306. Thousand Oaks, CA: Sage.

Scarry, Elaine. 1985. *The Body in Pain: The Making and Unmaking of the World*. New York: Oxford University Press.

Scheper-Hughes, Nancy. 1997. "Specificities: Peace-Time Crimes." *Social Identities* 3 (3): 471–497.

Scheper-Hughes, Nancy, and Margaret M. Lock. 1987. "The Mindful Body: A Prolegomenon to Future Work in Medical Anthropology." *Medical Anthropology Quarterly*, n.s., 1 (1): 6–41.

Schmidt Camacho, Alicia. 2008. *Migrant Imaginaries: Latino Cultural Politics in the U.S.-Mexico Borderlands*. New York: New York University Press.

Schudson, Michael. 1984. *Advertising, the Uneasy Persuasion: Its Dubious Impact on American Society*. New York: Basic Books.

Seremetakis, C. Nadia. 1994. "The Memory of the Senses, Part I: Marks of the Transitory." In *The Senses Still: Perception and Memory as Material Culture in Modernity*, edited by C. Nadia Seremetakis, 1-18. Boulder, CO: Westview Press.

Shohat, Ella, and Robert Stam. 1994. *Unthinking Eurocentrism: Multiculturalism and the Media*. London and New York: Routledge.

Silverstone, Roger. 1999. *Why Study the Media?* London: Sage.

Slattery, Dennis Patrick. 2000. *The Wounded Body: Remembering the Markings of Flesh*. Albany: State University of New York Press.

Soja, Edward W. 1989. *Postmodern Geographies: The Reassertion of Space in Critical Social Theory*. London: Verso.

Sol Arriaza, Ricardo. 1988. "Communication, the Church, and Social Conflict in El Salvador, 1970–80." In *Media and Politics in Latin America: The Struggle for Democracy*, edited by Elizabeth Fox, 93–102. London: Sage Publications.

Stone, Oliver, director. 1986. *Salvador*. 123 min. Hemdale Film Corporation.

Sturken, Marita, and Lisa Cartwright. 2001. *Practices of Looking: An Introduction to Visual Culture*. Oxford: Oxford University Press.

Taylor, Charles. 2002. "Modern Social Imaginaries." *Public Culture* 14 (1): 91–124.

Tsing, Anna. 2000. "The Global Situation." *Cultural Anthropology* 15 (3): 327–360.

———. 2005. *Friction: An Ethnography of Global Connection*. Princeton, NJ: Princeton University Press.

Urquiza, Waldemar. 2004. "Influencia de la cultura estadounidense sobre la cultura salvadoreña." *Cuaderno de Investigación: Emigración* 1 (1): 67–95.

Veblen, Thorstein. (1899) 1992. *The Theory of the Leisure Class*. With an introduction by C. Wright Mills. New Brunswick, NJ: Transaction Publishers.

Villalta, Nilda C. 2004. "Despiadada(s) ciudad(es): El imaginario salvadoreño más allá de la guerra civil, el testimonio y la inmigración." PhD diss., University of Maryland at College Park.

Waisbord, Silvio. 2000. *Watchdog Journalism in South America: News, Accountability, and Democracy*. New York: Columbia University Press.

Warner, Michael. 2002. "Publics and Counterpublics." *Public Culture* 14 (1): 49–90.

Way, J. T. 2012. *The Mayan in the Mall: Globalization, Development, and the Making of Modern Guatemala*. Durham, NC: Duke University Press.

Williams, Linda. 2001. *Playing the Race Card: Melodramas of Black and White from Uncle Tom to O.J. Simpson*. Princeton, NJ: Princeton University Press.

Wright, Melissa W. 1999. "The Dialectics of Still Life: Murder, Women, and Maquiladoras." *Public Culture* 11 (3): 453–473.

Zilberg, Elana. 2002. "From Riots to Rampart: A Spatial Cultural Politics of Salvadoran Migration to and from Los Angeles." PhD diss., University of Texas at Austin.

———. 2004. "Fools Banished from the Kingdom: Remapping Geographies of Gang Violence between the Americas (Los Angeles and San Salvador)." *American Quarterly* 56 (3): 759–779.

———. 2007. "Gangster in Guerilla Face: A Transnational Mirror of Production between the USA and El Salvador." *Anthropological Theory* 7 (1): 37–57.

———. 2011. *Space of Detention: The Making of a Transnational Gang Crisis between Los Angeles and San Salvador*. Durham, NC: Duke University Press.

Zukin, Sharon. 1991. *Landscapes of Power: From Detroit to Disney World*. Berkeley: University of California Press.

———. 2004. *Point of Purchase: How Shopping Changed American Culture*. New York: Routledge.

INDEX

Abelson, Elaine, 127
Administración Nacional de Telecomunicaciones (ANTEL), 23, 97
aesthetic: conventions, 106; of cynicism, 13, 77, 78; of violence, 81
Agencia de Promoción de Exportaciones e Inversiones de El Salvador (PROESA), 101, 161n8; creation of, 162n15; logo, 103; "Meet Your Roots: Work in El Salvador" program, 112–117; notes neutrality of accents in Salvadorans, 119; promotional materials, 103; website, 162n16
Aguayo, Fernando, 9
Akşin, O. Zeynep, 99
Alferoff, Catrina, 114
Alianza Republicana Nacionalista (ARENA), 85
Alisky, Marvin, 21
Anderson, Benedict, 31, 67, 72
Aneesh, Aneesh, 100
Appadurai, Arjun, 4, 15, 96, 127
Arias, Arturo, 81, 82, 83
arma en el hombre, El (Castellanos Moya), 84, 85
Arnau, Toni, 50
asco, El: Thomas Bernhard en San Salvador (Castellanos Moya), 8, 12, 73–92, 160n6, 161n8; addresses questions of how readerships and publics are formed, 77; aesthetic of cynicism in, 13, 77, 78; contempt for possibility of national unity in, 77; continuous politicization of universities and, 76; criticism of support for intellectual pursuits in, 83, 84; as critique of ideal of "inner cop," 85; denigration of materialism in, 75, 76; describes postwar disenchantment in, 80–86; emigration seen as status symbol in, 79; everything Salvadoran found lacking in, 73–90; fear of pollution and lack of control in, 89; identification with "inner cop" within all Salvadorans, 84; mockery of feelings of nostalgia in, 13, 74, 75, 77; negotiates truth and fiction in Salvadoran politics and culture, 77; points to lack of literature and history in El Salvador, 75, 76; questions why anyone remains in El Salvador, 76, 77; reluctant return to El Salvador in,

77; removal of reminders of Salvadoran identity in, 73–90; revelations of legacies of civil war in, 84; Salvadorans seen as "degradations of taste," 75; sensitivity to reader's way of seeing world, 77; sentiment of disgust in, 73–90; telling/retelling of character's relationship to Salvadoran national reality, 76, 77; view of emigration as solution to social and personal issues in, 79
Asdrúbal Aguilar, Lucas, 61
Ashplant, T. G., 48, 60
Asociación de Periodistas de El Salvador (APES), 19
Auyero, Javier, 142
Avila, Ernestine, 55

Baker-Cristales, Beth, 26
Bakhtin, Mikhail, 31
Ball, Kirstie, 95
Basaglia, Franco, 52
Benjamin, Walter, 139, 140, 141
"Bestia, La" (chronicle), 64
Beverley, John, 81, 82
Bhabha, Homi, 53, 63, 145
Binford, Leigh, 24
Boczkowski, Pablo, 68
bodies, migrant: compared to "credit cards," 50; *cuerpomátic*, 50; injuries to, 60, 64, 65; repatriation of, 55, 60, 66; stereotyping, 54; stigmatization of, 54; transnational, 50, 54
Booth, John, 5
Bourdieu, Pierre, 15
Bracero Program, 103
Breakfield, Charles, 99
Brown, Ed, 156n22
Buck-Morss, Susan, 139, 140, 141
Buff, Rachel, 3

Calderón Chelius, Leticia, 3
call centers, 93–124; advertising for, 14, 95, 104–117; age issues, 116–118; applications for work in, 14, 104; applications from deportees, 109, 110, 111, 112, 163n32; bilingual workers in, 8; business process outsourcing and, 100, 109; career aspirations at, 94; class identifications in, 98;

shopping malls (*continued*)
transnational imaginary, 15; private/public spaces in, 15, 16, 126, 130, 131; recognizing and engaging transnationalism and, 10; as reference points, 130; respite from street violence in, 130; secure spaces in, 8; significance of, 14, 126; socialization spaces in, 15, 128; as spaces of consumption, 9; as spaces of hospitality, 130; as spaces without qualities, 130; spheres of life and, 143–146; stereotypes of, 128; understandings of safety and, 15; unequal access in, 131, 132; unequal participation in spaces in, 127
Silverstone, Roger, 6
Slattery, Dennis Patrick, 65
social: change, 4, 7, 13, 96; class, 94; communities, 77; contradictions, 3; domination, 21; elites, 23; identity, 53; imaginaries, 4, 15, 36, 40, 47, 66; interaction, 15; justice, 156n19; landscapes, 15; language, 37; marginalization, 120; meaning, 47; memory, 4, 9; networking, 100; norms, 81; order, 37, 60, 63, 86, 90; organization, 26, 100; placement, 3; processes, 3, 10; production, 6; reality, 27; regulation, 5; relationships, 16; spaces, 69; standing, 90; status, 138; totality, 41, 48; transformation, 132; violence, 20
Soja, Edward, 131
Sol Arriaza, Ricardo, 21
Soteras, Eduardo, 50
space(s): of citizenship, 15–16; of constraints and contradictions, 94; construction of sense of place and belonging, 2; of consumption, 8, 15, 16, 126, 128, 141, 150; dangerous, 15; diasporic, 11, 25; discursive, 68; of fluidity and exchange, 51; of hospitality, 130; idealized, 15; of imagination, 126; of imagined community, 48; of infomation, 42; inhabited by migrants during border crossings, 12; of interpellation, 5; journalistic, 51; of knowledge, 42; for learning to self-regulate, 5; of leisure, 15; mediated, 10; movement through, 100; nationalized, 35; national/transnational, 7; online, 69; of opportunity, 94; of people, 25; political, 69; public, 126; relationship of private and public, 7; representational, 31; secure, 8; shopping, 126; social, 69; of socialization, 15, 126, 128; of transmigrants, 11, 12; transnational, 12, 32, 33, 51; of transnational imaginary, 55; where citizens do not necessarily live in geographic boundaries, 40
stereotypes: arising from fear or repulsion, 53; of call center agents, 95; construction of excluded as "other," 53; defining, 53; positive/negative effects of, 53; of qualities of Salvadoran migrants, 30, 51, 53; seeking to manage subjects by use of, 53; of shopping malls, 128; social production of, 53; used in media reports, 30, 36, 51, 53
structural adjustment, 35

Sturken, Marita, 51, 105, 157n25
subjectivity: experience shaped by, 70; fragmented, 15; media and, 20

Taylor, Charles, 4
Taylor, Peter, 156n22
Taylor, Phil, 99
technology: advances in, 5, 99; distances giving in to advances of, 40; media reliance on, 19, 29; as model for news reporting, 23; movements of, 100; recording, 19
technology, communication, 99; professionalization of, 21; transformative uses of, 7
Temas claves para el Plan de Nación: Consulta Especializada, 41, 97
Tilley, Virginia, 120
time: connected to space, 32; empty, 31; importance of, 31; importance to narratives of movement, 31; representation of, 31; significance to imaginings of national consciousness and distant communities, 31
Tipografía La Unión, 28
transnational/transnationalism: belonging, 7; creation of equal opportunities and, 5; engagement in, 10; exclusions from process of, 5; expectations of, 4; identity, 8; inclusion/exclusion from, 7, 11; labor, 94; lived experiences of, 2; movement, 40; practices of, 4; understanding dynamics of, 3
Tsing, Anna, 52, 59
Tyrant Memory (Castellanos Moya), 160n2

United States: assimilation in, 35; naturalized citizenship in, 2; Salvadoran communities in, 40, 41
Urquiza, Waldemar, 129

Valle, Adriana, 158n19
Veblen, Thorstein, 126
vendors, street, 143; Coordinadora Nacional de Vendedores (CNV), 144; emergence of, 16; in informal sector, 144; limits of malls and, 127; marginalization of, 16; as Metrosuelo, 144, 145; ordered removed, 144; selling fake products, 144
Villalta, Nilda, 81
violence: aesthetic of, 81; built on experience of separation, 55; conceptions of, 70; in contrast to world of patriotism and success presented elsewhere, 55; as determining factor in emigration, 69, 70; diffuse, 8; domestic, 49, 70; escaping, 16; experiences of, 52; of family separation, 11; forms leading to misrecognition, 39; gang, 12, 20, 61, 62, 63; generalized, 8; histories of, 7, 50; interpersonal, 81; intersecting forms of, 53; invisible, 11; against journalists, 20; memories of, 68, 69; in migration, 11, 12, 50, 54, 62, 70, 71; militaristic, 85; narratives of, 81, 147; normalization of, 53; political, 2, 3; as

ABOUT THE AUTHOR

CECILIA M. RIVAS is an assistant professor in the Department of Latin American and Latino Studies at the University of California, Santa Cruz.

Available titles in the Latinidad: Transnational
Cultures in the United States series: